HIEROGL WORDS OF POWER

"This is a work of genius! Normandi Ellis, the author of this mind-cracking, soul-shaking work, is a once and future priestess, poet, and practitioner of the mystery, magic, and spiritual arts of ancient Egypt. She illustrates the enormous difference between our material thought and what we might call our soul thought or hieroglyphic thought. The Egyptians lived closer to the depths of their intra-dimensional minds than we do. By learning to perceive hieroglyphically, we can tap the many levels of consciousness; we can accommodate ourselves to the many transformations of our time; we can discover the many meanings, the sacred ambivalences. By consciously shaping our lives through spiritual attunement by thinking hieroglyphically, analogically, and symbolically in charged multi-patterns with webs of meaning, we can begin to create changes in our own forms—in our bodies and our minds. Thus, we approach the enantiodromia, 'the big turnaround,' that leads to a higher and deeper culture for us all collectively."

JEAN HOUSTON, PH.D., SCHOLAR, PHILOSOPHER,
RESEARCHER IN HUMAN CAPACITIES, AND AUTHOR OF
THE PASSION OF ISIS AND OSIRIS

"Normandi Ellis dreams into the mind of ancient Egypt, and Egypt dreams through her. She is one of those who passed through the lion skin, as Egypt said of initiates, and now invites us to taste the mysteries. With *Hieroglyphic Words of Power,* this word priestess gives us access to ancient codes for creation through the heart and the tongue. She takes us on a tour of the magic library of Seshet—scribe, goddess, and celestial consort of Thoth—where gods and glyphs come alive. This beautifully designed book is a workout for the visual imagination and an invitation to awaken to the power of naming and constructing personal oracles from ancient words of power. Through essays on sixty medju neter (words of the gods), Normandi introduces us to 'hieroglyphic thinking' and leads us with poetic clarity through a profusion of deities, creation myths, and spiritual bodies. She leaves us with a reference book to which I will return again and again—a resource unlike others, because, beyond scholarship, the author's shining love for her theme blazes through every word."

ROBERT MOSS, AUTHOR OF
DREAMING THE SOUL BACK HOME,
THE SECRET HISTORY OF DREAMING, AND
THE DREAMER'S BOOK OF THE DEAD

"This book is almost as good as being in class or traveling with Normandi Ellis, as she shares her immense wisdom from her even bigger heart. As the class or tour eventually ends, this beautiful book ensures that the teaching does not—you can delve into it anytime to discover new layers and revelations. Normandi presents the hieroglyphs of Egypt as tangible oracular tools to navigate the magical cosmology of our existence and to divine ourselves as living images of the magic that created us. This book is not only about the magic; it vividly helps us to remember that we are the magic."

KATHRYN W. RAVENWOOD, AUTHOR OF
HOW TO CREATE SACRED WATER

"Normandi Ellis's latest book has given me something precious: access to a door that for years I thought had no key, behind which—I just *knew*—were wonderful things just out of reach. At last, with the surprising and multi-layered techniques given, I see a way to crack it open."

ALAN RICHARDSON, COAUTHOR OF *THE INNER GUIDE TO EGYPT* AND
AUTHOR OF *MAGICAL KABBALAH* AND *THE SEA PRIEST*

"As Normandi writes, 'truth is more than one thing.' To break the spell that reality is something fixed, Normandi conjures spells of imagery and poetry, tricking us into a larger truth. Don't be confused that in your hands now is a book of words. For if you dare suspend your usual perceptions and expectations, you may recognize that you're being handed a prism of realization—one facet, one image, one key to the kingdom at a time. Beyond the relative reality that we unconsciously construct moment by moment lives the imaginal realms. Step into these pages. Let go. Become ancient and available to the gods through your own nonrational self."

DEBORAH JONES, EXECUTIVE DIRECTOR OF
THE NINE GATES MYSTERY SCHOOL

HIEROGLYPHIC
WORDS OF
POWER

SYMBOLS FOR MAGIC, DIVINATION, AND DREAMWORK

NORMANDI ELLIS

Bear & Company
Rochester, Vermont

Bear & Company
One Park Street
Rochester, Vermont 05767
www.BearandCompanyBooks.com

Bear & Company is a division of Inner Traditions International

Cataloging-in-Publication Data for this title is available from the Library of Congress

ISBN 978-1-59143-376-7 (print)
ISBN 978-1-59143-377-4 (ebook)

Printed and bound in the United States by P. A. Hutchison Company

10   9   8   7   6   5   4   3   2   1

Text design and layout by Virginia Scott Bowman
This book was typeset in Garamond Premier Pro and Avenir with Aviano and Gill
Sans used as display typefaces.
Photography by Amy Auset Rohn
Illustrations by Lexas Hovis

To send correspondence to the author of this book, mail a first-class letter to the
author c/o Inner Traditions • Bear & Company, One Park Street, Rochester, VT
05767, and we will forward the communication, or contact the author directly at
https://normandiellis.com.

✦✦✦

For my brothers, Edward and Byron,
and my daughter, Alaina.

The imagination is not a state: it is the human existence itself.

WILLIAM BLAKE

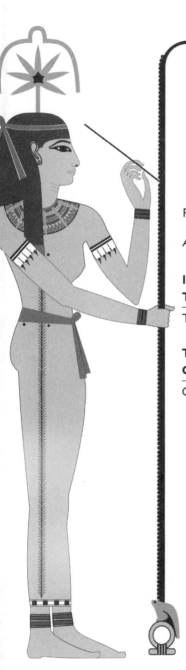

CONTENTS

FOREWORD BY NICKI SCULLY   xi

ACKNOWLEDGMENTS   xix

**INTRODUCTION
TO THE HIEROGLYPHS**   1
THE WORD OF GODS

**THE UNIQUE MAGIC
OF THE HIEROGLYPHS**   11
OPENING THE WAY TO MEANING

Familiarize Yourself with the
    Hieroglyphs in Meditation   15

Use the Hieroglyphs as an Oracle   18

Invoke the Hieroglyphs When
    You Dream   19

Engage in Ritual Work with
    the Hieroglyphs   22

Create Amulets to Access the
    Hieroglyphs' Healing Power   25

Use Number Magic to Broaden Your
    Understanding of Hieroglyphs   27

A Final Caveat   36

WORDS OF POWER

Akh	41
Akhet	45
Amen	48
Ankh	52
Anpu (Anubis)	55
Arit	59
Asar (Osiris)	63
Ast (Isis)	67
Aten	70
Atum	74
Ba	77
Benben	79
Blank	82
Djed	84
Djhuty (Thoth)	88
Dser	93
Duat	96
Geb	98
Heh	100
Heka	103
Heru (Horus)	107
Het (Khet or Khat)	112
Het-Hor (Hathor)	115
Hotep	121
Hu	125
Ib (Ab)	128
Ir-ma'a	132
Ka	136
Khaibit	139

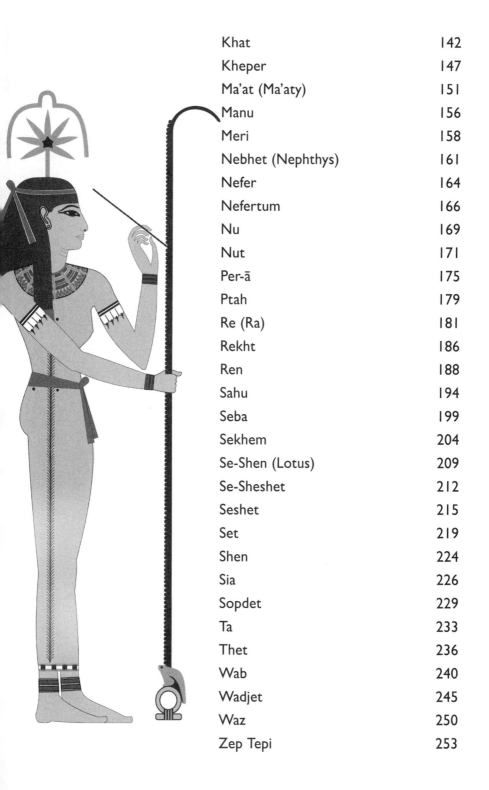

Khat	142
Kheper	147
Ma'at (Ma'aty)	151
Manu	156
Meri	158
Nebhet (Nephthys)	161
Nefer	164
Nefertum	166
Nu	169
Nut	171
Per-ā	175
Ptah	179
Re (Ra)	181
Rekht	186
Ren	188
Sahu	194
Seba	199
Sekhem	204
Se-Shen (Lotus)	209
Se-Sheshet	212
Seshet	215
Set	219
Shen	224
Sia	226
Sopdet	229
Ta	233
Thet	236
Wab	240
Wadjet	245
Waz	250
Zep Tepi	253

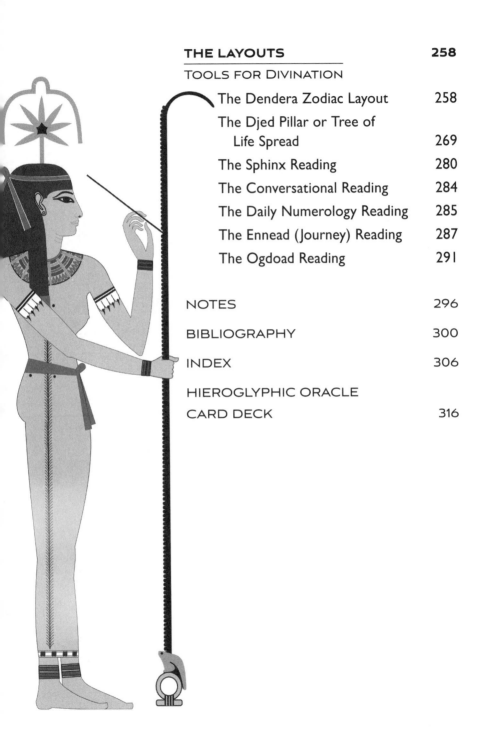

THE LAYOUTS   258

TOOLS FOR DIVINATION

The Dendera Zodiac Layout   258

The Djed Pillar or Tree of
   Life Spread   269

The Sphinx Reading   280

The Conversational Reading   284

The Daily Numerology Reading   285

The Ennead (Journey) Reading   287

The Ogdoad Reading   291

NOTES   296

BIBLIOGRAPHY   300

INDEX   306

HIEROGLYPHIC ORACLE
CARD DECK   316

FOREWORD

BY NICKI SCULLY

How many ways can you say *amazing?* In hieroglyphs there are glyphs that, when put together, give one a multidimensional, poetic view of what *amazing* really means. Suffice it to say that with this book, Normandi Ellis has done the amazing. Again. For this is not an ordinary book. Rather it is magical in the deepest sense of the word. It enables a person, even a nonscholar like me, to access the entire scope of the Egyptian mysteries, which, given the requisite time and attention, will open like the sacred lotus, revealing a new dimension one petal at a time.

Every journey with Normandi at the helm of it has been a constant source of insight and knowledge for me ever since I was gifted with her exquisite translation of the Egyptian Book of the Dead, *Awakening Osiris*. It was given to me by a dear friend in the early 1980s, and I was smitten. When leading tours to Egypt I used to draw from it to introduce teachings at the temples, often employing bibliomancy by opening a page at random and reading a passage or two. It was and still is my scripture and my constant companion whenever and wherever I travel.

I had to meet this "amazing" writer, and eventually I called the late author and Sphinx scholar John Anthony West to ask for Normandi's phone number, after which I made a cold call and received a warm reception. It was during a visit to her then-home in Kentucky that she and I experienced a magical connection that presaged two decades of our Egyptian Mystery School and ultimately led us to coauthor our recent book, *The Union of Isis and Thoth*.

Meanwhile, some years ago the *medju* Seshet started gestating in

Normandi's brilliant mind. I first encountered this when she and I were teaching together at a Women of Wisdom Conference in Seattle, February 2017. I knew that Normandi's interest in hieroglyphic thinking had taken her deeper and deeper into the mystical realms that only the literate—those who could read and understand this sacred language—could comprehend. And yet until that day, when I was introduced to what has become *Hieroglyphic Words of Power,* I hadn't realized that with this tool any person can become not only a hieroglyphic thinker but an oracle of great value as well.

I love teaching with Normandi because we push each other. I came from the worlds of alchemy and shamanism, yet I thought of myself as psychically blind. Normandi had "the sight" from birth and initially thought everybody had similar opportunities to speak with God, or in her case, "God's Wife." She spent hours upon hours of her childhood drawing and painting in the underground sewer pipes near her home and had a strong connection with a spirit guide whom she called God's Wife. She later learned this was Isis. Although raised as an Episcopalian, for years Normandi would laughingly call herself an *Episcopagan.*

Once, prior to an Egyptian mysteries intensive, my husband, Mark Hallert, had a vision wherein it became apparent that we were to learn to speak for the neteru family—the gods of Egypt and Isis in particular. Much to my surprise Normandi immediately and emphatically said, "No!" I was baffled when I hung up the phone, not at all sure what to do. Up until then, in my world, Mark's visioning had often marked the beginning of new teachings or detailed journeys, and it never occurred to me that he could be wrong. In any event, I didn't have to wait long (about thirty minutes) before Normandi called back to say that she was "in." She had found an old journal of hers from five years earlier. Its last page contained her musings that perhaps it was time to give voice to the neteru. As intimate as she had been with all of them, the idea of becoming an oracle had frightened her, and she had not pursued it. This time, however, she knew that she could no longer run from it.

So give voice we did, and of all the intensive Egyptian mysteries retreats that Normandi and I conducted over the years, I believe that more lives were changed by this one than by any before or since. In a dramatic and obvious way, our students, some literally kicking and screaming, allowed this "amazing" gift of becoming an oracle to be awakened or renewed in them. It really caught on, so much so that I could probably name at least a dozen books that were written—either directly or in a secondary fashion—as a result of this particular weeklong intensive.

Normandi is the only person I know who actually attended school to learn how to be a Spiritualist medium. The rest of us simply went with what we discovered along the way, and our skills grew organically. In the decades that Normandi and I taught and traveled together, I observed her endless curiosity in action. She constantly studied and learned new things, and when she wanted to learn something, there were no holds barred. The hieroglyphs are something she has been studying and teaching for many years. Indeed, when writing *Awakening Osiris,* she not only had to learn each hieroglyph and the meaning that was intended, she had to go through the Book of the Dead three times in order to complete its translation. Her thoroughness is such that the project, which was initially an undergraduate assignment for a translation class, took her ten years to complete.

I recall that the first time I was introduced to the hieroglyphs, Normandi said that her favorite word was *heka,* or *h-ka.* The word *hex* comes from that word, for *heka* means "magic," and this one word seemed to encapsulate the crux of Egyptian magic. Vowels are not used in the written language because they represent the breath of God and are thus considered sacred. Heka, on the other hand, expresses a whole sentence, an invocation or entire ritual that makes something come into being the way it's supposed to. In order to practice heka you have to have proper words, proper sequencing, proper intonation, and especially proper intention. Intention is the most important part of it. If you have clear intention as well as the will, and you can envision the proper sequencing of what is to occur, the divine breath then makes it happen. Therefore, a positive intention to use this magic for good is paramount, for to misdirect or misuse its power can be devastating.

Normandi has the gift of packing more information and wisdom in one sentence or paragraph than most writers put in a page, or several, yet she delivers directly from her heart, and her heart is the heart of a poet. As only a poet can, she describes how hieroglyphs are sacred words—"words of God"—with layers of meaning that may be revealed through deep meditation. For me, the most potent aspect of this oracle is the way in which she describes each hieroglyph in a precise fashion. The insights and wisdom of the hieroglyphs have been brilliantly unpacked by Normandi through the use of her great reservoirs of knowledge, both scholarly and mystical.

As she says, "The person who writes with hieroglyphs and understands them as god consciousness works as a technician of the sacred. Rituals, dreams, incantations, and shamanic visions demonstrate the power of poetry and of symbol." She goes on to tell us how the ancient scribe and modern shaman-poet share the ability to converse with Source, or the universal life force energy, through conscious focus or meditation on a single symbol.

If you follow the instructions in this oracle and meditate on specific images long enough to let them carry you into a different dimension, you'll be rewarded with more than a casual comprehension of Egyptian magic and oracular divination—you'll become the master of your own destiny, and you'll be able to guide others in this as well.

Normandi explains that hieroglyphs work on three levels and her thorough articulation of the nuances of hieroglyphic thinking can reach even the most novice of students and motivate them to create their own oracle deck. Many of the cards of the deck represent families that come in threes, such as Ptah, Sekhmet, and Nefertum—or Isis, Osiris, and Horus. These cards express both the principles and the aspects of the mythical story of each deity. Other cards and different card spreads or layouts (used when doing oracular "readings") relate to the ten spiritual bodies of the ancient Egyptians, providing a second interpretation of them. The ten spiritual bodies, as Normandi originally described in *Dreams of Isis,* are related to the ten bodies described in the sephiroth, the Tree of Life in Qabalah. These ten bodies are expressed in the Djed Pillar Reading discussed later in this book. (See the Djed Pillar Reading on page 269.) In this reading you can see the overlay and how the energy moves top-down from spirit to matter. (Normandi also describes how to use certain cards for healing, especially when paired with those cards that express the spiritual bodies.)

And as if that wasn't enough, Normandi goes on to add an overlay of numbers, which can be used in various ways, not only based on the number that might appear on a card, but also the number according to its position in the various layouts. She explains the meanings quite clearly, concluding that the "number magic" of this oracle adds a philosophical layer to the meaning of your spread. (Please know that there are many different ways to include numerology in your readings.)

A word of advice: Be sure to pay attention to your dreams when working with this oracle. Keeping a dream journal by your bed will help you connect the dots as time goes on. The neteru can, and certainly did for Normandi, present themselves in nightly dreams. They can help you to tap into the collective psyche's interpretation of these symbols over time. Please also know that the oracular messages that are conveyed in your dreams may become clearer as you reflect upon them in your journal.

Each of the sixty hieroglyphs that Normandi has chosen from the more than 700 most commonly used images are presented in this book in alphabetical order, starting with akh and ending with zep tepi. Thus they are easy to locate when you're looking for information about them. Consequently, this book is invaluable as a reference as well as a guide. The depth of information one is given about each respective hieroglyph helps to round out one's understanding of the ancient Egyptian cosmology involved.

In this book, Normandi carefully explains the myths and meanings associated with each hieroglyphic "word," and how the hieroglyphs were used for more than three thousand years when some form of this language was in use. And of course, she delves into possible meanings for specific readings or situations, allowing for multiple interpretations in accordance with how you choose to use the images and your personal experience of them.

For example, Anpu (Anubis) is one of my favorite neteru. Normandi not only offers up a full history of who he is and what he's most known for, she provides options for expanding your knowledge and experience of him and your ability to utilize his attributes, which are many.

There are a number of ways you can use this oracle. You can use one of the layouts Normandi has prepared and simply gaze at an image until it speaks directly to you. Intention is vital, so having a question helps the symbols speak to you in a way that allows the correct story to reveal itself.

Another interesting and unique feature of this book, as touched upon earlier, is the opportunity it affords of creating your own personal deck using the hieroglyphs. You can draw your own images on card stock or papyrus. Then shuffle them before choosing one of Normandi's layouts or pulling cards at random to see what relevant story wants to awaken in you. For clarification, you can draw extra cards to place upon or with others that you have drawn in order to extend their meaning.

Illustrating the images of the hieroglyphs on your own cards is the juiciest part. This engages your mind at a deeper level than if you were to just look at what someone else has written or drawn. With each new card pulled the entire deck takes on more meaning, as though the cards are talking to you the entire time. As you begin to unpack the layers of meaning of each hieroglyph, your inner conversations become easier and deeper.*

It's difficult to explain the feelings that arise when you draw or pull a card that has real meaning and resonance for you, and when it's put in context with other cards, a conversation takes place that addresses the initial question you posed in your reading. Whether you use one of Normandi's layouts, which are very helpful, especially for beginners, or whether you ask a question and see which cards turn up for you, you quickly learn to recognize when you are truly in touch with the Divine. The heart connection you make when you draw your own cards awakens and deepens every time that card comes up in a reading.

As Normandi states, "Every hieroglyph is a key to consciousness.

---

*Of course, if you are not inclined to make your own cards, you have the option of buying a deck. (See page 316.)

Every hieroglyph is actual. Through its art form, consciousness emerges. We use attention to work with the symbols of the hieroglyph to understand its meaning, to focus a meditation upon the outer symbols of our lives—because *everything* is imaginal. The world thus becomes a world apprehended through the senses." And this occurs through repetitive exposure, through drawing the images in a notebook, or by creating your own cards.

Anyone who works with archetypes knows that their deeper meanings are revealed through repetition. I am reminded of school when I was quite young and had just learned to write. Although usually punitive, we were often asked to repeat a phrase over and over in order to allow the full consequence of its meaning to literally sink into our consciousness as a way to change, and in many cases program, our understanding. Add your focused attention, intention, repetition, and gazing/meditating over time, and your imagination will awaken the appropriate senses for a deeper understanding of your relationship with the hieroglyph, and with the natural world around us. First there was the word. Following this, one's intention and attention add the motivating force that creates one's reality. Ultimately, when you apply your intention and attention to the study of the hieroglyphs in this oracle, you are using magical means to create the knowledge and experience required to make real change in your life.

Consider that this oracle is not just a way to do readings for others, it is a journey that will unfold for you in ways that only become imaginable with practice. To say that this is well worth your time and attention is an understatement and but a shadow of the praise this book deserves.

NICKI SCULLY has been teaching healing, shamanic arts, and the Egyptian mysteries since 1983. During her first visit to Egypt in 1978, Nicki experienced an epiphany that transformed her life. She deepened her focus on healing and began delving into the hidden shamanic arts of Egypt. She is now a lineage holder in the Hermetic tradition of Thoth, her teacher and mentor. With Thoth

she developed Alchemical Healing—a comprehensive healing form that is prac-
ticed by thousands of practitioners internationally. In the late 1980s, Nicki
founded Shamanic Journeys, Ltd., her venue for conducting workshops, retreats,
and spiritual pilgrimages to Egypt and other sacred sites. She is the producer
of numerous CDs and the author of eight books, including books on healing,
metaphysics, and the Egyptian mysteries. With Normandi Ellis, she coauthored
The Union of Isis and Thoth. For more information on Nicki, please see

www.shamanicjourneys.com

ACKNOWLEDGMENTS

Thank you, Jon Graham, for returning my call when I left a Sunday message on the phone saying, "I have this idea for another book," and described it. Thank you for calling me back on Monday. Thanks to my mentor Nicki Scully, for being my Anubis and opening the way for me to do my work, now every day. Thank you, thank you, dear sister. Thank you to my fellow travelers and cohorts in the work: Deborah Jones, Sandra Corcoran, Indigo Ronlov, Gloria Taylor Brown, and Kathryn Ravenwood. Thank you to every student who gave feedback on the process of using hieroglyphs as oracles.

Thank you, Lexy Reed Hovis, for attending one of the first classes on hieroglyphic words of power in which we drew the images of these magical words. Lexy, you have done a marvelous job inscribing the heka of the goddess Seshet into your heart. I can't thank you enough for the beautiful illustrations that grace this book.

And a huge thank you to Amy Auset Rohn who photographed the gorgeous temples of Egypt on two different trips with me. Thank you also for taking extra time to photograph the hieroglyphs themselves as we walked about the temples, adding a few more until we were done. This book would fall far short if not for your skilled eye. Thanks to Meg Wolsiffer for using your magical graphic designer's wand and creating readable photographs of particular hieroglyphs that were crumbling or too dim to capture properly.

This acknowledgment would not be complete if I did not thank my mentor and friend Jean Houston who, many decades ago now, lifted up a rock under which I was hiding and said "Hello, hello! Come out!" Jean, your generosity of spirit, your work with me in editing and creating "hieroglyphic thinking" in your book *The Passion of Isis and Osiris,* and the opportunity over the years to converse, speak, and tell stories has been the gift of a lifetime. All we discussed led to this book and helped me hone my thinking on the hieroglyphs that follow.

Jamaica Burns and Anne Dillon, my editors and lifesavers, I am forever indebted to your skillful ways of excising my jumbled thoughts (like upturned temple stones buried in the detritus of a lifetime!) and helping me to excavate the true meaning of the text we worked on together. Your patience with me was a blessing, especially when schedules overwhelmed and computer crashes impeded our progress. Bless your eye for detail and pattern that demonstrated exactly what hieroglyphic thinking is about.

And to my Egyptian friends—Emil Shaker, Hatem Aly, Ihab Rashad, and the late Mohamed Nazmy—I am forever indebted to you for making me a part of your family. It is you who are my Beloveds, my Habibis. When I walk on your sands, when I feel the sun and wind on my face, when my eyes rest upon the hieroglyphs that enter beauteously into my dreams, I know that I am home.

And to Egypt itself. I loved you before I knew you. You were in my bones; you were the neteru in the natural world. When I found you, I found my world. In a real sense, it is you who gave me the words.

INTRODUCTION
TO THE HIEROGLYPHS

THE WORD OF GODS

Words are magic. Thoughts create actions that manifest forms. No matter what language you are using—English, Chinese, or the language of hieroglyphs—thoughts are things. Ancient Egyptians knew this to be true. They called their sacred writings heka. The concept of heka contained all potentiality. It is consciousness itself. You are already inside the world of magic at this moment. The late Egyptologist John Anthony West was fond of saying that the ancients would have seen the entire cosmos as one monumental magical act; that is, the manifestation of consciousness as the material world.[1]

As a working definition, the ancients knew heka as a prescriptive language that created realities through the exact words uttered at the right time, properly intoned, and filled with heady intention. Heka was the alchemical energy of the ancient world. It was a basic metaphysical concept that our thoughts and how we speak them create our reality.

Like dream language and poetry, hieroglyphs work on multiple levels, encompassing all levels simultaneously. They are symbolic and sensory (image), and vibratory (sound), and filled with mythologies (narrative) that are embedded within the hieroglyph. The poet Ezra Pound called these three *phanopeia, melopeia,* and *logopeia*—the essential ingredients of poetry.[2] It takes intuitive leaps to make full sense of a single hieroglyphic "word," much less a sentence written in hieroglyphs. Hieroglyphs are an inherently poetic language, as well as a magical language, which creates "a spell" in those who understand it.

The high priests, who knew the ancient texts and copied the words of transforming death into life inside the corridors of Egyptian tombs and papyrus scrolls, also knew that hieroglyphs were oracular. They interpreted dreams and oracles in the same way that they used the language inside the scrolls.

What does it mean that thoughts are things? Thoughts are the DNA of the universe, containing the code that gives form to our physical life experience. Without sensation or substance we could not grasp any thought form, yet symbols are much more complicated. The Lascaux cave paintings of cattle, for example, contain complex series of dots that were discovered to contain star patterns of the constellations representing Taurus and the Pleiades. More than simply meaning "I am hunting a spotted ox," the paintings contain embedded information about the time of year that the herds were likely to travel along a particular path. Art affords more than quaint Cracker Barrel décor. It offers important recorded information about how to amplify one's quality of life while providing a sense of order and beauty.

But it goes beyond even that. As the American existential psychologist and author Rollo May has said, "What if imagination and art are not frosting at all, but the fountainhead of human experience? What if our logic and science derive from art forms, rather than art being merely a decoration for our work . . . ?"[3] My friend Cosima Lukashevich, a mixed-media artist steeped in Egyptian culture and the arts, offered an intriguing possibility in a private Facebook message to me dated September 20, 2017. She asked, "Could people (and I am suggesting here both artists and non-artists) use art to draw the world *forward*?"

I believe that was the case with the Egyptian scribe who engaged in three-dimensional art, language, and architecture. For the ancient Egyptian priests, scribes, and visual artists, the mantic arts they used built doorways into the ancient mystery of interlinked science, spirit, and consciousness. Humankind continues to move through these open doorways, now as then, to create new worlds. It becomes entirely possible that the hieroglyphs draw us into transformative states of consciousness these five millennia later, just as the hieroglyphs moved and motivated the ancient mind toward its return to Source.

We are no longer talking about art as an individual expression of consciousness, or even as a cultural phenomenon. We are talking about the artistic process as consciousness itself—the universal pattern of our creative human DNA.

P. D. Ouspensky, in his book *In Search of the Miraculous,* quotes G. I. Gurdjieff as saying, "Symbols not only transmit knowledge but show the way to it." In speaking of the symbol of the seal of Solomon, Gurdjieff went on to say, "The transmission of the meaning of symbols to a man who has not reached an understanding of them in himself is impossible. This sounds like a paradox, but the meaning of a symbol and the disclosure of its essence can only be given to, and can only be understood by, one who, so to speak, already knows what is comprised in this symbol. And a symbol becomes for him a synthesis of his knowledge."[4]

It is not really possible to say that "this" symbol equals "that" meaning. Symbols accrue meaning, expanding with endless, interrelated diversity and aspect. A symbol swims in the waters of endless possibility, and those who understand the power of symbol use it as a raft to float from meaning to meaning in a vast ocean of consciousness.

Where did this language that is consciousness come from? In essence, the mind of God. More than one Egyptian myth suggests that the thought forms of Ptah, or Atum, or Thoth orchestrated the harmonies of the cosmos. The Gospel of John 1:1–3 echoes this idea, insisting that "In the beginning was the Word and the Word was with God and the Word was God." *Medju neter,* the ancient Egyptian term for the hieroglyphs, meant the "Word of God." The Emerald Tablet of Hermes Trismegistus, a Greek magical text attributed to the Egyptian god Thoth, tells us that Egypt was built in the image of heaven, saying that the All is of one mind, and that which is below is like that which is above.[5] All created things originate from this one great thought.

Together Isis and Thoth created the magical, incantatory hieroglyphs, and any high priest, magician, or individual who knew and used them appropriately could command worlds, as did Thoth and Isis. The magical incantations written by Thoth were the laws of ma'at, the "Truth" itself. Forty-two of the most exquisite, powerful hymns and chapters in the Book of the Dead were originally written by Thoth "with his own fingers."[6]

The Cairo calendar calls Isis "Provider of the Book." The ancients believed that the words of Isis "come to pass without fail." At the Delta city of Busiris she was called the Great Word because of the ways in which the incantations from her lips healed the sick, raised the dead, and, with Thoth's help, stopped time by causing the boat of sun god Ra to sail backward. Both Isis and Thoth are associated with the wisdom and magic of books. In a Hymn to Isis, an aretalogy of the Ptolemaic era, the Goddess asserts: "I am Isis, ruler of every land. I was taught by Hermes (Thoth) and with Hermes devised letters, both hieroglyphic and demotic, that all might not be written with the same. I gave laws to mankind and ordained what no one can change."[7]

The scribe goddess Seshet, a companion of Thoth, establishes the foundations of temples, records the individual's life deeds on a notched palm frond, calculates time by the star logs, keeps the library, and manages the Akashic Records. Mentioned as early as the Old Kingdom First Dynasty, Seshet may be considered an early manifestation of Isis. While Isis was later associated with Sirius, Seshet was associated with the Pleiades. Both goddesses are linked to the cow goddess Hathor, the oldest known goddess. A primeval star goddess, Seshet was said to have created the story of the First Time (Zep Tepi).[8] Her library, per ankh or house of life, contained the scrolls of rituals and prayers for the daily morning, noon, and evening rites for every god or goddess and for every day of the year.

Without knowing it, I must have felt her influence in my life early on. When I was a child in Kentucky, I used to hide out in storm sewer tunnels (dangerous, I know) with my paints, drawing images and writing poems on the walls. I have no idea where this impulse to sit in a darkened tunnel to write and paint came from. I can only imagine it was left over from a former lifetime in Egypt, for in ancient Egypt, creative expression found many forms and there was little distinction made between writing, drawing, and painting. It may have been that this creative childhood penchant primed me for my later love of hieroglyphs and a deepened understanding of image and word that was to develop in me as an adult.

Perhaps we can follow Seshet's lead by seeing both writing and painting as ways to communicate, making no distinction between the symbolic and the real. What if the world was nothing but a set of symbols for a higher form of existence? What if our appearance on the canvas of Earth was the equivalent of our being living, breathing hieroglyphs for the gods to read and understand?

The first full shamanic, hieroglyphic religious poetry that we know appears in the disheveled pyramid of the Fifth Dynasty pharaoh Unas. These Pyramid Texts provide the earliest religious texts of transformation; they date from approximately 2460 BCE. They detail the intricate ways of resurrection of the soul; the shamanic mystery tradition associated with every high priest or pharaoh. The Pyramid Text is the first book of the afterlife and the original prayer book of a soul in transition.

Hieroglyphs are particularly and peculiarly difficult to translate with complete accuracy. One word in another language cannot substitute for a single hieroglyphic symbol. These hieroglyphs were perfectly executed, ritually infused, and considered holy. They were meant solely for the eyes and lips of the pharaoh, who was a high initiate of Egyptian magic. The images held a grammatical lyricism as well, making them the first sacred poetry known to man. A whole philosophy appears within each hieroglyphic image. Chant lines and repetitions, sound vibrations, and hypnotically recurring images were perhaps intended to induce a trance-like state in the individual, which allowed him to ascend into the heavens. Thus riding on this incantatory language was he able to converse with his ancestors and his Creator.

Not only were the hieroglyphs alive, sprung from the lips of the deity, but the whole world was alive—a living hieroglyph. Every frog, every tamarisk tree, every ripple of water was a living mirror that reflected the divine presence in the world. Divinities, like the things of the world, have their diversities in nature. The ancient word for a god or goddess, *neter,* was understood as "nature" and the laws of God were the natural laws of the world.

The consciousness of the creative intelligence that envisioned hieroglyphic communication operates in thought waves that defy logic. The mind-boggling symbol-infused reality of hieroglyphic thinking is probably why dreams confuse most people as well, and why most people confound most other people around them; because—when it comes right down to it—we are all likewise diverse and created from that enigmatic mind of God. That makes each of us perhaps as confounding as walking hieroglyphs.

Taking at face value any language and any religious text (ancient or modern) creates interpretive problems. Thinking "this equals that" misses the delightful fullness of what is being expressed. Beyond literal meaning, hieroglyphs express the kind of thought patterns that are the essence of creative thinking. The deeper truths we crave cannot be found in single-word translations; they must be derived from a core understanding of myth and mythic language. Myth unites the inner world of human experience with the outer world of the universe.

If we look at a single word we might understand how this concept of hieroglyphic thinking* works. Let's begin by examining my favorite word, *heka* (magic), which we will discuss further beginning on page 103. One needs five hieroglyphic signs to write the word for magic; only two of them, *h* and *k,* are phonetic. Yet all of these images work together to create the many concepts of divine magical utterance. The first hieroglyph offers a hard *h* sound. Most Egyptologists see that hieroglyph as a candlewick of twisted flax fiber. It looks like three criss-crossing loops, or perhaps three circles stacked on top of each other. A single strand of fiber, looped at the top, separates into two ends at the bottom. Actually, our Roman letter *h* also implies two strands that meet in the middle, like one rung of a ladder.

The Egyptian language used three distinctly different types of

---

Hieroglyphic thinking is a term that Jean Houston and I used when collaborating on her book *The Passion of Isis and Osiris.*

Heka

h sounds. There is a soft, breathy h—like a sigh or a breeze—and a throaty, combined kh sound that is more frequently used in Middle Eastern languages and in Hebrew. Then there is a hard, raspy, explosive $h,$ as if you put your hand over a lit candle flame and said, "Hot!" Potentially that hard h provides an aural impression of the word for magic.

The visual impression of the candlewick—a single twisted fiber with three loops—reminds me of DNA combining and recombining; DNA is the magic of Creation. Certainly it demonstrates separation and reunion, and again separation and reunion in fluid motion, which is a visual reminder of the natural laws of opposition, of attraction and of unity. Many metaphysical concepts are projected by this one image. For a novice, simply *learning* the power of these natural laws might seem magical.

The image also reminds me of the four planes of existence, the upper loop being spiritual and resting on top of the mental plane, the mental plane above the astral plane, and, finally, the two ends of the string like two legs standing on the Earth in the physical plane.

It might also be that magic is a kind of scientific phenomena that the ancient Egyptians understood. Did they know about the DNA double helix? To the modern mind, that image applies very well to a concept of magic—for what does DNA do? It creates life through the union of separate chemical strands that combine, separate, recombine, twist, and transform into matter. In addition, there is an explosive chemical reaction whose fire quickens and sets the life of the organism in motion. These energetic light codes at the moment of human conception are mirrors of the magic that created Egypt. Gods made the world by magical means, and shaman-priests used that formula to create and alter realities thereafter.

Now between the first hieroglyph, *h,* and the second hieroglyph, which is *ka,* we really don't have a sign for a vowel sound. Standard practice among early Egyptologists was to insert an *e* in almost every instance where a vowel should be but wasn't. Most Arabic, Hebrew, and Near Eastern languages contain a flame letter as part of their alphabets. These marks above the consonants inserted vowels where originally there were none. That breathy part of the word was connected to the breath of God, as in "In the beginning was the Word. . . ." The true name of the creator god is not to be taken lightly.

The inspiration, or the intake of the breath, and its exhalation, creates the spirit of the word. The vowel sound being unwritten allows for similar words to be implied. *H-ka-t* can be seen as another word for a ruler, a chieftain, a pharaoh, or a shaman. It can also be understood as Heket, the frog goddess of transformation who holds the ankh or breath of life to the nose of a child being sculpted by the ram god Khnum on his potter's wheel. An ancient Egyptian medicine man or woman knew that every embryo from chicken to child begins its first stage of life resembling a frog. All life moves from the zygote, subdividing and reuniting until it turns into an embryo that resembles a tadpole. Thus Heket, the goddess of magic and the goddess of Creation, holds the ankh, the key of life. Again we circle back to that idea that something invisible (a vowel) is still a primary part of thought; it is equally as invisible as a strand of DNA.

Now we encounter a second hieroglyph, *ka,* a bilateral sign that uses one sign for two sounds working together in the same way that *th* or *wh* work. Ka similarly signifies multiple things, depending upon how it is written. Ka may refer to an animal, specifically a bull, suggesting the magic of Creation, insemination, and conception. Apis bulls, or *kau*, were divine aspects of the god of regeneration Osiris and were buried in the Serapeum in Saqqara. All living beings contained the divinity of God. Because meat was often a sacrifice made to the gods, *ka* was another word for food and for that which nourishes and sustains. When we ingest any living thing, we partake of God because everything has its source in God. The ingestion and processing of food within the fire of the belly is also an alchemical, magical process.

The hieroglyph *ka,* written as a pair of arms extended from the chest at right angles with palms up so that the chest opens fully, was a symbol for spirit. The energy that inhabits matter and becomes its life force is ka. With both arms open wide to open the chest, the heart cavity opens fully to the Divine. Sometimes the ka was viewed as the double of a person or a god. Ka energy connects us to our ancestors, and to life through our desire nature, through our needs to be fed, to be loved and to feel connected to Source and imbued with purpose. All that is ka energy. Essentially this is the part of magic that implies a life-giving reciprocity between the human and divine worlds.

We have three more hieroglyphs, which are determinatives, in the word *heka*. These particular hieroglyphs are not vocalized but simply connote the flavor of the hieroglyphs that precede them. In the only determinative shown in this particular image (see page 7), we see a rolled-up scroll tied with string. Whatever text lay inside that papyrus was hidden from view, implying that magical knowledge was not for everyone to know. In the wrong hands it could be misunderstood or misused with as much devastation as plutonium. The natural laws behind the phenomenon of magic were powerful, inalterable laws not easily understood by all, and not always used with good intent. A priest-scribe had an ethical responsibility to preserve the mystery. While many stories abound that this was not always done, it is true that magic and sacred ritual need to be preserved to prevent their misuse. For this reason most sacred scrolls were kept in a temple library and not in the home or "at the office." A separate language, hieratic, was used as the everyday shorthand of the hieroglyphs.

Although not every scribe used every hieroglyph available to him, two other determinatives often appeared. The first would be a scribe's kit that contains a box with ink, reed pens, and an inkpot. The magic-making that this implies can be a human endeavor—a kind of craft learned through practice—the way a student learns to read and write. Highly adept scribes were high priests, doctors, and executive officers working on behalf of the common good. Or at least one hoped. The scribe's kit was used to both write and paint. In the Kemetic (ancient Egyptian) language there was no difference between writing and drawing or painting; thus a scribe used whole brain thinking and engaged both the logical and imaginative lobes of his brain to create sacred language. That image alone is a huge clue about the power of the ancient language and hieroglyphic thinking.

A final determinative hieroglyph depicted three seeds. Three of anything indicated a multiplicity of things, which is why the divine beings often appear in clusters of three. The holy family consisted of Isis, Osiris, and Horus, and the three sun gods Khepera, Ra, and Atum represented the dawn, noon, and sunset. In this case the seeds represented multiple ways of making and creating magic. It also implied multiple outcomes with innumerable intentions. This idea of multiplicity carries with it a responsibility. In other words, "As ye sow, so shall ye reap." The meaning of the seeds is not only the idea of producing a harvest generation after generation, but it reminds us of the caretaking required in planting and magic-making. One must use one's magical invocations carefully. Another way of saying that would be "Be careful what you wish for because you may get it."

THE UNIQUE MAGIC
OF THE HIEROGLYPHS

OPENING THE WAY TO MEANING

Hieroglyphic language works on multiple levels. It does come from the real world of symbol but it is not imaginative in the way that common social critics speak of inventive imagery. *Medju* (the word) is language that is a precursor to heka, and heka, in essence, is a magical formula defined by Egyptian metaphysicians as "the proper words in the proper sequence with the proper intonation and the proper intent." Through it one could create worlds. Heka is the magic that is calibrated from medju neter. Isis embodied the power of the sorceress and was called the Speaker of Spells. That was speaker of spells in a good way—for healing, for protection, for resurrection, for stopping time, and so on.

Medju is "the Word" emerging from divine lips into form. Magic is the god's fuel. Vibration creates all things. Those who use color and sound as artists—musicians, painters, writers, actors, scientists—are all magicians who use the precision of sound, light, and intention to create and see realities. Medju neter becomes transpersonal in the way that divine beings used it. Medju energy flows out into thingly-ness, riding on a wave of energy put forward by desire and will (intention) and the passion for creation (life force energy, or will, or chi).

The person who writes with hieroglyphs and understands them as god consciousness works as a technician of the sacred. Rituals, dreams, incantations, and shamanic visions demonstrate the power of poetry and symbol. All of these ways and many others provide unique opportunities to work with the hieroglyphic words of power as a meta-physical tool. How much you get out of the glyphs depends upon how much you meditate with them and work with them. The ancient priest-scribes became adepts in part because they worked with the energies on a daily basis.

As an aside I want to tell you about a dream I had—because hiero-glyphs work in similar ways to dream images. I dreamed that I sat in an open-air courtyard with a group of students listening to a scholar in a toga expound on the meaning of a particular tarot card image. This card included a lion-headed fountain in which water streamed from the lion's mouth into a basin. In the background a distant doorway opened into empty space and rolling sands. The painted card represented an actual place. The scholar told the group that the lion fountain could be found in Egypt. Ever the traveler, even in my dreams, I raised my hand.

"Where in Egypt is the fountain?" I asked.

He pointed to a lion fountain inside the courtyard where we sat, saying, "There is the fountain."

I said, "No, I mean, 'Where is the lion fountain *in Egypt?*'"

Again he pointed to the fountain where we sat.

Frustrated, I leaned over to the gentleman seated next to me, and said with exasperation: "He doesn't understand my question."

The man smiled, pointed, and said, "No. You don't understand the answer. *There* is the fountain. And there is the door we came in through."

I woke up thinking that I understood what the dream message meant: Time and space inside our dreams are always shifting realities.

Some years later while traveling in Egypt, I walked around behind the Temple of Hathor in Dendera. For some reason I had never been behind the temple before, and I discovered there both the doorway and the lion fountain—except, in the dream, both had been covered in deep sand and appeared to rest on the same ground where I was seated (in the dream). In reality, modern excavations had removed the sands behind the Temple of Hathor, making the lion-headed downspout on the top of the temple about one hundred feet over my head rather than at eye level as it had appeared in my dream. Yes! There was the fountain! My reality just shifted several times.

Every hieroglyph is a key to consciousness. Every hieroglyph is actual. Through its art form, consciousness emerges. We use attention to work with the symbols of the hieroglyph to understand its meaning, to focus a meditation upon the outer symbols of our lives—because *everything* is imaginal. The world thus becomes a world apprehended through the senses.

Neter and nature are the same. Ted Andrews, author of *Animal Speak,* reminds us, "No matter how much we cloak ourselves in civilization today, we will always be a part of Nature. . . . Animals and humans are inseparable." The natural world plays a strong role in shaping our reality through the unconscious. Animals and all things of nature appear in dreams, meditations, and clairvoyant readings to offer guidance and to work on our behalf as allies. Andrews goes on to say, "[A]ll animals speak to those who listen. When we learn to speak with the animals . . . the animals are no longer our subordinates. They become our teachers, our friends, and our companions."[1] Closely studying the behaviors and traits of those elements and creatures of the natural world provides insight into the way their behavior and action may be at play in situations around us.

When John, in the Gospel of John 1:1, offered the formula that we call the Word of God, the author alluded to a metaphysical understanding of how reality had manifested. God had spoken it into being. That speech was a language vibration of light and sound. It spoke us into being, becoming a part of our spiritual DNA. We have a similar capacity to co-create with the Divine.

So not only does attention to the symbol of the hieroglyph matter, but intention becomes a primary part of manifesting through language. Say what you mean and mean what you say. It is best if we can work with attention and intention as we approach an understanding of consciousness. A magician is a living model of both and if you can consciously attend to your intentions, you are a classic alchemical metaphysician. By attending and intending, you can alter realities; and you can alter other people's perceptions of *their* reality. Doing that you can create real change through magical means.

Alchemy, of course, is an Arabic word that describes where this magical dictum comes from, this turning of lead into gold, this transforming consciousness. It is *Al-Khemy,* using the ancient hieroglyphic word *Khem,* meaning "from the Land of Egypt." The term *black arts* has been applied to the idea of alchemy, not because alchemy is bad, but because alchemy derives from Egypt, a land rich in fertile black soil caused by the flooding Nile.

Hieroglyphs incised in stone create a permanent record—not simply a historical record. They bring consciousness into a poetic, symbolic, physical form in order that the thought might be repeated and intoned over and over so that thought will alter physical reality. The law of environment, one of the lesser known but equally powerful natural laws, means that whatever appears in our environment becomes a focus of our attention and describes who we are. In addition, what we need to evoke will appear in the surroundings around us.

Well-crafted, mind-blowingly beautiful hieroglyphs written in stone on temple ceilings, columns, and walls were painted in vivid colors derived from ground-up, powdered gemstones. Each color still held the crystalline structure of the gem itself. The deep blue of Hathor's temple derives from crushed lapis lazuli, a stone that holds the power of dream, astral flight, and enlightenment. The bluish greens of turquoise and malachite mined in the Sinai Peninsula offer protection, healing, abundance, and joy. The earthy reds of powdered carnelian became the lips of the goddess Hathor. The mask of her dazzling golden face, of course, has since been stolen and carted away by thieves in antiquity, but the rest of the images remain. Beyond simple colors, these gemstones impress a kind of crystalline memory upon the environment. These gemstone colors last for thousands of years because they were painted with the intention of revealing magic and the magical means of attention to detail that is part of creating a "Heaven on Earth."

Once a temple was created through the magical means of stones and incantations, images and hieroglyphs, and the adoration of the priests and the intonations that accompanied the daily prayers, the temples exuded an eternal magic. Yet over several hundred years, any house (divine or otherwise) falls into disrepair and when floods, mud, and war ravage the original structure a new one must be built to replace it. Every time a temple needed a refresher, the mason-priests used a seed stone (often the phallus of the god of Min) taken from the original temple and reinserted it in the new temple being built on the foundation of the older temple. It was a way of preserving the magical essence of the structure. (For more information on how you yourself are a temple of the Divine in a physical structure, see *The Union of Isis and Thoth*.)

The hieroglyphs that covered the temples from floor to ceiling, and including the ceiling, were intended as eternal praises and prayers, not simply decorations. Every time a priestess walked through the temple columns and cast her gaze upon a row of hieroglyphs, she vivified those living prayers. There are a number of ways the modern practitioner can use the hieroglyphs in a similar fashion to elevate her work and vibration. Herewith are a few suggestions.

FAMILIARIZE YOURSELF WITH THE HIEROGLYPHS IN MEDITATION

The modern shaman-poet and the ancient scribe-priest know how to hold an entire conversation with the universal life force energy by meditation on a single hieroglyph—the same way some people meditate with a mantra or a picture image held in the mind, which is more or less the same thing. In fact, that is actually how this book began. For nearly two years I used the hieroglyphic symbols as a focal point in my ongoing meditations. I drew the images that I was invoking onto blank papyrus, which I'd bought in Egypt and cut into strips, placing them where I could see them during meditation.

Selecting a hieroglyph to use in meditation is an appropriate way to begin working with the hieroglyphs presented in the following chapter. The act of drawing the hieroglyphs can itself be a meditative practice. The more you copy a hieroglyph with attention, the more you will come to understand its powerful *intention*. This would be the same as saying the more you work with any tarot energy, the more you understand the vastness of that particular card.

As you write or copy a hieroglyph in a notebook with your own hand, you inscribe the image into your own flesh. The more often you work with these symbols, the more you will expand your consciousness, your understanding of life, and your ability to create a life around yourself through your attention and intention. The magic is inherent in the hieroglyph itself and lives within you. In other words, each word written in hieroglyphs offers a world to be explored.

Drawing the glyph invites comparisons and a discovery of patterns coalesced around the images. For example, Sir Alan Gardiner's *Egyptian Grammar* demonstrates that there are more than seventy different bird hieroglyphs, and not all of them mean the same thing, nor does a single image mean the same thing every time it is repeated. Sometimes it is a sound, sometimes a symbol (determinative), sometimes a concept.

Saying the word aloud as you meditate activates the auditory pathways. It's a calling down of that energy being vocalized. Sound meditation can be an avenue for expanding our consciousness, especially when we pay attention to the vibrational patterns, the tones, the rhythms, and the musical intervals. The French mystic and symbolist R. A. Schwaller de Lubicz detailed the sound formulas used by the ancient Egyptians. He suggested that not every sound formula had an equivalent definite translation. Rather he believed that the magical, sacred utterances were intended to excite the nerve centers of the brain and body to create physiological and psychological effects. Sound healer Jill Mattson and the poet John Fox have similarly described words as medicine.

Meditating with the hieroglyphs can also have a healing effect on the practitioner. Simply saying the word creates within the speaker certain vibrational patterns that carry the energy of the chakra systems. Tonality and musicality of the spoken word all have their effects, which is no doubt why the ancients had hidden the vowel sounds from the uninitiated eye. Thus there is much dissension among scholars over the pronunciation of certain words. Is it *Re* (ray) or *Ra* (rah), for example? In my opinion (being the Southerner that I am), sound is also a cultural thing. We acclimate to the words of our mother tongue even in the womb.

Examine within yourself your purpose for wanting to learn to use hieroglyphs as part of a magical practice. There is a great deal of energy that has been built up over the millennia, surrounding the mysteries of Egypt, which people are endlessly fascinated by. As with any magical practice there may be benign motives behind their use as well as malevolent ones. As well, motives that are *unclear* may result in results that are not crystalline. Meditating on hieroglyphic cards can carry you along unexpected avenues.

Wanting to wield power over others has long been a part of Egyptian lore, of course, but it's an impure motive. Many Egyptian magical stories about such practices abound. It is not my purpose to take you there because of the types of soul energies that are attached to such practices. A good use of these hieroglyphs is for the unfoldment of the individual consciousness and the appearance of the solar angel. (Loosely defined, I see the solar angel as the incarnated soul's awareness of the nature and quality of its truest Self.) In my opinion, there is so much work that we have to do on ourselves that if we wish to progress our own souls, we have little time to waste in trying to manipulate others.

Meditative Practice Examples

- Copy your chosen hieroglyph over and over in a notebook—or better yet, on a piece of papyrus—to bring the sound into manifestation through the fingers. Saying the words and feeling the energy of that hieroglyph travel down your arm as you speak brings the lessons of the hieroglyph home. Repetition will assist in your understanding of the energies.
- Say the word *sahu* aloud and repeat it slowly as you meditate on it. The sibilant and breathy vocalization of it, which brings forth the energy of the ascended master or light beings, has a stimulating effect on our meditations. And it calls forth the divinity of that being.
- Meditate on a single word for ten minutes a day. Especially effective

just before bed or just after rising, this practice can help develop the neural pathways in the brain, aiding understanding of the concepts and making connections to the synchronicities of that image appearing in a reading, in a daily walk about town, or in a dream.

If you spent three days on each of the sixty words in this book, you would find yourself engaged in a six-month study of the medju neter. For meditation purposes, this provides enough time for initiation, development, and registration of your depth understanding of these hieroglyphs.

USE THE HIEROGLYPHS AS AN ORACLE

In my thirty years of working with the hieroglyphs, I began to see them as more than an abstract language suggesting thought processes. They became living expressions of divine energies, in the same way that tarot cards express universal energies. Some myths of the tarot tell us that they originated in Egypt. Although they were inspired by all things Egyptian, they did not begin there. Knowing that, I thought, why not create an oracle deck that *was* from Egypt, using those hieroglyphic images frequently found in papyri, temples, and tombs? There have been many Egyptian oracle decks featuring gods or goddesses, but few that used the hieroglyphs as the actual oracular language.

The sixty particular hieroglyphs presented in the following chapter came to mind; they were word images that began to float through my psyche and enter my dreams. One night I dreamed these same words were stitched inside a long flowing robe that I was wearing. The wind blew the coat open and the hieroglyphs tumbled out. I called that dream my dream of Prospero's coat.

According to some sources, there were more than two thousand names of gods and goddesses in the ancient world. It would be impossible to work with that many hieroglyphs or cards. The stories of the ancient gods and goddesses that are chosen here represent those that are more well-known and that highlight our own developing consciousness—the ups and downs of life, the psychological states of being through which we all must move and progress. When you draw a card that has a connection to a particular god or goddess, the aspects of that particular myth play a part in understanding the hieroglyph as well as the sign.

Cards that represent gods or goddesses, called neteru, act very much like trump cards in a regular tarot deck. They carry a certain transpersonal and psychological weight that is deep and multifaceted. Occasionally problematic cards arise, such as the hieroglyph for Set, a neter, or the hieroglyphs for the word *khat* or *arit*. Hieroglyphic oracles, however, never predict a devastating circumstance without offering advice as to how to deal with it, or how to move through the obstacle. Reading the hieroglyphs in combination with a secondary glyph helps to fully integrate its message.

Hopefully you've sketched the hieroglyphs already in an effort to familiarize yourself with them. I now suggest that you create an oracle deck from the sixty hieroglyphs presented in this book. To do this, I suggest that you draw each glyph on papyrus, if you can, or on card stock (blank index cards would work well too). Copy them by hand. Then study the oracle hieroglyphs as you hold each card, imbuing it with your energy and deepening your own understanding of its multiple meanings. (Some meanings are articulated later in the book, beginning on page 41.) If you prefer not to draw the oracle cards yourself, you can purchase a deck of hieroglyphic oracle cards. Information on how to order is provided at the back of this book.

INVOKE THE HIEROGLYPHS WHEN YOU DREAM

Ancient Egyptians had the same fascination with dreams that we do. Indeed, they utilized dream guides, dream omens, dream divination, and books of dream interpretation. The hieroglyphs *rswt* and *qed,* depicted as an open eye and a bed, referred to dreams. The words meant to come awake or become enlightened within the sleep state—in other words, lucid dreaming. The Coffin Texts equate sleep and death in this spell for a safe passage into the afterlife: "O sleeper, turnabout in this place which you do not know, but I know it."[2]

During sleep the ba soul travels through the astral realm. This human-headed hawk floats above the sleeping body, goes where it will at night, and returns in the morning. This realm of sleep was considered similar to the halls of the underworld that the soul walked after death. One of the magical tales of Khaemwast and his son Si-Osire depicts them as two ba souls flying together into the duat to see what happens after death. Their journey is similar to the parable Jesus provides in Luke 16:19–26 about the rich man and the eye of the needle, and the poor Lazarus entering the underworld, meeting their fates after death.

Not just once but many times Khaemwast and his son Si-Osire travel about in their dream bodies, becoming the archetypes for future dreamworkers to engage in shamanic flight and conscious dream travel. The priests and priestesses who followed such practices operated as remote viewers, telepaths, seers, sibyls, and shamans who established mental telepathy between distant temple centers and the palace. Like trained CIA operatives, they engaged in operations to secure the borders of Egypt.

Not only were high priests "equipped" souls in the astral realm, but so must the pharaoh be equipped with heka because he was a divine son and considered the highest of high priests. If one became initiated into the Egyptian mysteries it was necessary to enter the astral realm in a deep, shamanic, and occult state that allowed one to see clearly. Being conscious in the workaday world is not necessarily the way to understand symbols. Rather, through the lens of the dream, when the waking, rational mind can be circumnavigated, the depth qualities of the imaginal reveal themselves. Initiates entered a dream-induced trance in order to contact the sahu and the akhu of their ancestors and the neteru. With the divine plan downloaded in their dream state, the awakened individual might be able to bring up the powerful messages that lay in the depths of the psyche, and in the depths of the anima mundi. (More information on shamanic flight and the ancient Egyptians appears in *Shamanic Wisdom in the Pyramid Texts* by Jeremy Naydler.)

Most Egyptian temples, especially those dedicated to Amen in the New Kingdom, employed priests as dream interpreters (so-called masters of secret things) for the service of healing. Individuals traveled to the oracle temples attended by priestly dream interpreters and slept inside the temple on a dream bed. These temple priests helped one to contact a loved one in spirit during their dreams and they interpreted any messages from the gods. A collection of Greco-Roman dream spells provided herbal recipes, rituals, and invocations to the dream deities.

The dream book of Qenherkhepshef, a priest from the Valley of the Kings community, contained 108 ancient Egyptian dream interpretations. These were categorized as being either auspicious or inauspicious dreams. Much of the interpretation had to do with the punning quality of a dream image. For example, dreaming of a man on a donkey doesn't seem to be a fortuitous dream until one realizes that the words for "greatness" and "donkey" were similar. Why? Because in ancient times, important people rode into town on animals rather than walking.

It is not unusual for those who have travelled to Egypt to return with Egyptian imagery instilled in their dream lives. This comes as no surprise. Collectively the ancient Egyptians lived with these symbols and meanings for well over three thousand years. Surely those images have been imprinted upon the collective psyche and are readily available to any who wish to use them.

The most important work of an oracular priestess or priest was to be able to "dream true," or to have precognizant or clear dreams. The ancient Egyptians called it *ir-ma'a,* meaning "clear sight" or "true vision." You can practice techniques for dreaming true. For instance, you might sleep with a hieroglyph (written on papyrus or card stock) tucked beneath your pillow. Be careful of the card you decide to use. Choose it with utter clarity of intention. In your dreamtime, unless you are a well-accomplished lucid dreamer, you have less control over the visitations from ethereal beings who might see your calling card laid out plainly and decide to drop in to see what's up. Not every entity wandering about on the astral plane has spiritual illumination as its intention.

Before actually choosing the card ir-ma'a as your dream intention, work with the neter to whom you feel most bonded and secure. Thoth and Isis initially came with me on my nightly sojourns, then Sekhmet and Anubis. Sekhmet and Anubis make for strong protectors in the astral landscape of the dream. The lion goddess Sekhmet and the dog god Anubis can keep you safe from spirit entities surfing the astral plane. I also recommend them as protectors of the bedrooms of children who experience nightmares.

Once you have made a strong contact with a dream guide, such as Seshet, Isis, or Thoth, you might ask for specific images to explore in your waking meditations. Or you could request synchronicities to inform your work with a particular hieroglyph. Ask your dream guide to begin showing you images.

One can see then that dreaming of hieroglyphs and their associated symbols can be an important way of receiving oracular information. Of course, the implicit meaning will differ for each individual. As you work with these hieroglyphs you will continue to accrue deeper levels of meaning for each symbol. That is why keeping a dream journal is the best way to receive the fullest oracular messages from your dream guardians and guides.

I highly recommend the dreamwork practices outlined by my former teacher, the late Jeremy Taylor, in his books *Dream Work* and *The Living Labyrinth*. These transpersonal psychology books complement the completely shamanic and creative approach to dreamwork in *The Dreamer's Book of the Dead* and *Dreaming the Soul Back Home* by dream teacher Robert Moss. In particular Moss offers techniques for dream recall, dream intention, dream recovery, and lucid dreaming. All of these techniques offer ample opportunities to take hieroglyphic images that appear in dreams and explore them in depth over a lifetime.

ENGAGE IN RITUAL WORK WITH THE HIEROGLYPHS

When working to invoke the deities of a particular place or pantheon, one might place the neteru cards only on an altar in order to invoke the energies of particular deities. (See below for lists of the neteru families.) Or one might wish to incise a candle in the particular color of a god or goddess. For example, you may wish to invoke Nut and the energy of her fecund cosmos by writing or inscribing her name on or into an indigo seven-day candle, and the energy of her partner, Geb, the Earth, on or into a green or sand-colored candle. You can also incise the hieroglyphs in clay tiles, which is another very effective way to communicate with their energies.

These "glyph families" will usually appear in threes. They include a god, a goddess, and (often) a child. Sometimes there appear to be no progeny, but typically there are three energies; two that work together to create a third. Some of these divine beings have stories that intersect with those of other gods or goddesses. The families of the neteru are:

Kheper—Ra—Atum: one being with three aspects of the solar energy in Heliopolis

Nut—Geb: the polarity of Heaven and Earth and male and female principles in Heliopolis

Osiris—Isis—Horus: primary agricultural family of father, mother, and child

Set—Nephthys—Anubis: secondary hunter-gatherer family

Hathor—Horus: lover and beloved, primarily in Dendera

Ptah—Sekhmet—Nefertum: creative triad of Memphis and Karnak

Thoth—Seshet—Ma'at: cosmological origin of universe in Hermopolis

Other particular hieroglyphs offer symbols representing the spiritual bodies of the ancient Egyptians. These operate with energies similar to the sephiroth of the Qabalistic Tree of Life. (See the Djed Pillar Reading on page 269 for a more complete image of how the energy moves up and down the Tree of Life.) These ten bodies operate on four planes of existence: the material, the astral or etheric, the mental, and the spiritual. One body appears at each sephira; they operate as spheres of life force energy. The upper sephiroth are primarily spiritual, acquiring more density in form as the energy descends from the top to the bottom of the tree. The lower spheres can be seen from the earth plane, vibrating at higher and less dense frequencies as they move upward. Each could be understood as developing states of consciousness as the individual grows in spirit. The very bottom physical sphere represents the living container for all of the other nine states of consciousness above it.

Ancient Egyptian magician-healers understood that all is vibration and that the frequency of vibration determined the form of spiritual matter. As we work with these bodies,* we understand how the body is a temple for the spiritual states of being; that is, it is the abode of the invited divine being.

> The bodies in the upper spiritual plane—*ka, ba,* and *khu*— correspond to Kether, Chokmah, and Binah.
> The bodies in the mental plane—*ren, sekhem,* and *ab*—correspond to Chesed, Geburah, and Tiperath.
> The bodies in the emotional or astral plane—*sahu, khaibit,* and *khat*—correspond to Netzach, Hod, and Yesod.
> The nine astral, mental, and spiritual bodies coalesce into one physical vessel—*aufu*—which corresponds to Malkuth.

One meditative ritual practice might involve having a friend help you draw an outline around your body with a crayon as you lie on a long roll of bulletin board paper. Next draw the ten sephiroth of the Tree of Life and their hieroglyphs on the corresponding points of your body: kether/akh at the top of the head; chokmah/ba at the right ear and binah/ka at the left ear; chesed/ren at the right shoulder and geburah/ sekhem at the left shoulder; tiperath/ib at the heart; netzach/sahu at the right hipbone and yod/khaibit at the left hipbone; yesod/khat at the genitals; and, finally, malkuth/aufu beneath the feet. You may wish

---

*Deeper details on the Qabalistic Tree of Life and the corresponding meanings and appearances of the spiritual bodies of the ancient Egyptians appear in part 2 of my book *Dreams of Isis.*

to lie down upon the drawn hieroglyphs and feel into each one of them, or simply place the hieroglyphic card upon your body as you meditate on how the hieroglyph feels there. Sometimes after a deep meditation it feels important to begin to draw silently on the body, telling your life story as connected to a particular sephira or glyph in words or images.

CREATE AMULETS TO ACCESS THE HIEROGLYPHS' HEALING POWER

Yet another level of interpreting the hieroglyphs involves their use as healing amulets. Probably the most well-known emblem of divine protection and the most copied amulet of the ancient Egyptians is the wadjet, known as the Eye of Horus. It originates in the story of the wounded eye of the god Horus, which had been gouged out by Set during battle and healed by the love of the goddess Hathor. (See the description of this glyph in the next chapter for more of that story.)

It is not uncommon for me to be lecturing somewhere and later, quietly and shyly, be shown the wadjet hieroglyphs tattooed across a woman's chest as a healing amulet after her mastectomy. I have also been shown the outstretched wings of Isis spread across the back of one in need of her protection after an accident or an attack.

In the ancient world craftsmen shaped amulets of faience, gemstone, or metal for various purposes, including protection of the dead, conception of children, healing of illnesses, protection of houses, growth of crops, ritual music-making, divination, and, of course, as beloved offerings to the gods or goddesses. My own altar contains a magic wand of hollow copper that contains specific amulets, sands from Egypt, gemstones and crystals, as well as prayers written on strips of papyrus. The hollow tube has been hermetically sealed. Just as women in the ancient world did, I have created chalices and cups for holy water. These chalices are decorated with the hieroglyphs of the goddess Isis as Sopdet, the god Hapi, and the hieroglyph zep tepi to bring to it the energy of the inundation and the creation of the world in the beginning.

Grave goods often contained marvelous amulets, many of which were wrapped within the mummy linens to facilitate spiritual healing in those locations where incisions had been made to the body during the embalming process. Every mummy was buried with the ubiquitous scarab placed over the heart. On the back of it were incised words from the Book of the Dead, known as the Negative Confession. These words magically protected the heart as Anubis weighed it on the scales of ma'at in the neterworld.

Given the frequently fraught and harried lives we lead in this modern world, and especially in times of difficulty, it makes sense to invest one's energy into carving in wood or stone a scarab whose underbelly at the very least bears one's name in a cartouche, accompanied by words of protection. As you read on in this book you will learn more about the words you might wish to use and place inside the elongated shen emblem, that is, the cartouche.

In brief, you may wish to study the following hieroglyphs for use in healing and ritual.

Ankh: supply of life force energy and abundance
Djed: stability of the spine, the body, or a situation
Hotep: peace and sustenance in community
Ib: attaining desires; strengthening the heart and emotions
Kheper (dung beetle): emotional protection during transitions
Sekhem: willpower and strength; healing on all levels
Shen: angelic and divine physical protection; setting boundaries
Wadjet (the eye): healing, protection, and clarity on all levels
Waz: mastery of a physical block or interference

Shaman-healers often wrote healing prescriptions for individual ailments on the arms of the one who was ill. The magical charm was written in a medicinal ink made from crushed healing herbs or plants that was then painted onto the patient's skin. Once the patient completed the recitation of this healing prayer to Isis or Thoth or Sekhmet, he or she licked off the magic spell, ingesting the healing potion. It was the combination of thought and medicine that healed.

Anyone wishing to use amulets for healing should consider reading the books *Practical Egyptian Magic* by Murry Hope and *Isis Magic* by M. Isadora Forrest, as well as *Sekhmet* by Nicki Scully. It would be redundant for me to recite all of the valuable advice in these books here.

USE NUMBER MAGIC TO BROADEN YOUR UNDERSTANDING OF HIEROGLYPHS

Around 520 BCE, Pythagoras, a young man from the Greek island of Samos, was mad for understanding the mysteries of the ancient world. He wandered Egypt for twenty-two years, determined to pry from the lips of its priests the secret magic of temples and hieroglyphs. His persistence eventually paid off. Through Pythagoras we moderns come to understand geometry, mathematics, and astronomy in the same ways that the ancient Egyptians did.

Pythagoras wandered temple complexes in the Land of Khem, staring at hieroglyphs that he could not yet read. In the hypostyle halls he sat gazing up at what must have felt like the waters at the dawn of Creation itself. Patterns on papyrus column after papyrus column repeated with slight variations, but the cosmic rhythm was apparent to his emotional body, if not yet to his mind. He gazed longingly upon the temples the same way one might gaze upon the stars at night—noticing their eternal presence and their changing vibrations. He gazed agape at the hieroglyphs he could not decipher. *What am I seeing?* he wondered.

The priests, it was said, often laughed at the traveler standing wide-eyed and agog. After a time they sent the foreigner away empty-handed. When he begged to be taught how to read hieroglyphs, they told him to go to this other Temple of Thoth (in some far-off city) and study with those priests. So Pythagoras set out for the distant city of Hermopolis. One day, finding Pythagoras wandering through their temple, again staring at hieroglyphs, the priests of Thoth told him to go to the Temple of Amen (in Luxor, yet a further distance away) and study there. Thus,

Pythagoras went from temple to temple and from priesthood to priesthood because he desperately wanted to know the meaning of these magical writings. Finally the priests of Ptah in Memphis and Heliopolis were instructed by the pharaoh himself to stop shuffling responsibility to another temple, and just teach Pythagoras the meaning of the hieroglyphs.

What Pythagoras learned, he learned "mouth to ear," the way real initiates learn the mysteries—that is, through oral transmission. The most important requirement of such teaching is being able to listen and to intuit. None of these teachings were written down (other than being represented by the written hieroglyphs themselves). Pythagoras, himself a teacher in the mystery schools of Greece many years later, taught his students by way of the oral tradition. Nothing of his teachings were written down. His philosophy survives because the students of his students took notes, which were passed on. Some thirty years after his sojourn Pythagoras taught the hermetic principle that "All is number."

He returned to the Greek island of Samos where he'd been born and began his school of philosophy, cosmology, alchemy, astrology, music, harmony, geometry, mathematics, and mysticism. What we know of Pythagorean temple teachings we have read in the works of Plato, Aristotle, Diogenes, Porphyry, Iamblichus, and others.

The ancient Qabalistic practice of converting words into numbers is demonstrated in particular in the Book of Numbers, but also throughout the Hebrew scriptures. The chapters and verses of various books emphasize particular spiritual qualities. The use of recurring numbers as quantities also holds deep significance. For example, the forty days and nights that Christ spent in the desert, the forty days and nights that Moses spent on Mount Sinai, and the forty days Elijah fasted without food or water appear as signposts of each individual's initiation. The number forty becomes a numerical symbol of trial and testing. Forty refers to the manifestation of the enigmatic god principle (zero) as it enacts the foundation and formation (four) of matter and life experience.

Gematria, as it was called, may actually be *Khem-matria,* the matter of numbers that Jewish scholars learned from the Egyptians. The word *gematria* itself indicates that the origins of this mystical tradition came from Khem (or Gem), meaning the "Land of Egypt." Geometry and gematria are linked. Architecture and number, as demonstrated in Egyptian temple structure, creates spiritual resonance through the use of proportion. Although gematria has been attributed to the Assyrian, Babylonian, and Greek empires, most likely the study came from those Jews who lived in Egypt prior to the great Diaspora. Primarily, this means Moses, the reputed author of the Pentateuch, who was raised a son of the pharaoh and trained in the temple as an Egyptian initiate of the mysteries. When they left Egypt, the Jews and Moses took with them the temple wisdom of gematria and geometry. In the same way, later Greek philosophers carried the hermetic knowledge out of Egypt and copied it down in their history books.

One of the things that became apparent to me while working with the hieroglyphs is that each word has a power and aspect all its own, which can be qualified by a number placed in conjunction with the glyph. Those numbers can be acquired and applied in differing ways. For example, if you are giving a card reading to a person whose birthday you know, you can add the month and day together to find their birth path and then read the hieroglyph description with the birth path number—a number usually between one and nine.

How the Ancient Egyptians Used Numbers

Let's look briefly at how the Egyptians used numerology. First there was no zero per se. There was an ouroboros named Mehen, a great serpent coiled into a circle, which had swallowed its tail. Basically Mehen was the god force depicted as the beginning and the end, the alpha and the omega of the Egyptian pantheon. It may be connected to the idea of creation and the hieroglyph nefer. Some Egyptologists believe the word *nefer,* which means "beautiful," looks like an upside-down penis or a cross surmounting a circle. During the Thirteenth Dynasty of the Middle Kingdom, the *nef* hieroglyph was used as a zero in accounting sheets. However, one can argue that nothing can come from nothing and into that zero is placed the tail of the serpent—or the numeral one. The nef works simply as a placeholder or an indication of the next level to the number. In numerology, the number ten is counted as $1 + 0 = 1$. So we are back to the original number one.

1 • All numbers and all spiritual matters derive from the unity of the One, of God Supernal. The unity of the One is perfect, eternal, and undifferentiated consciousness. It is the thing itself. A single line beneath the sun disk becomes the name of the sun god Ra, or light itself.

2 • The One and the Other become the polarized energies of divinity, the law of polarity, and the law of cause and effect. All things exist in pairs. There is no doorway through which to pass unless two pillars stand in opposition on either side to create the doorframe. Duality combines male and female, negative and positive, light and dark. All life, according to the mystical equations of Thoth, evolves from a divine pairing of opposites. Egypt was known as the Two Lands: the fertile Black Land of Osiris and the Red Land, or desert, of Set. Heaven and Earth are unified oppositions. Another way of saying that would be "As above, so below; as within, so without."

Life is impossible without the notion of duality. Two strands of the twisted chain of DNA combine in the same way that there are two sides to the ladder of heaven held up by Horus and Set in the Pyramid Text. These paired opposites unite to create a deeper expanded consciousness. The mystery of the *djeba,* or twin souls, speaks of how the gods Osiris and Ra combine in the underworld, in the psyche, and in the spiritual alchemy of life and death.

3 • The metaphysical role of the Trinity is recognized in nearly every religion. Certainly the Christian idea of Trinity is based in the Trinity of the God, the Goddess—in this case the Virgin Mary—and the Holy Child. Most commonly the Egyptians honored that Trinity as Osiris, Isis, and Horus, but every ancient Egyptian theological center had its own trinity. The spiritual relationship of love that occurs between masculine and feminine, or spirit and matter,

reconciles what exists in opposition. That is the creative force of the universe. Any time a word is written to indicate its spiritual generative properties, its hieroglyph shows three seeds. For example, seeds next to the hieroglyphs for truth, or ma'at, mean that truth is sometimes more than one thing.

4 • The four elements of air, fire, water, and earth represent the foundation for understanding the cosmos. In Thoth's heavenly cauldron of creation four principalities bubbled: infinite space, infinite time, infinite darkness, and infinite light. In the physical world they appeared as the four pillars that held up the sky in the four directions. They represented four sacred centers of spiritual life assimilated on Earth. Called the Four Sons of Horus, they were: Hapi, the hamadryas baboon who protected the lungs; Imsety, the human god who protected the liver; Duamutef, the jackal protector of the stomach; and Qebehsenuef, the falcon who protected the intestines.

5 • All human beings exist simultaneously on Earth and in Heaven as the five-pointed star soul in the belly of the sky goddess Nut. She and her husband, the earth god Geb, birthed five divine children: Osiris, Horus the Elder, Set, Isis, and Nephthys. These five spirit children manifested in earthly form as deities and as the first earthly humans. Five is the intermediary number between one and nine. Five was considered a number of destiny, for it was the ideal of the realized man to become a star in the company of Ra. In Hymn 467 of the Pyramid Text of Unas the soul returning to his heavenly home proclaims, "Here I am, O Ra . . . I am a soul, a star of gold."[3]

The five-pointed star, or pentacle, warded off evil. The number five appears as our five fingers. Indeed, the Pythagoreans showed one the open palm of the hand as the symbol of the power of five to ward off the evil eye. Because of its importance the pentad was used as a secret sign among the Pythagoreans, enabling them to distinguish themselves and recognize other members. Directly related to the geometrical importance of divine proportion and related to the value of phi (Φ), the image of the pentacle is found in nature's leaves and flowers. The Greeks believed each point of the pentad represented an element, and the all-important fifth element—the idea.

6 • The cube became the model for time and space. A cube requires six directions: up and down, backward and forward, left and right. When pharaohs and their queens are shown as Divine, they appear seated upon a cube that placed them squarely at the juncture of mind and matter. The temple in Egypt is also viewed as a cube of space, which is the model of the universe. In addition, time is divided into quantities of six. An hour is sixty minutes long; the minute is sixty seconds long.

7 • The union of spirit and matter (3 + 4) is 7. A pyramid sits on the ground with a square base symbolizing the four elements. Its triangular sides symbolize the trinity of Spirit. There are seven chapels honoring seven deities in the Temple of Osiris at Abydos. There are seven Pleiades, seven petals in Seshet's headdress, and seven Hathors. The seven Hathors are the musicians at the Temple of Isis and the fairy godmothers who attend every Egyptian birth. Seven becomes idealized and represents perfected spiritual attainment in the Egyptian system.

8 • In her essay on genesis and number, Lucie Lamy, the stepdaughter of alchemist R. A. Schwaller de Lubicz and the daughter of Egyptologist Isha Schwaller de Lubicz, identifies the properties of the numerical stanzas of the Creation Hymn to Amen at Medinet Habu.[4] Stanza 80 of Thoth's myth recounted in his temple in Hermopolis describes how the Ogdoad, or the primary eight divine essences, mysteriously came into existence. The text identifies the progenitor as Atum. It reads: "First I was one, then I was two, then I was four, then I was eight; then I was one again."

This mantra was uttered in Thoth's cauldron by the Ogdoad, those eight paired gods and goddesses who represent darkness, time, space, and light. The number eight provided the Egyptian magician with the magic and mystery necessary to create matter out of cosmic, spiritual substance. The eight beings become the chain of DNA with its four paired chromosomes. It emulates the way a fertilized egg cell divides and multiplies to create life in the womb of the mother, just as it did in the great cauldron of Thoth. Therefore, eight—a lemniscate on its side—suggests eternity, secrecy, mystery, and incredible powers of organization.

9 • The Ennead represents a family of nine gods and goddesses who oversee life on Earth. The identities of these deities sometimes vary, but they always represent three trinities of creative gods, goddesses, and their offspring. For example: Nut, Geb, and Ra; Osiris, Isis, and Horus; Set, Nephthys, and Anubis. The most popular representation of the Ennead begins with the god Atum, who is both male and female. He becomes Shu and Tefnut, who are then joined by Geb and Nut, creating air, fire, earth, and water. These give rise to the two pairs Isis and Osiris and Set and Nephthys. Nine marks the transition from one scale of numbers to a higher scale of numbers using two digits, beginning with ten, when the holy child Horus enters the picture after nine months of gestation.

Use Numerology as the Ancient Egyptians Did

Numerology, per se, was never meant to be used to foretell the future, because time is always what is happening in the present. The law of cause and effect indicates that actions taken now determine what will be. So number magic provided more or less a philosophical understanding of the meaning of a symbol and its varying influences on us at different times.

Say, for example, you wish to quickly glimpse the particular energy of a particular day. You might determine the number of the month and day (August 27, for instance: $8 + 2 + 7 = 17$, which is reduced to 8). Then drawing one hieroglyph, say heka, you could look at the eighth point of interpretation and see that August 27 would be a marvelous day to use your magic and ritual to restore the balance of Heaven and Earth by bringing peace to a difficult situation. The practice of compassion and forgiveness are advised (see pages 106–7).

Another way to use the hieroglyphic gematria, when reading for someone else, is to determine that person's life path by adding up the numbers of the month and day of their birth. Note that only the month and day are used—not the birth year. For example, my birthday is September 24. My numbers are 9 + 2 + 4 = 15. The number 15 is reduced to reach the final number: 1 + 5 = 6. No matter what card I draw from a deck or stack of hieroglyphs, the six number will always be a reflection of the hieroglyph's energy for me. If I ask a question, such as "How do I gracefully move out of a restricting situation?" and I draw to myself a blank papyrus card, then the answer lies in emptiness. I pause, my mind blank. I sit. I wait for the first thought to arise. In the emptiness of my mind I see a bubble rise to the surface. I know that numerologically six is about being in relationship and also about healing oneself and others through the energy of spirit above and earth below. Imagine a six-pointed star, the Star of David; one triangle of healing points upward, while the other points downward. This is a perfect image of as above, so below. Being in the stillpoint of that Star of David between the two triangles is standing within the chrysalis of energy awaiting transformation. My intuition tells me then that I may want to pay attention to what my body needs to move out of the situation. A purge may be needed. I might also need to return to a balance point with another individual. Blank suggests to me listening rather than acting.

When you work with these hieroglyphs, ask yourself how this symbol, and any associated number, may be used to their highest capacity to increase the quality of your life journey. Conversely, how might this particular symbol and number negatively hold you back?

Each individual hieroglyph has its own number, which is dependent on its spelling and which will open up a deeper understanding. I worked with this information intuitively using the traditional spellings for the hieroglyphic words, as well as offering some alternative spellings. The reason I alternately explored the Greek, Roman, Old Kingdom, and sometimes New Kingdom spellings of the ancient words is because I believe language is fluid. Over time, environments change and even commonly used words develop alternative definitions and meanings. Words with similarly intended meanings in differing languages often show slightly different colorations. The Greek Isis differed from the ancient Egyptian Ast. We can discover these differences by comparing their names through numerology.

For example, the Greek Isis (9 + 1 + 9 + 1 = 20) is a goddess of divine partnership. Throughout the Greco-Roman world she is primarily seen as a partner, even a savior, of Osiris, and a mother to Horus. She becomes defined as mother and wife, which is the nature of the number two. In the ancient Egyptian world she holds an altogether different energy. Sometimes the Egyptians call her Ast (1 + 1 + 2 = 4). Her name literally means "the throne," upon which her child, the pharaoh, sat. Four in numerology suggests a solid foundation, the building of a culture upon natural law and principles. Ast is "the Goddess," not some whimsical femme fatale. Sometimes her name was spelled Auset (1 + 3 + 1 + 5 + 2 = 12 = 3). The number three suggests that this divine feminine is the creative matrix implying the mother's womb. Lady Isis is "She of Ten Thousand Names" and qualities—her many epithets and names alone could be a study of the numerical meaning of her many names.

Other Ways to Use Numerology with the Hieroglyphs

One can use the numbers that accompany the hieroglyphs in this text in several ways. Seven layouts appear at the back of this book; they are based on images from Egyptian hieroglyph and myth. Perhaps you wish to use a familiar Celtic Cross Reading. In that case, you may read the meaning of each hieroglyph with regard to the position in which it falls; the positions are numbered one through nine. When a card falls in the tenth position, then read the meaning associated with the number one (10 = 1 + 0 = 1), and—because zero is the reflection of god-force energy—add an emphasis on the spiritual meaning of that position. (Perhaps the best way to think of zero numerologically is to see it as a lens that creates a focal point of god energy onto matter, like the center of a magnifying glass.) In an astrological reading, like the one that appears in the Dendera Zodiac Layout, likewise interpret the readings of the houses according to the number, with houses ten, eleven, and twelve being reduced to one, two, and three respectively.

As mentioned above, when I give one-draw card readings, I ask the person to provide me with their birthdate. The month and day added together will suggest the highest vibration of their birth path this lifetime. Knowing their birth path will suggest to me which numbered interpretation of the hieroglyph may be appropriate to discuss. Or perhaps you wish to use the numerology of your name, or your personal year, to find which aspect of the hieroglyph resonates most closely with you. To determine the personal year, add the birth path number to the number for the current year. For example, the year 2020 is a four year (2 + 0 + 2 + 0 = 4). So you would add the number 4 to the birth path to find the personal year.

A FINAL CAVEAT

On occasion I have received disparaging comments about the Christian themes and tones that sometimes appear in my books. You will find a few of these Christian references here. In my opinion, truth is more than one thing. (See the hieroglyph ma'at, for instance.) My inclusion of these themes and motifs is only objectionable to those who do not understand that the "Gentiles" of the Christian scriptures appear as the early Christians because the belief systems of the Essenes (initiates) and pagan (ancient Egyptian priests and scientists, mathematicians, et al.) were co-opted. The gnostic gospels are, in fact, very Egyptian, and the Eastern Orthodox Christian religion, especially the Coptic faith, has its roots in ancient Egypt.

"Why does this seem so foreign to people?" my tour guide friend Noura asked, and then responded to her own question: "The Jews and the ancient Egyptians lived side by side for eons. Jesus and his family hid in Egypt when he was an infant. He ate his first meal and drank his first water in Egypt. He took his first steps in Egypt."

A few Jewish friends have questioned my use of Qabalah with the Egyptian hieroglyphs, finding this upsetting because their people were enslaved by the Egyptians. Frankly, Moses learned a great deal from Egypt. And I suspect that as the purported author of Genesis, Exodus, and the Pentateuch, the Egyptian influence on him explains why Christian and Jewish creation stories are so similar to Egyptian creation stories. The many crossovers into the Hebrew scriptures as well as the Christian scriptures verify that those religions learned a great deal of the mystery religion of their adopted homeland, then took it on as their own after they left. The archaeology of Elephantine Island, where Jewish and Egyptian temples to similar deities are found, is sufficient proof that there was such an overlap.

I think that my citation of Egyptian, Christian, Jewish, Islamic, and even Hindu similarities to alphabets and meanings is completely justified.

That said, it's up to you to find the appropriate ways to use these hieroglyphs. They are an open door to an ancient cosmology and, as such, are replete with multiple meanings for you to interpret and benefit from as you will.

THE HIEROGLYPHS

WORDS OF POWER

I began writing the oracle descriptions in this chapter after a few months of meditation about the matter, several related dreams, and some encouragement from my spirit guides. Students began to ask if I would teach them the hieroglyphs and I said, "No. There are too many of them, but I will teach you hieroglyphic thinking." I began to teach classes in hieroglyphic thinking, showing my students my papyrus slips. Thus was born the use of hieroglyphs as oracles. But truly, I can't really say these are *my* inventions. The Egyptians were using the hieroglyphs as dream oracles for three or four thousand years before I began to teach them. The particular use of them as described herein, however, and the descriptions that follow, are my own.

As outlined in the previous chapter, there are a number of ways to use these hieroglyphs. Before you begin, as with any oracle deck or magical tool, I recommend that you get in touch with the power of each word image. Sit with your chosen hieroglyph in meditation. Invoke Thoth, author of the hermetic wisdom of the Emerald Tablet, to be with you. Invoke the goddess Seshet, keeper of the records, to be with you. See yourself standing before her library, the per ankh, which the priest-scribes called the house of life. Ask her permission to receive the wisdom scroll of one particular hieroglyph so that, one at a time, you can study each hieroglyph in meditation.

Invite the divinities Sia, Hu, and Heka to stand with you as you study. They are the gods of insight, utterance, and magic whose presence attended world creation. You might even begin by choosing one of these three hieroglyphs to acquaint yourself with. Gaze upon the image, then close your eyes and see your chosen hieroglyph projecting itself from the back of your head to a movie screen behind your closed eyelids.

Hold the image steady and breathe it in deeply three times. Then breathe it out, articulating the word again three times. Additional images may arise as you practice this exercise. You might find the words become like flames, or you may find that the hieroglyphs become enlivened and move about. Work with them in whatever way they show themselves to you. If you plan to spend hours working with the cards, it might be wise to draw your own oracle cards, or incise the hieroglyphs in clay tiles, as mentioned previously in this book.

About the Imagery

I invited photographer Amy Auset Rohn to accompany me to Egypt and through its temples, to take photographs of the images on their walls. She actually went back a second time in order to get some additional images that we needed.

Frankly it was pretty hard to take consistent photographs in a way that would make all of the artwork look similar: some of the images were incised and some were bas relief, so they didn't always match. And some of the writing in the images was inscribed in granite, which is hard to carve but long-lasting. Other hieroglyphs had been carved into sandstone, which is very soft and disintegrates more easily.

In any event, we ended up with a span of hieroglyphs that dated from 2640 BCE to 300 BCE. Temples dating back that far had become dilapidated, and as a result, the stone surfaces of some of the glyphs had become uneven, parts of them had flaked off, and some of the glyphs were scratched, having been purposely mutilated. A second problem was that, over the course of four thousand years, the style of the hieroglyphic language itself and the writing of it had changed. In terms of an American analogy, look at the English script that was used to document the Declaration of Independence in which the letter s looks like the letter f throughout.

Given all of this, it was problematic to make the hieroglyphs stylistically consistent. In other words, the glyphs did not present as having a mechanized typescript, similar to the typescript that is featured in books by E. A. Wallis Budge, Alan Gardiner, R. O. Faulkner, or any other number of Egyptologists. Therefore it became necessary to hire a graphic designer, Meg Wolsiffer, to pull together the broken pieces of the hieroglyphs presented here and manipulate the images so that they appeared to be whole—at least as whole as they had been when they were originally created.

Additionally, Lexy Hovis drew the hieroglyphs to use as her own oracle deck and she has kindly let us use those images in this book so that readers can see how to draw the images themselves. The photos and line drawings do not always match each other exactly. They are sometimes examples of variant spellings; for example, the way we spell *catalog* and *catalogue,* or *color* and *colour.* Egypt was greatly influenced by other cultures throughout its history. There were especially novel ways of writing words when the Greeks added the sounds of their mother tongue in the Ptolemaic temples.

What follows is a brief explanation of each of the sixty hieroglyphs, as well as nine associated points/interpretations of each one. They're provided in order to solidify your understanding of each respective hieroglyph. Note that the nine definitions may be used to enhance the meaning of a reading through the use of numerology as discussed on pages 29–36.

AKH

Hieroglyphs have been called the language of birds. Indeed, fifty-four bird images appear in the hieroglyphic sign list of renowned British Egyptologist Sir Alan Gardiner. The importance of birds may be that the winged ones are our closest emissaries to heaven and take the form of spirit messengers, even as the gods and goddesses often appear winged. Birds link our waking life with our dreaming life, our imagination to our daily world.

To the ancients, the crested Egyptian ibis appeared black, with a pronounced curved beak and stork-like legs. According to the Greek historian Herodotus, in the spring the ibis rose up against those winged serpents that were trying to invade Egypt.[1] The sacred ibis, *Threskiornis aethiopicus,* which was white with a bald head and neck, honored the bird form of Thoth. Another species of ibis, *Plegadis falcinellus,* appeared black and iridescent, with a radiant headdress or crest. The Egyptians—seeing this bird as a symbol of magic, healing, and protection—equated it with the akh.

Sometimes the akh bird is linked to the myth of the phoenix (also called the *bennu*), which was a large bird, perhaps a heron. Two long feathers protruded from the crown of its head. At other times a sun disk appears atop its head, indicating the first appearance of the sun when it rose from the Earth mound after the Flood at the dawn of Creation. Thus began time, and thus is this same bird likewise associated with the god Thoth who measures the hours and the days, and keeps an account of the cycles of moons, suns, and stars. In order to teach the magical arts, Thoth took on the form of the akh bird. So revered were these birds that the Serapeum in the ancient necropolis of Saqqara contained one and a half million of them, all of which were mummified.

Herodotus went on to say that the phoenix came from Arabia carrying its father's body embalmed in an egg of myrrh. This bird exhibited brilliant gold-and-red plumage. It built a nest of incense twigs in the ancient city of Heliopolis and from the ashes of its old body, it emerged transformed.[2] The akh bird was thus associated with Osiris; its curved beak was said to penetrate the heart of the god, thus leading to his resurrected state. An alchemical symbol of transformation, death, and rebirth the phoenix was never or very rarely found in Egypt. Apparently, again according to Herodotus, the bird returned to the ashes of its nest every five hundred years—although, he says, he had never seen one, except in paintings.[3]

To dream of a phoenix or an akh may indicate the need to leave "the little self" behind because that is a self we have outgrown. In the ancient world becoming "akh-effective" meant to do a meritorious work that lasted, such as building a temple or monument, or to defend those who were weaker and less fortunate—for example, elders and children.

Akh begins in initiation through incarnation and becomes the highest and most perfected of the spiritual bodies. As our highest self, it draws from the inexhaustible splendor and abundance of the universal mind to provide us with everything that the heart, body, and soul need. Akh is the goal, but it is not easily attained.

The Egyptian Book of the Dead contained a chapter on the transformation into an akh bird. This chapter guided one in attaining the luminous body vessel that would exist as a permanent part of the cosmic landscape. "These stellar rituals also conferred the wisdom of parthenogenesis, a knowledge of bringing forth from one's self both the divine and infernal forces that engender existence in the cosmic worlds," says

Rosemary Clark, an independent scholar and interpreter of Egypt's sacred traditions, in her book *The Sacred Tradition in Ancient Egypt*.[4]

An imperishable body and the idealized state of being, akh was one's link to the circumpolar "Imperishable Stars"—those stars that circle the North Pole and never set. Other spiritual bodies are used temporally while we are alive, but the akh is an eternal body that one might properly think of as the god seed of life. Flashes of brilliance, radiant being, the crown chakra, the aura being filled with light—all these are part of the akh energy. The resurrected body of Christ, for example, is perfect, radiant, and glorified, as is the akh.

The Coffin Texts speak to the mystery of becoming a living star in the afterlife. "For any person who knows the spell, he will become as Ra in the eastern horizon, as Asar in the duat. He will go down to the circle of fire without the flame ever touching him."[5] The hieroglyph for akh used the image of the golden-crested ibis, with its shining feathers streaming around its body from its crown. One can see that akh relates to conjuration, that is, extremely powerful manifestation through the high spiritual work of a light being. It is through the akh body that miracles are performed.

The akh bird, or phoenix, symbolizes the enlightened, perfected soul. By looking in the dark, fishing, and peering into the shadows under its wing, the ibis makes visible what lies in the depths of the river. Always something swims about in the depths of the unconscious; you can never see all of it. Yet you can focus your gaze to peer into the depths of mind, and find the fish—those slippery, quick little phantoms so hard to see.

Be still. This is the art of meditation. This is the art of self-analysis. Do you spend enough time in contemplation, sitting for development, analyzing yourself or working your magic? All of this is what you came here to do. If you are overly social, you will lose energy, time, focus, and direction. The akh bird reminds you to go fishing in your meditations. Ask specific questions and see what rises to the top.

Akh is the light itself. While shining your light is one of the greatest forms of leadership, sometimes you need to dim the light a bit so that it doesn't scare the other fish. You may be brilliant—we all are in some way—but it's often best not to think of yourself in those terms. In stillness and silence you can see more clearly into the depths of what lies under you. We see now the source of that word *under-standing;* it means a foundation of support.

1. Never ever forget that you are the light of God cloaked in flesh. Others may forget it, but you must not. You are intended to lead. It isn't necessary to shine your light; simply *be* the light. Let no man or woman dim it. Remember that you came from the light.

2. Receive unexpected visitors and let your prejudgments fall away. Lean into a conversation and deeply listen. An angel is trying to speak, to work with you in dreams and meditations. A time of initiation draws near.

3. Use the power of a clear mind and the energy of your heart to utter and create your highest possible life desires. The way has been prepared and your creative potential is meant to come to fruition.

4. If you want more light in your life, enact a plan to create more light. Go fishing for the next great project by preparing the tools of your tackle box, so to speak. Work always for the global good. It is especially wise to work for the world and for that which will benefit you at the same time—because it should be the same thing.

5. While all seems in motion and everything is change, learn to calm your heart and mind. Learn to see far and wide by studying remote viewing to use in your meditations.

6. You are already a divine being—whole and perfect. Align to your true self. Open up and tap into the energies of higher beings on the upper planes. It is time for hope and to connect with the sacred heart of the universe.

7. Devote yourself to your inner life work by way of your dreams and meditations. Read books that inspire and evoke more light in your life. Do rituals of cleansing and releasing. Align your priorities so that they reflect your true purpose on the physical plane. Study your symbols for their messages.

8. You do not need to work yourself into exhaustion. Projects move forward by negotiating deals from a win-win perspective. Ask your guides to help you check off a number of details on your to-do list.

9. Truly learn to see beyond the limitations of the *form* of life. It is temporal, but you have the power to envision what you want now and to swiftly act to attain that which is for your highest and best.

AKHET

Good morning from the world of Spirit—Light Land, or the Land of Akhet as the ancients called it—and good night. We speak here of two powerful horizons, of the beginning and the end. The hieroglyph Akhet depicts both a sunrise and a sunset. This horizon symbol indicates the place where Heaven and Earth meet, where light descends or ascends on the earth plane.

All of the spirit beings in Akhet are clothed in raiment of white light like the robes of Jesus or the gowns of angels in Renaissance paintings. Really, these bodies of light are pleated like rays of sunlight in the atmosphere. We stand in Akhet in the light of the Divine; blessed and at peace. Akhet is not just a reception hall in heaven or a place where angels and ancestors hang out. Yes, there is peace and contentment; however, in Light Land, there is work to do—council meetings to attend and plans to devise. Akhet is also known as the city of gold or Shambhala. Here everyone's light shines to illuminate the darkness on Earth.

Akhet is not reached immediately after death, but is a place where one's highest consciousness resides. One can attain it in the living via deep meditation—Buddha did; Prince Arjuna in the *Bhagavad Gita* did; Mahatma Gandhi, Teresa of Ávila, Teilhard de Chardin, and others did. Akhet is deeply satisfied and compassionate living, not just for other souls on the planet, but for the planet itself, and for those in Spirit. Akhet is the possibility of living in perfect harmony. It was Akhet that I saw on the morning of the Harmonic Convergence in August 1987 when a city of gold appeared upon the horizon above Denver.

Akh is the name of the phoenix rising, the shining intelligence of the bennu bird, which is the highest spiritual body, the god spark itself. Akhet is the place of splendor where the phoenix resides and from which reside flames before the throne of God. The bright fiery intellect of mortals, immortals, and spirits comes from this place.

The word also defines a place of being in beginning. This is our source and spirit in the body of God from which we flow forth. Akhet is the season of inundation as well, the beginning and the place of return. It is abundance manifested.

Legend has it that Akhenaten, the son of the Pharaoh Amenhotep III, was spiritually led to his infamous city at Tell el Amarna. This desert plateau was ringed by mountains, and amazingly, as Akhenaten was sailing by it on his boat on the Nile, he saw the hieroglyph of the Akhet casting its rays of sunlight above the horizon. The globe of the sun lay precisely between two sloping hills, resembling the living hieroglyph of akhet. He recognized this as a sign that his god Aten had given to him. Thus he shuttered the famous Temple of Karnak in Luxor. Then he moved to this desert outpost, which apparently was in the middle of nowhere, and built his holy city. He called it Akhetaten, meaning "the horizon of Aten."

In addition to seeing the oracle of the Akhet that led Akhenaten to turn his back on Amen Ra, it is believed that a second hieroglyphic image of Akhet led to the downfall of his city of light. According to Alan Gardiner an eclipse that occurred in the first year of Nefertiti's co-regency and the thirteenth year of Akhenaten's reign may have been visible in Egypt. Pawah, a lay priest and scribe of the god Amen's offerings in the Temple of Ankhkherpherure in Thebes, was said to have inscribed on a piece of ostraca a record of an ominous solar eclipse that occurred during Akhenaten's heretical reign. The inscription read: "Thou causest me to behold darkness by day."[6] Indeed, the totality of the solar eclipse that occurred in Egypt on November 13, 1337 BCE, lasted an exceedingly long eleven minutes. Akhenaten died about a year after.[7]

I offer this story to suggest that every coin has two sides. Imagine when the waters of the Nile lie across the land like a great mirror. When the sun rises there is no apparent difference between beginning and ending, or between Heaven and Earth: As above, so below.

1. God's light shines on you now and you are able to begin to implement a new plan. Others will follow you because they can see you know how to proceed in a spiritual way.

2. Join forces with other light workers to create a community of light beings who serve Spirit. Even if only one other person is in your tribe, the divine light is there also.

3. An *aha!* moment arrives. You have a new idea or sudden awareness, a stroke of creative insight. The light force energizes you to continue and complete this work within three months. Be confident in moving forward.

4. Shambhala, the city of gold, appears on the horizon as an inspiration for building a spiritual community. Study this pattern of following the light through meditation and by writing in your spiritual journal. Build a strong foundation of communal trust, of shared goals, of shared work, and of nurturance and compromise when following a higher power.

5. A sunrise moment. The sun's rays break through the clouds and a storm has concluded. You will be able to see something that you haven't seen before.

6. The family is blessed by a new light coming in. Family members and ancestors gather. Plan a physical reunion and let shared food, shared love, and shared memories shine forth in all that you say and do.

7. Know that you are a divine child. The masters see your light and join in your meditation. The solar power of Ra aligns with the light of the master teachers. One of them will step forward to make his or her presence known.

8. Abundance comes. The season is upon you and the plans you have made must be tended now. After the seeds sprout the true work begins—weeding, cultivating, and fertilizing. This work may involve your mental or physical body. Ask which seeds need your attention. Some buds must be nipped and decisions must be made about what to bring to maturity. Harvest in six to eight months.

9. One who has crossed to the other side uneasily now breathes in peace at last. They send you their praises and thank you for your devotion to them. If we have lived a compassionate, light-filled life, at the end of our days we will understand that we have lived well and our work is now complete.

AMEN

Sometimes spelled *Amun,* this god was originally one of the primeval, invisible gods who paired with a goddess named Amentet. The female counterpart became the embodiment of the hidden Land of the Dead. Amen personified the unknown creative life force energy. Amen attained his prominence in the New Kingdom, elevated to great heights by the priesthood in Thebes.

At that time Amen was equated with Ra as a force of light. However, Amen was also a god of the air—invisible, all-seeing, and everywhere at once. Acquiring the powers of the older deity Shu, Amen's energies complemented those of the great vulture goddess Mut. Mut took on the lioness attributes of Shu's sister Tefnut. Amen personified the great powerful, invisible blast of dry hot winds that roil through the western desert; these winds are known as the khamsin and their power is mighty. In her book *Soaring Stones,* innovator Maureen Clemmons theorized that the harnessing of wind power was one of the creative tools that the visionary priestly architects of Amen and Mut employed to move (fly!) stone obelisks and thus build the monuments of Egypt. That's a mighty god of air!

While the hieroglyphic images primarily indicate sounds, it doesn't hurt to meditate on them as part of the additional understanding of the interpretation. Amen is a perfect example of that. We see the reed (or perhaps feather) as the *a* sound and the ripples of water as the *n* sound. What do these two things have in common? The same unseen wind ripples the water and blows through the reeds (or uplifts the bird with the feather). The invisibility of air, the hidden power of its vibratory energy upon these things, makes me think: *Yes!* Shu and Amen are mighty and powerful, as is the invisible atom and the vibration of all being that is a part of the natural world.

When Christians and Jews add a tag line to their prayers to give them a certain oomph, Amen—the Egyptian god's name—is invoked. In a similar way Amen was employed in ancient Egyptian prayers and supplications. He was equated with invisible magic that, when invoked, sealed the deal. He was the unseen yet divine presence within oracles. Indeed, his oracular priests carried a golden statue of the god enclosed in a naos. They used this to make predictions for those mere mortals who paid a handsome price to the temple priests to see what the unseen god envisioned in their future.

When the invisible god appeared on temple walls, he often took the form of a man wearing a solar headdress with two plumes. During the New Kingdom, Amen appeared as a ram-headed sphinx, several hundred of which lined the nearly two-mile corridor between the Temple of Karnak and the Temple of Luxor. A being of protection and fertility, this ram held an image of the pharaoh tucked under his chin. Amen's ram's horns curve around and under his ear, signifying that he seems to be particularly good at hearing and listening to those prayers and petitions directed to him.

Appearing inside Thoth's cosmic cauldron with his consort Amentet, Amen (Amun) was one of the eight progenitors of Creation emerging from the Ogdoad. Together, the pair represented the co-creative aspects of obscurity, darkness, hiddenness, water, and infinity. Primarily because he was a god of obscurity and infinity, he was given the power to attain whatever form he pleased, including merging his energy with the sun god Ra and becoming the all-powerful, ever-present light in all things—whether that light was visible or invisible. His popularity rose in the New Kingdom, taking over the epithets and traits of the preceding gods until he came close to becoming a single god whose names unified all the others.

One of the more well-known sites dedicated to Amen is the oracular temple in Siwa Oasis. During the Twenty-Sixth Dynasty of Egypt this temple was already said to be a famous and ancient oracle. One myth of its founding tells us that two dark-skinned priestesses (Nubian?) from the Karnak Temple of Amen were banished to the desert. One of them fled to Greece and became the voice of the oracle at the Temple of Dodona; the other established the oracle in the Libyan desert at Siwa and became its sybil.

Probably its most famous visitor was Alexander the Great. After meeting with the priests of Amen, they conferred the title of king upon him, saying that indeed he was divinely created because his mother had conceived him in a conjugal dream visitation of the god Amen in that very temple. Thereafter, Alexander depicted himself as king of Egypt by wearing the ram horns.

1. Amen is the Divine within you. When you conclude your prayers by saying Amen, you are waking up that energy inside you. In this case, shine forth your light like Amen Ra and do not hide it.
2. Celebrate your capacity as a co-creator of the life you live. The divine being within you hears your thoughts, knows your feelings, and creates

the world that you prescribe. Know that God is manifested in the life you see before you.

3. Work with the co-creative, hidden power of love to craft a life that makes you and those around you happy. As Amen is the sun, so is his son Khonsu the moon who reflects the light of his father, bringing joy and light in the evening.

4. To see God in heaven look at the world around you. Every being—every tree, every stone, every cloud—is the physical face of God. What does it know? What are its powers? How does it influence your life? All things reflect a light vibration, the unseen energy of the universe.

5. God is an eternal being. All is change and changing. Just that. What you seek to know now is not knowable now. The changeable nature of a divine being cannot be seen but is everywhere and nowhere like the wind. Amen conceals his light within us, a light we sometimes forget and hardly dare believe in. Yet, Amen's life force is essential to the universe. His changeability underscores the freedom of religious expression and acknowledges that our ideas of God are both personal and mysterious.

6. Amen and his vulture goddess consort, Mut, embodied the process of life and death—ultimately two mysteries that often strain the human mind. Trust in the divine process allows us to live lives that matter. Love abides and creates communities in which our influence and presence lives on after us.

7. Transcendental and self-created, Amen was the living light whom nearly everyone in Thebes served in some capacity, either as laypeople or priests. Look within to see whether or not you are being called to serve as part of a spiritual community.

8. Although we cannot see God, we continue to create awesome beauty that reflects the power of the Divine. We build cathedrals and churches and we bring people into their chapels to defy the emptiness. We light candles to chase away the darkness. Spirit manifests through our hands, our minds, and our love.

9. That which is unknowable remains unknowable. Faith guides our footsteps. Grace is the wind that touches our foreheads. We cannot see in the dark except by holding up the lantern of the god within our own hearts. Hold it high and shine it on the path for others.

ANKH

This ubiquitous, well-known hieroglyph offers messages of renewal, fertility, and eternal life. Nearly everyone who has ever seen the key of life knows immediately what it means. Most gods and goddesses, the pharaoh and his queens, and many of the comforting beings in the underworld clasp or offer the ankh. It is the key to the mysteries, the key of life, and the breath of life.

The ankh particularly invigorates those who have entered the afterlife. For example, the goddess Hathor fondly offers the ankh to her newly departed companion Nefertari in the duat. The goddess holds the ankh to the queen's nose so that she may breathe in the fragrant renewal. Whatever seems to have died—person, project, love—it shall be renewed and live again. Like the sa hieroglyph, which the ankh resembles, it offers magical protection. Some suggest that the ankh may represent a sperm penetrating an ovum at the beginning of life. I do not dispute any of these ideas, believing that these similarities are the way one's mind constellates a fuller poetic meaning of a simple, albeit somewhat abstract, image.

Other scholars suggest that the ankh may be the full breast of the goddess or the teat of the cow offering its life-giving milk. Schwaller de

Lubicz indicated that the word also meant "sap of life" and referred to both milk and milky alabaster quartz, such as is found in the Pyramid of Unas or in the Fifth Dynasty sun temple at Abu-Gurab.[8]

The ankh, often offered by the hands of goddesses, becomes an especially feminine symbol. Like the thet, the ankh represents the mother and the womb through which every one of us are connected. That protective, nurturing spirit of the Divine and its emblem of self-sacrifice—that is, giving one's life to a higher purpose—reappears in later Christian traditions as the sign of the cross. The physical world appears as the cross, or four directions, surmounted by a circle of the eternal.

A woman's mirror was often made of highly polished copper in the shape of an ankh, as a kind of pun to reinforce the idea of being the living image of the individual. Pharaoh Tut-ankh-Aten's name meant to be the living image of sun god Aten (until, of course, the priests of Amen changed it). Some Greco-Roman magical texts suggested that oracular priestesses use a mirror made into the shape of the ankh and dedicated to Hathor to scry into the future. In some myths, both Hathor and Sekhmet were known as the Eye of Ra, thus their divinations of the past and the future were powerful.

Other scholars suggest the ankh holds images of a sun rising across a flat horizon. In astrology the planet Venus is signified by an ankh. Life and love are the "high doing," that is, the spiritual work of learning through life experience, which leads to tremendous wisdom.

Egyptologist Alan Gardiner imagined that the ankh was actually a sandal strap, but it is more likely that the sandal strap was made to conform to the shape of the ankh. There was an ancient Egyptian inscription in the Temple of Abydos that called Ramses II "Lord of many provisions and abundance of barley . . . there is a plenteous harvest wherever his sandals may be."[9] The sly double entendre refers not simply to growing fields of grain, but to the more than one hundred children that Ramses sired because he parked his sandals under the beds of more than fifty wives and concubines.

1. Through all of our incarnations we attain one life eternal, but in this particular body we have one physical life. Live yours to the fullest.

Gather wisdom from all of your experiences. Become a shining example to others. God gives you life from Life.

2. Live for others. It's all about how we on this planet treat each other and all life-forms. The Golden Rule—Do unto others as you would have them do unto you—applies. You understand that we must all live in like manner, nurturing others as well as ourselves. Listen with your heart.

3. A new creation is coming straight out of your being. You will need to nurture it as it grows. Eventually you will release it and it will live on after you. This could be a creative project or a child. The work takes on a long arc; this is only the beginning of it.

4. Put your work under a microscope. Investigate what will make it pulse with life. Listen with a stethoscope to what you have not been hearing. Hear it now in order to fix any irregularities. Work the "Big List" of things that you need/want to accomplish today, this month, this year, in your life. Doing is being.

5. Live in the moment. Change things up. Go to the window to gaze out over an expansive vista for inspiration. Life is meant to be enjoyed. Let go of the melodrama. Read some inspiring books or poems, then go about living inside them, or write some poems or paint some pictures. Your life is grand theatre; enjoy the play. Resurrect some forgotten themes.

6. Our family connections are lifelines to the world. Keep those connections love-light clear. If there are family riffs, release and forgive. Life's too short for anger. Your body is a temple for Spirit. Care for it. Let hope in. The ankh here may indicate an addition to the family.

7. God is love. Even when you are alone, your spirit guides love you and work with you to keep you connected to Source. Isis cradles you in her arms. Live an inspiring life to others. Read and emulate someone else's inspiring life. God wants you to embrace your true calling. The power of the ankh celebrates "high doing." This means engaging in the spiritual work of learning through life experience, which leads to tremendous insights and spiritual wisdom.

8. God is in the details. If you are living a life of purpose, every day is a particular day in which particular energies are occurring and particular things are happening that will never be the same again. You may wish to track them through astrology, numerology, or even the colors you wear. Do

something that matters for others, for your work, for yourself. In all things, express gratitude.

9. Get rid of distractions that keep you from living in the now. Whatever is passing will transform when you let it go. Something new is rising. The seed must be planted in the dark, which requires radical trust. Prosperity waits in the wings.

ANPU (ANUBIS)

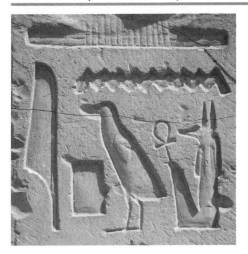 

Another name for the jackal god Anubis is "Opener of the Way." Whenever this hieroglyph appears, Anubis will lead you into alternate realms for the purpose of your ultimate transformation and spiritual growth. He opens the gateway to spirit communication and even to poetry. He opens any gateway you intend to cross and does so in a magical manner, almost as if he were padding just ahead of you, then turning to look over his shoulder and peer into your eyes to ask, "Are you coming?" or "Come on, I dare you." In the photo above, we see Anpu just to right of the ankh depicted.

The kohl-outlined eye of the jackal indicates a keen vision and psychic insight. The jackal's long, pointed nose helps it to discern various scents. We see images of airport security guard dogs trained to sniff out contraband. Similarly, jackals in the desert were known to sniff about, finding the tombs of mummies or the burial grounds of sacred creatures. The gift of clairvoyance (clear seeing), clairaudience (clear hearing), clairalience (clear smelling!), and clairsentience (clear sensing) are the magnificent gifts of Anubis.

This jackal protector helps us find what has been lost, what is missing, and whatever long-buried issue needs to be unearthed. There is a mythic psychology to that. As the accidental child of the union of Osiris and Nephthys, Anpu was abandoned by his mother in the desert. Thus sometimes Anubis appears to indicate that there is a strained relationship between parent and child. Yet the saving grace of this whole situation is that Isis becomes his surrogate mother and raises him with love, without judgment, and with nurturing understanding. In other words, sometimes when the time is not right for one thing it is right for another.

While this particular book on hieroglyphs only deals with Anubis as Anpu, a second jackal guardian named Upuat often joins him. Sometimes Upuat is said to be the son of Set, while Anpu is the son of Osiris. When appearing as a pair, Upuat guards the eastern gate and Anubis guards the western gate. Anubis amulets were made for powerful protection and transformation. Many an individual who uses Reiki in their healing practice might find a close relationship with Anubis as a guiding companion in the work.

Because Anubis guarded the entrance to the underworld, the jackal appeared black as inky night, with a grave, sometimes snarling and frightening countenance. As with most guard dogs, he may growl as we approach the entrance to an abode. That's his job—to indicate whether passage is to be allowed or to indicate whether one should turn back. Often in Egyptian shamanic work, one needs to ask Anubis whether or not to proceed upon a certain path.

At Hatshepsut's temple at Deir el Bahari he stands between her mortuary temple and the tombs on the other side of the mountain, which is the valley where the pharaohs of the New Kingdom were buried. As the embalmer of his father, Osiris (both eviscerating him and protecting him with balms and herbs), he often appears in a reading to indicate that the time has come for something that you once valued to pass away. This is not always a human life that dissolves, as it was when Osiris passed into the spirit world—but it can be. However, there is protection on all levels as this transition occurs and everything is in divine order.

Most often Anubis comes to assist in releasing attachments to contracts that no longer serve us in this life. That may mean that relationships will dissolve or decay, sometimes jobs, sometimes our attachment to places or other people. He may appear in past-life regressions, for he is very good at recalling what the soul knows but the body in this incarnation has forgotten. In ancient Egyptian iconography he always appears in the underworld in the Hall of Ma'at when the departed individual's heart is weighed upon the scales of ma'at in the judgment scene. Perhaps what passes away is a false hope or a misunderstanding of how things are "supposed to be." The work of Anubis is always to determine what is right or correct for our soul's progress.

Anpu symbolizes deep initiation on the spiritual path. He expertly guides the soul through the hidden passageways between light and dark, between the conscious and unconscious states—even the subconscious and superconscious minds. Linked to the modern dog, Anubis can assist us in not losing our way on life's path. He guards, guides, and initiates us through the mysteries of occult practice. His legacy and wisdom are intimately linked with the Dog Star Sirius, which is also equated with Isis. Long before recorded history, the Dogon tribe of Mali knew about the appearance of the double stars inside the Canis Major constellation. Sirius A and Sirius B consistently rose in heliacal fashion before the sun, predicting (or opening the way for) the annual inundation of the Nile and the beginning of the New Year. Sirius A marks the appearance of Isis and Sirius B was Anubis, her foster son and constant companion. He follows Isis, who guides the celestial boat of Osiris along its night sea journey. (See Sopdet on page 229 for more information on Sirius.)

To dream of following Anubis as a jackal or dog signifies a readiness for initiation. He appears as a messenger from the unconscious.

Depending upon the dog or jackal's actions, the message may indicate tenacity, sniffing out quarry, or a return to one's animal or physical self. It may symbolize a coming transformation, as when the jackal sits atop the Wheel of Fortune tarot card.

1. An opportunity presents itself to open you to a new understanding of a project or a life purpose. A new way of being and walking in the world unfolds before you. Step into a new light. Allow yourself to be seen. Speak up.

2. Pay attention with your physical ears to the messages of others. Sniff out the truth—what is really being said? An unexpected visitor appears; intuitively you know whether to welcome or deny your guest. Explore your alternate self to more deeply see what is really going on.

3. Work with your wolf pack to explore new, creative, and connective projects. A mystery unfolds. Your mind opens and information floods in to offer new ways of seeing. A creative approach becomes the fertile channel of a new understanding.

4. Shut the door behind you and work. There is much to do behind the scenes. When baking a cake, you can't keep opening the oven door. Protect your privacy. Invoke your helper and guide Anubis but be sure to release him when you have completed the work.

5. Prepare to travel suddenly to unexpected places. Magic is afoot. Take off on your own to a new adventure. Channel as you write. Whatever is passing away, say thank you and let it go. Anubis takes what is no longer working but still has value and helps you create new forms. Find new ways to reconstitute and re-energize memories from the past.

6. Open the door to family and friends. Be with your pack. Eat well, feed each other, and howl together. Share the wealth. Create a safety net and retreat. Repair any broken bonds. Get a physical check-up. Your doctor works with Anubis to sniff out any health problems.

7. Open the portal and be ready for the download. You connect with alternate realities—to Sirius, to angelic forms, or to those from alternate dimensions. In meditation connect with your guides and the Seven Ray energies. Anubis demonstrates hands-on healing and works miracles

when he stands beside the living physical form. With the dead, he heals the spirit into its perfected essence as light.

8. Open the Akashic Records and read. Get ready for some serious soul-developing business. Be open to new negotiations in the material world too. Dig a little to find answers. Find a hidey-hole and bury some precious resource you've been saving. Revise a will, sock away funds, invest in insurance. Be discerning.

9. Things come to a conclusion. Release resentments and old ways of thinking and acting that no longer serve you or anyone else. Put an end to suffering over a situation. Open the cage door and go free into the world, howl at the moon, or go on a vision quest. With Anpu, you move as an emissary of peace between worlds. Are you part of a pack or a lone wolf? Either can be right if it serves you.

ARIT

An arit is a passageway or doorway. In the astral realm many gates and doors lead one through the underworld and the hours of the night. As it is in death, so it is in life. We pass through many doorways, endure trials, and encounter opposition. These impediments are represented by the doorway or house around which flames or serpents are depicted. Other Egyptologists suggest the image depicts battlements around the entire portal similar to those seen on castles. Imagine that in either case, one's forward progress might be impeded either by fire, striking cobras, or arrows.

These images bring to mind the dilemma of Shakespeare's Hamlet who asks: "Whether 'tis nobler in the mind to suffer the slings and arrows of outrageous fortune, or to take arms against a sea of troubles, and by opposing end them?" Doing nothing gets us nowhere. Passing through an arit in life or in the underworld requires a changing state of consciousness. The power of the hieroglyph arit comes from learning to walk through our trials without feeling the need to criticize either ourselves or others. It means moving forward despite obstacles and without any assurance of what may exist for us on the other side. Crossing this threshold means passage without fear. Practice saying Psalm 23: "Yea, though I walk through the valley of the shadow of death, I will fear no evil." In self-doubt or self-criticism, we lose our way—in life as well as in the underworld.

What can we see on the other side? Imagine entering the kitchen from the living room, then stopping to wonder, "What did I come in here for?" That can happen when we go through a doorway unconsciously. How frustrating that is! Imagine how frustrating it must be when in the underworld (unconscious mind) you forget what you came in for.

Guardians, heralds, and messengers stand before each arit. To pass into the next phase of transformation, address each one, for knowing them leads to resurrection and ascension. In Saqqara at the edge of the *heb sed* courtyard that lies before the Step Pyramid, there appears a façade of an arit guarded by hooded cobras—goddesses identified as "ladies of flame." (See facing photograph.) The cobra reminds us to prepare ourselves before the sacred entrance into alternate realities. It's not an easy passage. Psychologically the arit may be equated with paralyzing self-doubt, self-criticism, and fear. If we do not move beyond these blocks we are lost; or more precisely, burned by tongues of fire. To get clear we must rely on the inner sight—the insight of our imagination, inspiration, and memory.

Hooded cobras carved onto the lintels above the doorways guard the entrances into the heb sed courtyard at the necropolis of Saqqara.

1. How comfortable are you in your body? You may have some negative feelings around your physical existence. It could vary from thoughts like *I don't like the way I look* to *I can't wait to leave the earth plane; I hate it here.* If you are ill, take a look at that. Your body is a temple of the spirit and if you dislike it or don't take care of it, that needs to be addressed. You create your own reality. Learn to love your body and your life.

2. The words we use, the thoughts we express, and the heart's desires open doors into many halls. Watch your language; through your speech you create your reality. Saying "I always pick losers" means you will always pick losers. You just told your soul to do so. Obsessive thinking clouds the mind. Practice thoughtful talk. Practice changing your speech into positive, life-enhancing truths.

3. How we dress, how we move, and where we live reflect our being. Look

around. What do you see in your bedroom when you first open your eyes? Does it reflect you? If something doesn't feel right, change it. Clutter hides the spirit. How do you interact with your world—rushing through traffic lights, scooting past people in the grocery aisles, slamming doors, giving "the look" to someone who is annoying you? Passing through this arit requires becoming a focused observer and seeing yourself as if from the outside.

4. The fourth arit is the foundation of every life. Daily actions become ingrained thought patterns. This is not a bad thing. If you manage your responses to life well, it may be just fine. If you engage in negative self-talk, emotional greed, or the like, spiritual impoverishment may result. Discernment means not following paths that lead to depression or inertia.

5. Your body language reflects your emotional state. To pass through this arit, pay attention to your posture. Are you slouching? Are you tapping your fingers or swinging your feet? Do you look your conversation partner in the eye? How often do you give or receive hugs? Smiles? While you may be saying one thing, your body may indicate another. How do you carry yourself?

6. Do you trust your intuition and rely on it daily? When you do that, you exude a magical power that pulls you into the right places to meet the right people at the right time. Trust your gut. Continue to develop your clairvoyant gifts, for developing one's intuition leads to enlightenment.

7. Balancing physical, emotional, and mental energies eases stress, increases vitality, and deepens a sense of living in concert with Spirit. Happiness and success derive from gratitude, not striving; appreciation for life now lowers your stress. Peace comes when we trust in a higher being.

8. Know thyself. Study the laws of pure thought, conscious speech, and compassionate action. You cannot be turned away from the gift of divine love. In thought, word, and deed, rest your life upon the unalterable laws of truth.

9. Remember this: What you do to the least of my children, you do also unto me. It's best to focus on what you do for others rather than on what you mustn't do. Create a life of value by affirming the value of the lives of others. Humanitarian work marks your passage through the gateway.

ASAR (OSIRIS)

Osiris, the Egyptian god Asar, became the first divine human to live, to die, and to be resurrected. All of the Book of the Dead is dedicated to exploring and maneuvering the complicated hallways in the underworld where Osiris reigns after death, seated on his throne as in the image above. While the shepherd's crook beside Osiris in the photograph hieroglyphically indicates a part of the *s* sound in the name Asar, it is often seen as one of the implements held in the hand of Osiris, the god of agriculture and animal husbandry. The Egyptians saw him as a benevolent shepherd, and we were his flock. In these underworld Halls of Osiris, one's heart is weighed to determine one's fate on Judgment Day. He embodies the pre-Christian resurrection mysteries to show us the metaphysical workings of the psyche.

Osiris has many forms and names: Lord of the Underworld, the Good Being, Lord of the Universe, Lord of the Boundaries, Lord of Eternity. His white face denotes the shining divine power of renewal and eternal life; his black face reveals death and mysterious potential; his green face offers renewal and rebirth. In the afterlife he sits on a throne beside his celestial father, the great progenitor Atum, the throne becoming a symbol of his authority. Christ sat at the right hand of his father; Osiris and Atum sit back-to-back. They merge with each other, becoming an alpha and omega.

Osiris's story includes his murder by his brother Set, his being suspended inside a Tree of Life, his first attempted resurrection in which he inseminates Isis, and his second death in which his body becomes dismembered and scattered.[10] The story of Osiris is the story of everyman. We have all been betrayed by someone we trusted. We have all stopped short of our goals, our plans suspended by indecision or a failing vision. We have all undergone trials that either partially succeeded or totally failed, and yet we gathered ourselves to begin again. We have all relied upon the spiritual fortitude of others (sometimes crying out for divine intervention) to pull us through when we were too exhausted to continue the fight.

In Osiris's story, his beloved wife, Isis, gathers all of his parts, creates a ritual of "re-membrance," and gives immaculate birth to his son. For his part, the Osiris who thought he would live eternally with the love of his life, contented in his garden, is dragged into the underworld, dying without warning. There, seated in the darkness beside Atum, a father god he cannot see, Osiris rules over the Land of the Dead. This is not so much an underworld as an "other world"—a deep, hidden place that is a state of consciousness we can barely fathom. Seated side by side with Atum in the underworld, he must learn to respond in faith to his father's directives. Osiris is the way in which we, having been defeated, come to live again.

The Egyptian Book of the Dead compiles the rituals and hymns designed to raise one's consciousness to the light, so that we understand death is not the end. This sacred, magical text teaches us to turn death consciousness into life consciousness. The sign of such a transformation was the appearance of the constellation Orion in the night sky. It seemed to rise over several weeks, lifting up out of the waters of the Nile at midwinter. The three stars in the belt of Orion (or knots in the girdle of Osiris) were represented on Earth by the three pyramids on the Giza Plateau.

Of course, Asar was the first king of Egypt, the one of whom the gods might have said, "We have made man in our image." His symbol is not simply about death; it also speaks of possibility—the growing plants, the sensual earth, the embodiment of life in a physical form. All tactile things of Earth were living beings of the divine body—Spirit clothed in the physical world. These aspects of Asar might be called the *paut*, meaning the *prime materia* out of which all life is formed and which is part of the body of the gods.

While he was alive Asar gathered about him a community with whom he shared the bounty of his garden, which included knowledge of the divinity of all things. Thus he created a civilized culture. As he did so, he used the power of the crook and flail to gather back into the fold those sheep who had strayed, and to separate the wheat from the chaff. All these talents as an agriculturalist become the spiritual lessons he demonstrates in the afterlife. Later they become metaphors for the parables about the spiritual life proclaimed by Jesus, the Good Shepherd. Osiris is a direct link to our understanding of spiritual truth, reflected in the stuff of life. The Heavens, and the Earth below, and the realms below the Earth, all respond to the same spiritual directives and natural laws.

1. Awaken now to your true power as a divine being in a human body. To realize your dream, you must first awaken to it. Awakened to it, you must enact it. A divine task is at hand.

2. Osiris and Isis represent a spiritual partnership. So much a team are these two that they become like two hands working together, creating a spiritual family of harmony and compassion. Your heart's desire elevates to a spiritual principle. While you live and work on Earth, do not become ensnared in the illusion of perfection. Instead, live in perfect harmony with natural laws and the choices you make.

3. When the Green Man Asar first stepped on Earth, all grains and vegetation erupted under his feet. When his coffin landed in Byblos, a tamarisk tree sprang up. Life is eternal; form not so much. Diligent work will grow your garden in the world and renew it for those who come after. Make some plans, resurrect a dream, or cultivate a planetary ideal.

4. The four planes of existence are the backbone of Osiris. Investigate how the concept of divinity occupies your physical, emotional, mental, and spiritual work. Explore your daily thought processes and ideas. Examine the ways in which emotions and dreams weave a tapestry of your divine life. In what ways can you bring Heaven to Earth daily?

5. Family dynamics seem excruciatingly complex. Just ask Osiris about his experience of sibling rivalry. Express radical forgiveness in a situation, without expecting particular results. You will make mistakes and others will too. Change what is yours to change and accept what you can't change and move on with your life.

6. Osiris loves deeply. Sometimes he loves in error, but he always acts on his feelings to make the world manifest through love. He guides humanity by his willingness to sacrifice. His love is a mystical bond. Where in your life do you feel eros, philae, and agape?

7. Through dreams Osiris taught his son Horus how to become a future leader and hero. How do dreams inform *your* daily life? Do you interpret the synchronicities of your life as waking dreams? Consider what the poet Langston Hughes asks, "What happens to a dream deferred . . . ?"

8. Don't try to be everything to all people. Your authentic self is the best anyone can offer. If you succeed, give Spirit the glory. If you need help, ask Spirit to guide you. You can succeed as a leader even if you aren't perfect, because like Moses, you do the work Spirit asks you to do. The number eight becomes a lemniscate on its side, showing us an eternal balance of the energies of Heaven and Earth. Honor both spirit and form.

9. Someone in the spirit world draws close now. You see signs of their presence in your life. Some anniversary of their earthly time (birth, anniversary, death date, favorite holiday) pulls that dear one's energy near to say: "I am fine now. Your love sustained me. I watch over you, guide you, protect you, and enfold you in my arms."

AST (ISIS)

The ancient Egyptian goddess Ast (sometimes referred to as Auset or Aset), became Isis to the Greeks and Romans. The Virgin Mary later assumed many of the epithets, myths, and symbols of the Goddess. Isis immaculately conceived and birthed the holy child Horus, who succeeded Osiris and ruled his father's kingdom. Isis also raised Anubis, the illegitimate son of Osiris and her sister Nephthys. Both she and Anubis are linked to the double Dog Stars of Sirius. As we know, these stars heralded the annual flooding of the Nile and began the Egyptian New Year during the "dog days" of summer.

The many myths of Ast (Isis) shed light on what it means to be a strong woman, a sister, a beloved wife, a creator, a teacher, a mystic, and a community leader. The Goddess struggles to survive in all these roles, as well as in the roles of working single mother, widow, outcast, and magical being. In them, she wrestles with overcoming difficulties and doing her spiritual work. Myths of Isis in these various iterations, as well as that of companion to many goddesses, appear as early as the Fifth Dynasty of the Old Kingdom and run throughout Egyptian history and beyond.[11]

The hieroglyph for Ast is a throne or "a seat" from which her name derives. We can see this throne represented as the glyph on the left in the photo above. The child of Isis seated in the lap of his mother is none other than the pharaoh sitting on the throne that *is* his mother. By suckling his mother, the Horus child ingests her wisdom. Aset also indicates true belonging and literally means "the place," as in "Home is where the heart is."

Isis embodies female creativity in all forms. She acquired the magical name of Ra (some say she stole it!) so that she could create with the same magic that the sun god did. Because she is linked with the Great Mother goddess Nut, the sky that birthed the sun, the myth implies that Isis already knows Ra's magical name but only makes him admit it. Her true divinity is occluded by her physicality, but her magic is all-pervasive.

Thoth performed many feats on behalf of his protégé Isis. For example, he caused time to roll backward to save the Horus child from death. On another occasion Thoth sent an entourage of scorpions to help Isis escape from Set's prison. As one of the mythological companions who accompanied Thoth as they escaped from a sinking Atlantis, Isis brought with her a knowledge of healing and agriculture. Through her loving attention she taught humanity and became its civilizing influence. A humanitarian, the wise elder performed compassionate, spiritual work in the world. No task was too great. That included searching all of Egypt to find the scattered pieces of Osiris. In the process she created life out of death. She used her magic by raising her kundalini energy and, while attempting to resurrect Osiris from his morbid state, she conceived a child, the future hero of the land.

The word *ast* also meant sanctuary, shrine, or holy place. The womb of Ast is a hidden holy place when she sits on her throne, but it is also the gateway to the stars. Called the Queen of Heaven and Earth, Isis appears in Greco-Roman statues with her feet on the world and her head crowned by stars, similar to depictions of Mother Mary. In the tarot Isis appears as the veiled High Priestess, as the pregnant Empress, and as the great mystery unveiled as the Star. Ancient prayers call her She of Ten Thousand Names. Her name was spelled many ways by many people, offering differing vibrations for whatever was needed in life: healing, fertility, magic, dreams, companionship, divination, vindication, or protection.

1. Say "I Am. I Am Isis. I am the divine feminine." Being a divine woman does not mean waiting for another to fulfill your dreams. It means actively engaging in the magic of creating your own reality. Express yourself. Be in harmony with the body of the Divine. Knowing who you are and what you want, go for it. Make some magic happen.

2. Twin flames meet. They don't ascend in love but mostly fall in love. That is a truth. Love means sacrifice. What are you willing to do or not do for the sake of love? When you grasp this concept, then fall in love and accept its gift because love also heals and sustains. The compassion of Isis raises us to its highest level. She carries high spiritual wisdom and intuition, and elevates partnership to a spiritual dimension. Intuitive and cooperative, Isis is the duality of spirit and matter.

3. Birth a new thought or a new, magical life. What your heart desires, create it. Isis midwifes all creative projects, whether they are physical children or children of the mind. She nurtures, offers joy, and celebrates as life comes into being. Some of our greatest creations come from deep longing, or even a sense of loss. Isis midwifed others until she could birth her own child. First she engaged in communal and planetary growth before entering the fullness of her own co-creative abilities. You, like Isis, are pregnant with something wonderful.

4. Isis had to leave the prison in which Set ensnared her before she could birth her true work. It's time to break free of your limitations and give yourself permission to create the life you want. Set your own rules. Awaken to your true nature as a child of the Goddess. This means more than taking power for oneself. A true mother nurtures and empowers others to follow in her footsteps. Isis rocks the cradle that rules the world, taking care of the details and setting things right.

5. You embody Isis. Hold that thought in your mind. Whether you are male or female, a loving, nurturing, magical potential stirs within you. You have a choice. Decide what you want. Choose your destiny. Employ prayer, affirmation, and work your altar. Awaken to your fullness.

6. Care for yourself, your family, and your partner. Celebrate the world with a

sensory feast of beautiful meals and nourishing food. Give lots of hugs and receive them. Plant flowers by your front door. Health, love, and friendship are part of the divine plan for all of us. We must step back at times in order to care for ourselves. Isis nurtures us through our own hands.

7. You are not alone. There are appropriate times to draw into yourself and contemplate your true nature. What does Spirit ask of you? How can you develop a closer relationship with the Divine, with the Goddess, with Source? Study how natural law works in your life as Isis reveals it to you.

8. Success is your legacy. Take the strength and power of all of your life lessons and begin to use that to create the reality you wish to inhabit. Care for the Earth. Make your place in it a magical place of gardens, abundance, and beauty.

9. Meditate with the Goddess. Be loving and creative as you move and work in your community, helping others, supporting their dreams, and making peace. Offer justice and empower those without voice—women and children, the homeless, the incarcerated. Create a place of worship within yourself, your home, and/or your community.

ATEN

The New Kingdom pharaoh Akhenaten believed the bureaucratic priests of Thebes were pocketing the offerings for Amen-Re, thereby enriching themselves. Thus he refused to pay the priests of Amen for the right to pray to his god. When his brother died before him, Akhenaten became pharaoh. He used his theological training in the power of light vibration to promote the idea of one god with many hands—the god Aten. The unity of divine power was a cosmic truth even among Egyptians, but the concept often creates a world of trouble for those who believe that their vision of God is the sole true vision. The one and the many are the same.

This hieroglyph represents a winged disc of light. Akhenaten believed that love and light knew no boundaries. They stretch everywhere, touching all points on Earth. This feathered sun disk symbolizes light as a vibration that moves through the air, surrounding us with an invisible life force energy that is both singular and multifaceted. The cupped hands at the end of each light ray profess the extension of divine, nurturing, spiritual love.

The hieroglyph for aten also meant "mirror." Depictions of Akhenaten's family show them reaching up to touch the hands of the living sun that extends its hands toward them. Even the pharaoh's name refers to this mirroring: Akh-en-aten means "In the image of the living sun god Aten." In the Gospel of Thomas, the gnostics express a similar idea wherein Jesus says, "If they say to you, 'Where have you come from?' say to them, 'We have come from the light, from the place where the light came into being by itself, established [itself], and appeared in their image.'"[12]

Although it seems counterintuitive when we observe the way diaphanous light slides through our fingers, we can see that light is the basic foundation of the universe. Light gives form to life. Everything that exists is a form of light vibration, which is the seed atom of all Creation. Just as the rays of the sun disk are many, Akhenaten believed that the one God could be seen in many things. Akhenaten left the cult of Amen because it had become exclusive rather than inclusive. He built his city in the desert at El Amarna (the ancient Akhetaten).

Akhenaten and his family feel the embrace of
Aten's great spirit as it touches and enlivens them
and their daily offerings.

There he worshipped Aten and composed the Great Hymn to Aten
that demonstrates a direct link to the Hebrew people who carried
forward Akhenaten's idea of monotheism. In a line-by-line compari-
son between Psalm 104 and the Great Hymn to Aten, one can see
the author praise the invisible one God whose powers and aspects
are many.

1. Light itself reflects the power and life force energy of God. Lift up your face. Let light shine on you. Feel that light and know that you are chosen. You embody light itself.

2. Love calls you and you enter a sacred partnership, a blessing you are meant to share. This may be a talent or a gift you will share with another. Your life energy is the god within you.

3. The hand of God reaches toward you; a great creative force touches you. You need only to reach up to receive inspiration from Spirit. When the gift is in your hands, apply yourself.

4. God has many hands; you have but two. You and three others, however, have eight hands. Gather your community and energetically work together toward a common goal to benefit all. When others see how four people can create a magnificent foundation, they'll want to assist.

5. Hindu gods and goddesses have many arms, holding many implements for creating, building, separating, playing, and working. You, too, have many things to do. Multitask the work, but only if you can focus first on two things at a time, then on three things. You can do well working five major tasks a day—not more. May the force be with you.

6. In the art at El Amarna, Akhenaten and Nefertiti kiss and cuddle their children beneath the rays of the sun disk. Recognize that the light in your own little family shines as it does on this tender ancient family. A child or parent needs your care and attention. As God reaches out to touch and bless you, reach out to touch and bless them.

7. Spirit offers you many insights. Outdoor meditations will inform you, especially if you stay awake to and aware of the symbols and images of the natural world living and moving around you. Feel joy. Sunrise and sunset are particularly potent times.

8. Express deep gratitude for the many gifts Spirit has given you. Do not rest on your laurels. Always continue to use your gifts. Share your talents and time abundantly. Organize your life and the people in it to serve the divine plan.

9. The bird opens and closes, opens and closes, opens and closes its wings as it flies, in order to attain great spiritual height. Accept the law of polarity. Something ends and, in the next motion, something begins. Let this

knowledge allow you to soar. Bless all that passes away as you continue to move toward the light.

ATUM

Atum sometimes appears as an old man walking with his cane, as is seen on the right of the photo above. As such, he represents the conclusion of a life. The sled too signifies endings, as it transported the mummified body and its grave goods across the sands to the tomb at the end of life. Imagine that sled as indicating not a grasping for ephemeral material possessions at the end of life. Imagine rather the greatest treasure is a state of being that includes our eternal values and philosophies. In every moment we carry with us all that we are.

Every end signifies a beginning. We know that energy is never destroyed, thus there is no death. There is renewal and reconstitution. In this case Atum's cycle of energy is drawing to a close, like a sunset. Even a peaceful sunset may leave a hint of sadness, for we know that something beautiful has passed. We often want what is good and blessed to stay in our lives forever, but no form does. Ashes to ashes, and dust to dust. Even the apparently eternal heavenly orbs of sun, moon, and planets wax and wane in their energy, manifesting their cyclical returns.

A god of the waning light, Atum also appears as the invisible god of Creation. He lives in the darkness and emptiness of space, inside the cloying, stifling darkness of the tomb, beneath the earth in the caverns of the underworld, and inside the unmanifest. Back-to-back with Osiris, who is a god of potentiality and the seed of future incarnation, Atum passes eternity. In funerary texts Atum is the ancient one whom none can see but whom all the divine ones call their father. He tells Osiris his son, "For you, the sky is given. For you, earth is given. For you, I light a fire in the sky. My love dispels darkness. Behold, you shall endure, one of the shining ones forever."[13]

Atum also means "to be perfect and complete." It means everything in its entirety, and it negates it all. The alpha and omega of the life force energy, Atum is an eternal principle that cannot be destroyed but which underlies the natural law that the universe is in constant motion. Form comes into being and goes out of being even as it comes back into being, like the murmuration of starlings that shapeshift as they fly. We see this image as a deep philosophical and scientific connection to the concept of the atomic ideas of Lucretius, the Roman philosopher, who said that the spiritual atom returns to its source, which is Atum. He believed that the atom (Atum of the ancients) created everything and was the source of all life. "Nothing is seen so swift as is the mind, when first it forms a plan, begins to act," he writes. "The mind you see more rapidly is stirred than aught we see in nature, and it must therefore consist of atoms very small to be so easily moved."[14]

The hieroglyph atum also indicates all mortal humankind—mortal being the definitive form that indicates dissolution, reformation, and evolution. Sometimes the god Atum is drawn hieroglyphically as a single feather, like the single ostrich feather of the goddess Ma'at, the foundation of all cosmic order. Atum, like Amen, is not the feather but the unseen air that moves the feather. He is the wind in the sail that moves the boat forward. In the myths of the vulture mother Mut, Atum, like Amen, becomes the unseen wind that fertilizes the egg. To dream of wind may mean that there is energy available to you for launching a new project or beginning a new phase of your life. If the wind is chaotic and extreme, it may indicate the dissolution of a project.

1. All experience is contained in the seed. We do not get to the seed until the former incarnation of the plant completes its life cycle. You have just ended something. Now comes the time for beginning again. The atomic seed is potential life.

2. This is the relationship of support—the old man with his cane at the end of life, or the two fingers of the father or mother who hold the child who is learning to walk at the beginning of its life. The key idea is support in both cases. Stay grounded. Be mindful of your step.

3. Sunrise, noon, and sunset. Beginning, middle, and end. Where are you in your creative process? Chuck those things you no longer need. Check those things that are just beginning and need a little extra nurturing. Stand in your power. Live a creative life.

4. Move toward your destination methodically. Allow yourself to plan a trajectory and then only do one thing at a time. Place one foot in front of the other and you will reach your destination. Stake the plants in your metaphorical garden so that all receive the light equally.

5. When the tide goes out it sometimes reveals things like starfish hidden beneath the waves. In the same way, the stars in the night sky burn all day long behind our back, even though we can't see them until just after the sunset. Then suddenly there they are! Magic is all around you. It's in the air you breathe. Be aware of it.

6. Think of ways to honor that which is passing away. The ancient hieroglyphic word *sir* referred to Atum as an esteemed elder or noble old man. This indicates that the elder tribe of your family and community has come into focus. Honor the legacy and tradition that one has carried.

7. Let the elders and your ancestors teach you until you reach your own power. Know that life eternal is the baptism, and Atum is that seed atom of life—the nature of reality. Spirit and natural law occupy your thoughts as you observe how all of life is a circle tied together.

8. Great gratitude for all the lessons of life must be expressed, even for a difficult past. It is not only okay to rely on others, it is a great benefit. Much success comes. Many hands make light work.

9. Something has come to a natural conclusion—a person, a project, a place, a life work. Glean its teachings. Feel free to mourn its passing and begin anew.

BA

The eternal soul, inked on papyrus and inscribed on temple walls, usually appears as a human-headed hawk. However, it may take the form of whatever bird it likes, always possessing the face of the person whose soul it represents. Naturally, soul is that which is developed through the process of living, accruing experience, and moving through successive fields of consciousness.

This ba develops over lifetimes. Soul lessons are never forgotten. We carry them with us into the next life. Those soul lessons become a part of us. One soul contains the record of many lifetimes of a particular individual. Yet with all the talk of what is contained in our Akashic Records and how many past lives we remember, there is no life that is more important than the one we are presently living. Through it we live out the karmic lessons of *every* life we have ever known and we are creating the future life by how we respond in this life now.

In *The Union of Isis and Thoth*, Nicki Scully and I described using the Egyptian ba during a particular soul retrieval process. Even the living, eternal ba may experience soul fragmentation. A particular painful memory may separate from us and need to be reintegrated in order for us to experience completion and enlightenment. The soul is considered migratory and can have its own agenda. For that reason, the books of the afterlife contain a protective "spell": "Grant thou that my soul may come to me from any place wherein it may be."[15]

Because the ba soul is eternal, it knows no death. It remains throughout our lives and goes with us beyond the grave. It enters eternal life to commune with other divine souls, or it may return to Earth to this body in this time, or in another incarnation. The ba connects us to the absolute. It is now as it was from the beginning. "My ba is the ba of the gods," says the Book of the Dead, "the ba of eternity, the ba in the body."[16]

1. "My soul doth magnify the Lord," says Mary in Luke 1:46. We grow in spirit by following our divinely ordained tasks. You have been chosen for big work that others will notice and follow in kind. This is work that your soul has been developing through many lifetimes.

2. The story of your life is written in the least sense according to what you do for yourself, and in the greater sense according to what you do for others. You take the needs of others to heart, and so your soul record contains stories of your generosity. Keep doing unto others.

3. Your soul is built upon three things—what you think, what you do, and those emotions that you may or may not be aware of. Flying between the planes of existence, the ba carries information from the physical to the astral (or emotional) world, to the mental world, and up, taking all life experience back to Spirit. When you love anyone or any being, you touch all worlds at once.

4. Because the soul receives impressions from the external world, it is important to build homes and communities in places that inspire you, making your aspirations soar. At this time, you are creating a foundation for future manifestation.

5. All things progress through constant change. Now is a time of change, when you are undergoing a deep transformation. You move from a lower consciousness to a higher consciousness. As you progress you are helping the planet to progress—because it, too, has a soul.

6. When we release the idea of limitation, we can realize the perfection of our souls. Salvation comes not simply by piling up good deeds, but by first recognizing that all we do is redeemed by a spiritualization of our bodies. We make use of our errors by understanding them and by working to incorporate those lessons into every subsequent act in our lives.

7. The soul touches both the inner realm of Spirit, from which it receives inspiration, and the external world, from which it receives impressions. As you bring into expression the original purity of divine consciousness, your soul is purified.

8. This body is a temple for the soul. Its presence there forms our ideals and informs our worlds. As it grows, we evolve. Release your attachment to this particular physical structure where your soul now resides. That bird will fly in and out of many temples. The most important thing is for you to feed your soul with spiritual food in whatever temple it exists in.

9. Human consciousness undergoes perpetual consciousness. Spiritual consciousness is eternal. The soul continues to fly higher up the ladder toward heaven until it can truly identify with Source. "The Father and I are one."

BENBEN

Beginning with the Third Dynasty of the Old Kingdom, the pharaonic tomb was built in the shape of a pyramid, a labor-intensive project. We see this image of the pyramid with its capstone in the image on the previous page. Later, during the New Kingdom, grand obelisks were erected by a number of different pharaohs to honor the sun god. Benben indicated the capstones of both the pyramid of a necropolis built on the western bank of the Nile and the obelisk of the temples built on the eastern riverbank. The capstones of obelisks often were mirrors of light reflecting the power of the sun god throughout the temples. They caught the dawn light at the moment that the sun crested a hill. The gilded capstone of a pyramid reflected the rays of the setting sun, and with it the promise of the sun's return tomorrow after its journey through the night. The capstone often became the focal point of a complex of buildings, such as the Great Pyramid in Giza, the Step Pyramid in Saqqara, or the obelisk stones at Karnak. In a land that celebrates divine beings creating the world by their utterances of light, the gilded and polished capstones reflected the extreme reaches of the spiritual sun.

Benben identified that mound of earth that arose from the dissipating floods at the dawn of Creation. In Genesis 1:31 Yahweh looked down upon what he had created and he saw that it was very good—not just good but *very* good. *Ben* in the hieroglyphs also means "what is good, true, and right to seed the future." Perhaps it relates to our words *beneficial* and *benevolent,* which derive from the Latin *bene.* Benben means that something is considered to be not just good, but doubly good, or as my Egyptian tour guides would say, *meya-meya,* meaning literally "two thousand percent."

The bennu bird, or phoenix, early on entered into the mythology of the venerated each day at Heliopolis, the capital city of Ra on the east bank of the Nile. The bustling modern city of Cairo has overtaken its site. Only the limestone capstone of Chephren's pyramid (sans gold) remains in Giza on the western bank. The Pyramid Texts in Saqqara, however, recount the importance of the pharaoh identifying with the cult of the phoenix, or bennu, in nearby Heliopolis.

Egyptologist Barry Kemp identifies the phoenix, or benben, with the hieroglyph for the way in which the rising sun, *weben,* sent forth its rays toward the west, illuminating the benben pyramid stone on which the bennu bird lives. Utterance 600, line 1652, of the Pyramid Texts says at the dawn of Creation Atum arose as the benben in the Mansion of the Phoenix in Heliopolis.[17] Benben as part of a spiritual complex may also refer to the body as a temple, for it houses the bodies of our spiritual development and enlightenment.

Can you see also the pyramid as our eternal home—the light of the divine soul that is connected to each of us? It is the seed of light within. The pyramid is also connected to astrology, to the timing of things according to the movement of the spheres and thereby vibrations. Consider that the obelisks operated on both sound and light.

1. Accept your own divine light. Remember that the divine spark of God—the phoenix—resides inside you. You may know this but often forget it. Any time you find yourself lost, remember that the light inside you is just a breath away. Breathe on that spark until it glows again.

2. As above, so below; as within, so without. This hermetic dictum assures us that earthly life reflects spiritual light. The light we make here shines in the heavens above us. Heaven and Earth are mirrors for one another.

3. The Trinity of Father/Mother/God or of Spirit/Mind/Matter appears in the symbol of the pyramid. This is the creative child in you, me, and all of us. A candle flame reaches up to connect with the light of heaven, dancing with the power of Spirit.

4. A pyramid's foundation resides in solid earth—not on the earth, but in the earth. Chambers of initiation in the Great Pyramid extend well into the earth. Your spiritual work needs these same practical, foundational roots. Reach into the depths to feed your soul. Quiet contemplation, especially when you are faced with difficulties, is the foundation of spiritual ascension.

5. A pyramid contains magic. Those who chant within the King's Chamber of the Great Pyramid may hear overtones of song from ancient masters that seem to emanate through the walls. The Grand Gallery of this pyramid is said to hold the history of the planet with constructions so accurate that the numerical vibrations create in living stone a predictive pattern for future events.[18]

6. Take care of your home and private meditation space. Remove any mental, emotional, or physical clutter for better access to Spirit. Ask what thoughts are hindering your progress. Keep your mind free of that clutter. Do not attach to what you don't need.

7. Ground your intentions to move your energy upward to see what the divine plan of your life may be. Before you do anything to distract you from spiritual goals, sit in meditation and look for the divine plan. Work with the oracles of your choice.

8. Creating a pyramid takes energy, time, and a division of labor. At this time examine the particular things necessary to accomplish a large overall goal. You can't build it alone. You are the overseer, like the chief vizier of the pharaoh. Spirit takes the credit. Allow Spirit to use you.

9. The benben is a place of death and renewal where atop the pyramid the phoenix builds his pyre. That is actually a golden moment to be attained, like reaching retirement in a blaze of glory and passing on what you know to the next generation. Celebrate something well-done so that you can go on to a new life and reawakening.

BLANK

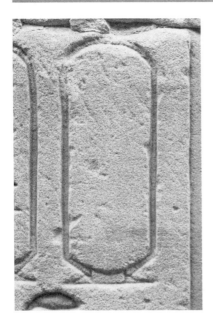

Emptiness is the hallmark of beginnings and endings. Imagine the universe handing you a blank scroll on which to make your mark. The next step determines the subsequent steps. There is no void that will not be filled. It is not possible to take no step at all; something is about to happen. Not taking a step means missing an opportunity. In some of the temples built during the Greco-Roman period of Egypt one finds empty cartouches where the name of the pharaoh was to have been inserted, but the pharaoh may have changed before the work was complete. The emptiness created a kind of placeholder.

This blank space offers freedom of choice. You might think of it as a wild card. A statue is formed, in part, by empty space—otherwise it would remain a block of marble and nothing else.

Let there be some empty space on your canvas of life, a space for Spirit to enter. The air that we breathe is never empty. It is full of the sustenance of life.

Meditation is the prime work with emptiness. It allows us a container for being—not doing or thinking. It empties the clutter so that light (and enlightenment) may fill us. Light is not something we grasp with our hands; it is an etheric state of consciousness. If there were no spaces between the synapses of your brain, there would be no awareness, no movement, no spark.

Allow space in your life.

1. Someone needs to stop talking. If you ask a question, listen for an answer. One cannot lead without intending a direction. What is the goal?
2. Be willing to receive a message or a gift. Receiving well is a gift you give back to the giver.
3. Be open. Let yourself become one with the creative force of Spirit.
4. Make space in your life. Include rest as part of your daily life plan.
5. Wait patiently for divine instructions. When you hear them, be ready to act.
6. A cleanse is needed. It is time for forgiveness, healing, and paying attention to your body.
7. A miracle approaches. Spend time in meditation as you prepare to receive.
8. Plans will change. Be open and adjust.
9. Let go. Let things pass. Practice emptiness.

DJED

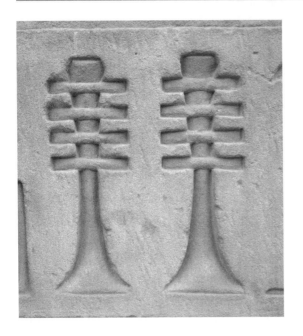 

The sensitive conduit of the spinal cord empowers the body to move, to receive impressions, and to express energy. The spinal column of stacked vertebrae protects this sensitive life force energy. The djed column represents the power of the backbone, the spine that gives stability to this kundalini life force. Be sure that the channel is clear and that the house is ready for the electrical cables. Pinched nerves and blockages of emotion become problematic in that they obstruct the flow of energy necessary for good health.

If one perceives kundalini energy as feminine, one can grasp how the ancient ones perceived the goddess Isis, and any other goddess, as a protective, projective cobra that rises up, spitting fire. The god Osiris, then, is the backbone that supports the life force energy. The djed symbol becomes intimately connected to Osiris who, in myth, was ensnared inside a tamarisk tree. The djed depicts the physical body as a container enclosing spiritual light. In the djed image, the limbs of the tree are severed. In the myth of Osiris, the powerful tamarisk springs up magically overnight around his coffin, which becomes the supporting pillar of a future temple. Life comes out of death. The djed symbol contains that mystery.

In the Qabalah, the Tree of Life represents four planes of existence: the physical, astral (or emotional), mental, and spiritual. These four

Isis, together with the pharaoh Seti I, raises the djed of Osiris at Abydos. Osiris is the god source contained within the body and on all four planes of existence—the physical, emotional, mental, and spiritual.

planes are similarly used in the ancient Egyptian djed symbol. The entire Tree of Life, which represents a full pattern for understanding consciousness, offers us a lifelong study. For our purposes, it is worth remembering that spiritual energy is what the poet Dylan Thomas called "the force that through the green fuse drives the flower."[19] The human body is the djed—the container and protector of the life force.

If the tree was rooted in the ground, its trunk would represent a living Osiris. The god/man's joy was represented as the verdant garden. What hangs from a living apple tree is fruit. The snake in the garden, the wise one, is Isis as a snake goddess. Adam and Eve in the Garden of Eden are the living Isis and Osiris in the gardens of Egypt's Black Land. The Tree of Life itself demonstrates the unfoldment of our developing consciousness. Working with that Tree of Life as the Tree of Knowledge in the garden helps us to discern intentions and the difference between good and evil. The apple in the sacred garden is secret wisdom. If the tree is cut down, there is no fruit.

What do you think the serpent knew?

Pruning the tree keeps it flowering; thus life and death are intertwined. We must prune and regrow so the heavy fruit will not break the tree. Ponder this: When it is time to exit this life, what might our legacy be? How have we lived to become pillars of the community? Can our lives be seen as supporting the structures of what comes after us?

1. Indeed, this tree in the garden represents the kind of renewal that follows a good pruning. You are getting down to the essential organic design of something. Be sure to root yourself firmly in the soil before what will be a rapid growth begins.

2. The djed speaks of male and female partnerships, of giving and receiving. The living Isis energy offers itself to Osiris. The protection of Osiris is offered to Isis. In true partnership two people uplift each other.

3. A new life plan begins. This new may not be a physical child, but a spiritual child, a product of a perfect union of masculine and feminine creativity.

4. It's important to work all four planes without forsaking one for another. Learn to feel creative energy (earth, water, air, and fire) moving up and down your spine in order to create a full, complex, living project, whether that project is a book, a family, a business endeavor—or you! Feed and water every aspect of your life with love. Support it from the earth plane by spending time in nature, and reach up into the air for Spirit by spending time in meditation.

5. Reach out. A windmill is a Djed Pillar in motion that generates energy through action. Let the energy of Spirit sustain you and move you to empower others. Communicate your intentions. Send out your messages. Generate some electricity in your peers.

6. Care for yourself by attending to the body's needs. Allow others to help you. When Osiris was trapped inside his truncated tree, Isis tended to him. Every temple in ancient Egypt contained massive stacked columns. Each pillar in these "Halls of Creation" told a different story, and all stories together tell the entire story of Spirit.

7. Ptah, the creator god, seems to be inert. He stands steady, holding a magic wand containing the Djed Pillar, his ankh, and his waz. Yet he created the world through voice vibration, by speaking it into existence. See your body as an instrument of chi energy. Watch Spirit move through you.

8. The energy of the caduceus—a single rod that supports two rising snakes—represents the entwined energetic channels of our DNA. The twin serpents form the rungs of the DNA chain. Cross-pollinated energies will integrate into one strong pattern.

9. It is time to get unstuck. How does the story of Osiris represent a part of your life? If you are stuck in a tree, where are you stuck? What has been cut off from you? How has your creative energy been blocked? What are the jewels hidden inside you? What do you dream of enacting, and what does your secret longing teach you?

DJHUTY (THOTH)

Thoth is the Lord of Time and the bridge to god consciousness. Part of his name is written with the hieroglyph of the akh bird (which we can see in the images above), or the shining intelligence, because he possesses the highest spiritual understanding. Thoth is the conduit for the great wisdom tradition passed on from the cosmos. His akh intelligence, active on the spiritual plane, influences manifestation. Thoth offers his wisdom and experience of the inner planes with flashes of insight—and frequently with trickster energies.

Some Egyptologists have suggested that the hieroglyph of the darkened circle is a placenta. I'm not in agreement. In my opinion, because it is most often related to the god Thoth, the *kh* hieroglyph is a darkened new moon. A lunar god would have begun measuring time beginning with the new moon. Typically, new moons are also the perfect astrological time in which to begin any new endeavor, which will grow as the light of the moon waxes. In that regard perhaps the *kh* hieroglyph of Thoth demonstrates the nurturing of life and any creation.

Using the principles of truth, order, and justice Thoth shaped the universe. These principles reveal themselves in the physical world as sacred geometry, higher mathematics, physics, and metaphysics. A messenger from the divine mind, he invented the hieroglyphs—the words of God. In this way he translated divine truth into concepts we can grasp. He used symbol as the form most easily understood in number, name, story, law, and humor.

One of the oldest creator gods, Djhuty, is lord of calendars and time, regulating the cyclical patterns of the moon that waxes, wanes, and returns to full. He epitomizes change as an eternal constant. In the creation myth of Hermopolis, his capital city, Thoth stirred the cosmic cauldron with his caduceus. The cauldron contained the eight beings known as the Ogdoad, whom we have discussed before. They were four male frogs and four female serpents. These pairs of oppositions defined the primordial principals of infinite darkness, infinite light, infinite time, and infinite space. Thoth's work was a mathematical construct in which unity, division, and multiplication constituted the powers of Creation.

As magician, sage, healer, scribe, and alchemist, Thoth often carries a variety of staffs and implements, all of which allude to his many diverse talents and powers. Some of these staffs are adorned with yet other hieroglyphic symbols, such as ankhs representing life, frogs representing multitudes of things, and shens representing eternity. With his caduceus, a winged staff on which two serpents entwine, we see Thoth as the ultimate healer. The magical rod of Moses, with which he brought forth water from a rock and parted the Red Sea, was alternately a serpent and a staff. The Greek god of medicine, Asclepius, carried a magical staff entwined with a single serpent. The snake-entwined staff remains a symbol of doctors and pharmacists today. Djhuty not only healed the gods of their injuries, his high priests became the chief physicians of the pharaohs. Some of the earliest medical texts were inscribed on papyrus by practitioners of the ancient Egyptian healing arts.

A master alchemist, Thoth was said to have authored many treatises on healing and magic. Among the most well-known was the Emerald

Thoth appears in Abydos. In his capacity as healer, he holds the caduceus with its serpent energies and touches the lips of the pharaoh to enliven him with the ankh.

Tablet (or Tablets), which details the natural laws that govern the universe. Of the many versions of the Emerald Tablet now in print, I prefer the version by alchemical philosopher Dennis Hauck. Thoth trained Egyptian priests as high magicians, sorcerers, philosophers, healers, alchemists, temple builders, Akashic recordkeepers, dream interpreters, and authors who worked with the gods Thoth and Ra to contribute the "Wow!" factor to civilization. The high priest Imhotep epitomized the Renaissance man of ancient Egypt. A scribe par excellence, Thoth authored the Egyptian Book of the Dead, writing forty-two of its chapters in his own hand. Considered the teacher's teacher, he continues to write and teach through his dedicated scribes who listen to his voice.

When Thoth appears in the natural world in his heron or ibis form, that sign is taken as tangible proof that one is being prepared to do an important magical work and to be initiated into the high mysteries. An ibis fishing spreads its wing to create a shadow on the water into which it peers, to see the fish swimming in the river's depths. Meditation is a similar place of shade in which Thoth wishes to appear. Thoth helps you to peer into the depths of your life to see what is hidden in plain sight.

1. Thoth says that it is time to start a new work. The next few months will begin your initiation into a deeper level of spiritual understanding. Great things have been planned for you.
2. As above, so below, says the first lesson of the Emerald Tablet of Thoth. Ask him how you can manifest Spirit in your life. The number two is a partnership number. Here it refers specifically to the partnering of the human and the Divine; thus it represents the power of spiritual initiation. Begin reading enthusiastically to renew and energize your spiritual studies. In meditation ask to be guided. Ask your spirit guides to accompany you in your endeavors.
3. Put creative works on the front burner. Write, plan, paint, and fire up your alchemical athanor. You may be asked to teach a younger person how to use their creative gifts or the spiritual powers of their mind. Even if this young person does not ask directly in this way, understand that this is what you will be mentoring them about.

4. Spirit sees and approves your commitment to building a strong spiritual foundation through a study of natural law. Prepare yourself by preparing your physical environment in order to better accomplish the coming work.

5. You experience an alchemical transformation under the direction of Thoth. Alchemical transmutations are not always easy, but they are a deeply powerful, sacred work that, in the end, sends you into the world more richly imbued with spiritual gifts than ever before. If your life is heating up in the cauldron of the cosmos, accept the process with gratitude.

6. Healing takes place on a deep level. It begins with a change in thinking and emanates through your DNA, through yourself, and it pours into every part of your body. When you sleep at night, clear your mind. Visualize this healing energy pouring into you through your crown chakra, surging through you with every breath. Release all toxins and negative thinking, then allow the healing energy to fill that empty space. Deep sleep rejuvenates you.

7. Thoth asks you to bring Spirit into form by entering the consciousness of Earth. He asks you to listen to what the Earth needs from humanity. You are a healer and a spiritual being. Thoth has a zest for spiritual knowledge. You will soon be guided by him in a sacred work.

8. Just as Thoth wrote the chapters of the Book of the Dead with his own fingers, it's time to put your fingers into the work. There is much for you to study—eight areas, in fact: numerology, astrology, natural law, life after death, alchemy, quantum physics, mythology, and dreamwork. By the time you finish all of these studies you will have attained the equivalent of a Ph.D. in metaphysical understanding.

9. The true name of the so-called Egyptian Book of the Dead was the "Book of Coming into Light." Thoth opens the door for you and ushers you to a new level. Moving through darkness into light initiates the transpersonal transformation of the spirit, mind, and body. Create a ritual around eliminating and burying the things that no longer serve you.

DSER

Dser, meaning "red," is the root of the word *desert,* which the Egyptians knew as the Red Land. Dser also indicated blood and battle—in other words, a time of testing and trial. In southern Egypt beyond the narrow green strip that bordered the Nile, the western desert rose into high reddish sand dunes, and on the eastern side, desert wadis ran endlessly through the land. These red sand hills are depicted in the hieroglyph and the valleys scooped out by the mighty khamsin winds sometimes reveal the bones of animals or travelers who died there. Recent shifting desert sands have revealed an ancient Persian army that perished and was consumed by a cataclysmic howling sandstorm in 524 BCE. Further in and far away from the sea lie the 40,000 year old bones of prehistoric whales that became trapped there. Where once there was a lush savannah and before that the bottom of the sea, mounds of red and yellow sand now flow. It wasn't always this way.

Recently I took a group of travelers to the predynastic city of El Kab, dedicated to the vulture goddess. High upon the desert cliff faces we saw Paleolithic images depict the great horned goddess blessing the animals—cows and gazelles. Herons waded beside the sailing ships and boats, which must have plied this second river, a mere phantom of the Nile now. Climate change has made a clean sweep and little remains of the desert's lush past. The desert holds many secrets. According to one myth, those Persian soldiers drowned in a sandstorm concocted by an Egyptian magician-queen.

This was the land of the god Set, whose dark impulses overtook him and caused him to murder his brother Osiris. There is little of permanence in the desert. You cannot build upon it because the sands shift. You cannot stay here. You must pass through without attracting attention, and the trek is arduous. Scorpions, vipers, robbers, and outlaws lie in wait. You run into obstacles. Your camel cannot carry too much; it and you will perish. Yet here and there a hidden river runs; an oasis pops up. You may refresh at the oasis, but you cannot stay. This is not your home. Kind strangers will refresh you but then you must move on.

When you hit a rough patch in life, you have wandered into the desert, becoming a stranger in a strange land. But in the desert wilderness Jesus underwent his trial by fire before he began his ministry. This is a rite of passage. There is still hope, dear traveler. The stars appear to guide you. Indeed, an end to the journey will come. Are you ready to begin again?

Both Moses and Akhenaten traveled an unmarked track, leaving the religion of their youth and going on a vision quest into the desert. Blazing a trail can be an impulse of the ego or full of illumination. It is imperative, however, to contemplate the obstacles that you and those who follow you will face. The Red Land stirs the primal blood energy. You might make this trek because you desire a change. It may be a mistake; or maybe not. It will be harder than you think. You will lose and find yourself. You will find your oasis and leave it. You will grow wiser in the end.

1. A long journey lies ahead. You know there is no way around it except to travel through it. Make your preparations. Carry only what is essential. Your inner strength and your trust in following the prodding of God will be the magic staff upon which you lean.

2. There are two rivers that are equally sustaining. One is the verdant Nile; the other stream lies hidden underground. Both offer life-giving water, but the hidden Nile is most precious for it appears unpredictably whenever it is needed. Find the blessings in your time of trial. Those will sustain you forever.

3. A creative person like yourself cannot constantly create. One needs fallow periods. Allow for some emptiness. Stop whipping yourself forward. Look for an oasis and rest. Go out and let the wind blow the burden and cares from your shoulders.

4. It's time to sort through your daily packs—what you try to accomplish, carry, or do. Pare down your to-do list. Commit only to the essentials for now. By making things lighter you gather your strength.

5. Stay flexible and tolerant of changes around you. You are learning what you never knew you would need to know—how to survive in times of trial. Keep your senses sharp.

6. Traveling the desert alone is difficult. One falls prey to many a mirage. When in doubt, rely on what you know, not on what you hope to find. Miraculous help appears when you need it.

7. It feels as if this long desert trek will never end. It will. Whenever possible, rest. Look at the stars that wheel through the night sky. Their patterns kept ships moving at sea and Bedouins crossing the desert. Stars led the magi to the Christ child. Study the stars and chart your course.

8. Keep your chin up. Do what has to be done. Money, sex, power—all these are mirages. Follow your deep soul dreams. Even nightmares can be useful instruction.

9. You soon reach the end of a long journey. Rather than trying to forget it ever happened, go back through this time to make a list of gratitude. Name what you have earned, what you have learned, and the qualities you have developed. Keep this wisdom list for future reference.

DUAT

That sacred place of darkness, the hidden world of emptiness before fullness and light, is known as duat, the womb of the goddess Nut. When you are in darkness and do not know what will happen next, be still. You are held in the belly of the Great Mother. In the darkness of the chrysalis the caterpillar is reshaped and divinely transformed into a butterfly. If you find yourself in doubt or worry, think of the stars and how their light encourages us to move in the darkness.

In the myth of Nut and Geb, all the stars in the Milky Way live eternally inside the body of Nut, Great Mother and sky goddess. Each star is a living, shining spirit of every person who was ever born, ever died, or has yet to be reborn. A star, of course, is like our sun, ever-changing and giving off energy. Energy can never be destroyed. It only changes form. Even in the dark times of your life, you are living, changing, and shining.

At night the stars demonstrate the vastness of the universe, shining like a thousand thoughts in the mind of God. These stars heal, bring peace, and offer a vision of the big picture. The big sky of the arid Sahara Desert shows us millions of glimmering lights. Think of duat as the master number fifty. Duat is DaVinci's perfected man standing within the circle. The five points of the star are his head, outstretched arms, and feet. The circle wherein he stands is the limitless beginning and ending presence of God. The symbol shows us how we and the Divine are co-creators of the world we inhabit. Look at this five-pointed image on the right-hand side of the photograph above, and meditate on it. As well, study the stars, which can tell us when and how to use our co-creative energies. Everything about this hieroglyph reveals a test of our powers.

Duat brings you to the edge of the mystery of life, death, and transformation. As with the desert, entering duat can be entering an unknown landscape. In the underworld, in the cavern, in the dark interior of ourselves, is the land wherein Osiris lives side by side with the mystery of his father, Atum. In ancient cultures, one met the gods inside the cave that separated us from the world we knew, and there we received their oracles—the words of one's destiny. The caterpillar does not know, but will soon learn, that this cavern of becoming will turn him into a butterfly. What was once his life will never be as it was before. Yet the life that is coming is utter beauty.

1. Because you lead others, your mind must be clear. When you enter a dark passage, few around you know what is happening. Continue to detach from ego and the drama of a situation.

2. You may have lost a twin flame yet your beloved stands beside you always. After Osiris passed into Spirit, he and Isis still worked together. Follow the guidance you receive from Spirit. The physical departure heralds a spiritual arrival. Feel love emanate from the spirit world.

3. In recent times light and clarity seem scarce. Perhaps you feel you haven't enough energy, time, money, or wisdom. Worry stifles creative flow. A shift approaches. Eliminate fear in order to prosper. Eliminate a block in some creative way.

4. Stay focused on the goal. When in darkness, use the power of your inner light—that is enlightenment. Do not allow fear or short-term gains to distract you. Focus in. The goal awaits.

5. You know this truth but may have forgotten: Everything has its cycle. The moon and the seasons demonstrate waxing and waning energies. All things die but leave a seed for renewal. Let nature be your comfort, hope, and lesson. What passes away returns. That is a natural law.

6. Someone near you passes through a dark time. In your own gentle way, help them negotiate the trouble. Do not fix it for them. Listen and make simple, affirmative suggestions. Ask them: What blessing disguised as a loss is being revealed, or what understanding has this situation taught?

7. You may be passing through or have just finished a time of trial. Do not pray for only the gift of things; make your prayers an adoration of God. What blessings did you receive? By blessing the darkness and thanking it (rather than cursing it), we turn our attention to our own light. While you wait for your answer, tend Earth's garden and set your heart in order.

8. Now is the time to stand up. Invoke divine help. Ask Spirit for clarity and assistance but take charge of any dark or stormy situation. Lead, but be clear in what you want to accomplish and how it will benefit those who come after you. Have courage. Know you embody a divine purpose.

9. Trust your feelings. Intuition and dreams will carry you to a distant shore and back again. Let go of the self-doubt generated by other people's opinions. Spirit supports and leads you.

GEB

The earth god Geb partners with the sky mother Nut. Whereas she holds the magic of the planets, stars, and constellations that pivot across the sky, he contains the magic of minerals, plants, vegetables, and herbs that arise from his body. Sprung from the life potential hidden within Atum, those seeds planted in the body of Geb spring into a playground of sensory delight. A fertility god, Geb offers the choicest foods of the Earth.

He rises up to meet his beloved wife, Nut, the way Earth's hills thrust up from the bedrock to bring us closer in rapture to the heavens. The longing of Heaven for Earth and Earth for Heaven is as strong as the longing of Osiris and Isis. The emptiness of the space that separates Nut and Geb is created by the god of air, Shu, who holds the sky goddess aloft. To some degree Shu represents the space that the mind requires as a conduit in meditation to calm the chatter of the material world as it tries to attain the spiritual dimensions.

Together, Nut and Geb are the powerful parents of the five great gods and goddesses: Osiris, Horus, Set, Isis, and Nephthys. Sometimes Geb appears as a man with a serpent head, but most often he is shown as a goose like his father, Atum (as in the facing image). Geb often appears covered in green shoots. He offers himself as the embodiment of all the fecundity of Earth. He has an intimate connection with Osiris and the souls of the dead that follow after. He embraces them as the Earth holds close the bodies of those souls who have passed on. He feeds them the cakes and fruits in the Field of Reeds, and in the underworld he observes the weighing of the heart along with the other gods and goddesses.

1. Praise to the Earth as it sprang from the thoughts of the Divine into manifestation. The appearance of Geb offers a strong ecological consciousness.
2. Heaven and Earth are mirrors of possibility. All that we shall become and which we grow into during a lifetime on this planet were planted as star seeds in the belly of Nut. Geb is our greening.
3. The Green Man of Egypt was originally Geb. His son, Osiris, likewise exhibited earth energy. Father and son both demonstrate the power of life transforming through photosynthesis. Geb is the natural Green Man of Egypt whereas Osiris is the cultivated green land.
4. Nut's heavenly body emulates the Milky Way. Geb's phallus becomes the hill that rises up to meet her. His green, languid body becomes the border of papyrus and bulrushes growing along the river. Earth is your domain. You have the power to demonstrate your creative aspirations.
5. Some myths describe Geb as the goose that laid the golden egg of the

world—not Mother Goose. On the other hand, Nut's hieroglyph sometimes contains a cosmic egg. I believe Geb holds the powers of male fecundity, which derive from love. Embrace your fertile masculinity.

6. Geb holds all the healing plants of the Earth. The Temple of Horus at Edfu depicts their medicinal powers. These plants and minerals were made into potions and oils. Explore herbal tinctures and oils as an avenue for self-healing.

7. One of Geb's chthonic powers is alluded to by his serpent head. While he may be the serpent of the underworld that curls around the dead, enclosing them in his body, he also aligns to the sexual magic of the kundalini rising up in the tantric union of Heaven and Earth.

8. At times called the Great Cackler, Geb laid the cosmic egg of the world and laughed so hard at his unexpected magic that he created earthquakes. Sometimes life takes a sudden, unexpected turn. There's nothing to do about it but laugh.

9. Both the male serpent Geb and Set represent the limits of the material realm. Rather than thinking of this as a limiting event or someone standing on your shoelaces (Set), learn to set your own limits (Geb). If you don't set limits for yourself, the universe may set them for you.

HEH

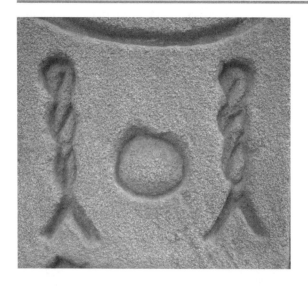 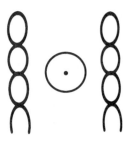

Heh represents the law of eternity. All energy circulates and that is what keeps us going. Blood circulates; nerve endings fire and travel through the body. The heart (the sun, the primordial fire) in heh pushes and pumps the energy that vibrates from within to without, beyond itself, ad infinitum. At times heh appears as a frog that indicates millions and millions of years. At other times, heh is the divine breath of Shu circumambulating the Earth. As the explosive sound of life and spirit emerging from the lips of Atum, we see that this image is similar to the non-egoic energy of the Qabalistic meaning of *He* in *Yod-He-Vav-He.* It is as if heh is the outbreath of light. The hieroglyphs show the heh symbol on either side of the sun.

The Roman letter *H* depicts parallel lines on either side of the letter, which to me conjures up the two rungs of the ladder of DNA. The crossbar is life force fire flaring between them. The hieroglyph of the *H* indicates a twisted fiber that becomes a wick to hold the candle flame. In sacred ceremonies, the candlewick is the human form upon which the fire of Spirit burns. The burning of candles in Christian ceremonies speaks of the light as Christ consciousness, but every spiritual tradition celebrates a festival of light. Our earthly bodies are but wick and wax. In this doubled image the wicks seem to burn in both directions (past and future), while the solar fire of the present holds the center. If the fire principle is too intense, it results in burning one's candle at both ends. The poet Edna St. Vincent Millay said that candle flame "will not last the night . . . but it makes a lovely light."[20]

Past and future are implied, but the fiber twists upon itself as if it holds a partial secret about cyclical return. Three circles stacked upon each other operate as a triune god force. Energy flows through three levels of the creative world—Yetzirah, Briah, and Atziluth—the formative, creative, and archetypal worlds on the Tree of Life that precede manifestation in the material world. Creation happens when worlds fertilize each other, when they come together, separate, then move back together again, like DNA recombining in various forms. What matters is the present light shining in their midst. Only in the presence of God do we shine.

Time exhibits a similar system of organizing the ebb and flow of energy, of doubling back upon itself. Ultimately, though, time is a mental construction that illuminates how things occur in ways that affect us on mental, emotional, and physical levels. In the spirit world time does not exist in the same way. Composed of light that has been constructed differently, it is a creation of consciousness called eternity. Consciousness exists across galaxies that interact with each other, creating their own kind relationship, just as cells communicate across the synapses in our brains. Time moves instantaneously; its momentary passage is an illusion.

1. The eternal godhead represents truth and all time. Focus on increasing your light in the here and now. In that way it has far-reaching effects into the future.

2. Pasts and futures interweave as part of the convoluted dance of time. Time twists and turns like these fibers on the candlewick. Do not rely on memory or expectation. Rely on what is in the heart, which is the core of one's being and spiritual light. There the flame burns brightest.

3. The cycles of time repeat as beginning, being, and ending, like a thread and needle moving in and out of the fabric of the life. See yourself as an eternal being having a temporal experience.

4. We are born into the infinities of cosmic law: infinite time, space, light, and darkness. Use your ability to manipulate time wisely. Practical use of time is only needed for where you are now. Your future life shifts according to your needs. If a demand is made on your time, create an opening and use the time wisely. Don't fret over time lost.

5. You may feel as if you are in a spin. But truly, everything happens at once—even multi-dimensionally. Time is an illusion. If you feel as if you don't have enough time, consider your focus of attention. The problem may be that actually you are aware of too many clocks running all at once. Focus on one thing "at a time," so to speak. Possibilities abound.

6. When we do what we love, time relaxes. A heart at peace and in joy creates a pattern of acceptance and comfort. Our heartbeat actually creates the illusion of time. We can speed time up or slow it down according to

our actions. Meditation stretches time; multitasking diminishes it. Listen to your heart; follow your joy.

7. Eternal being of light, be here now. Live your truth. Live your eternal, not your temporal, nature. Find time to meditate on being at the center of divine light—at one with the One. Feel love stretch beyond time and space. Reach out in love to your ancestors and descendants.

8. Many things are possible. You have lived many lives before this one. You have experienced relationships with many people. Nothing is random; all is interconnected. All is as it should be.

9. Bob Dylan encouraged us to "Stay forever young." Endings are illusions; all begins again. None of us are separate from each other. Life holds no strangers. Through community—even by simply sharing this Earth—we are all connected. We breathe the same air, drink the same water, are warmed by the same sun. Every being belongs to a family whose members resonate to the same stellar-born energy. Look for that resonance in all situations.

HEKA

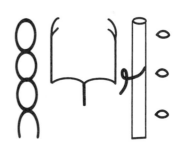

Magic is a divine act. By the time of the Middle Kingdom, magic was perceived as a divine being—creator, sustainer, and protector. In the Coffin Texts, the god Heka proclaims to the other neteru, "I am a god greater than you because I came to be before any of the other gods came into existence. I am Heka."[21] Most Egyptologists translate *heka* as "magical incantation," however, heka embodies the idea that thoughts are things. What achieves the outcome in affirmation, invocation, prayer, or thought is the desire for it to be so.

Even from his corner of the Egyptian Museum in Cairo, this Middle Kingdom statue of Heka, the god of magic, clearly demonstrates how alive he remains. When you pass by this lifelike representation, the energy is still palpable.

When personal will aligns with divine will and the will to manifest accompanies inspiration, then the metaphysical passion to make something happen fills the atmosphere; and so it happens. That is the power and magic of thought manifestation, which is a demonstratable law of mind. The greatest magic of any kind comes from Infinite Intelligence, whose thought brought the world into form. From the beginning it was meant for this power of the mind to be available to man. The master Jesus told his disciples in John 14:12 "All these things I do, you can do also, and even greater than these."

A caution accompanies this capacity. Because humans were also given free will, we can choose to use that metaphysical power wisely or unwisely, evoking good or ill, according to the will, the desires of the heart, and the power of thought. This is why Swiss Egyptologist Erik Hornung called magic "the nuclear energy of the early civilizations because of its dangerousness and its power to transform the world."[22]

The hieroglyph shows two arms reaching out (or up) as if longing to embrace God or another person. It implies that the power of all-embracing love manifests intention. Many cultures assume an attitude of prayer with two arms reaching up toward Spirit. When we reach up in that gesture that pulls our arms out from the chest, we open the heart to be penetrated by a divine love light.

In some of the New Kingdom papyri the word *heka* ends with a hieroglyphic rolled-up papyrus scroll tied with string. The ancient lector-priest-magician untied the scroll whose words were so powerful and sacred that it was ordinarily kept sealed. He read aloud, *verbatim,* the magical utterance and prayer with powerful intention. In this way he revealed the true meaning of the divine incantation unknown to ordinary man. Only a pure one dared to reveal the divine truth and use the mental power.

1. Follow your heart. It will never lead you astray. If you have the slightest doubt about whether it is right, however, don't do it (whatever "it" may be). Rely on divine guidance. Always trust your heart. You already know what is right for you, for its secret is already written in the scroll of your heart.

2. Perhaps you want more love in your life, a deepened relationship. Feeding one another feeds the body, mind, and spirit. You and a companion may share a heartfelt conversation over a good dinner. Be open to hearing what is in the other's heart.

3. Follow your bliss; your joy ignites and manifests your deep desire. You attain your life's purpose when you put passion into your work and relationships. If a hobby brings you joy, do more of it. Suffering isn't always necessary and joy is our natural birthright. Stay positive. Hold good thoughts as you work. Speak up. Share with others what you need to succeed.

4. Your prayers are heard. Now work the magic. Work hard for world peace, compassion, enlightenment, love, and abundance, so that all may attain the same. By seeing and treating others as yourself, you open the door to creative solutions for them and for you.

5. Now is the time to work for positive change. Create an altar space and make time in your daily life to invoke the changes you want. Even lighting a candle and saying an invocation before you sit down to work can have dramatic results. Let go of perfectionism that leads to procrastination. Do. Be. Engage in the work ahead. No need to control everything. Let Spirit do the steering.

6. Peace becomes you. Resolve any arguments through loving, well-chosen words. Vow to speak healing words consciously with a pure heart, and act compassionately toward others and toward yourself. We could affect world peace if we truly used the magical powers of conscious thought, word, and deed.

7. The first relationship to develop is between yourself and Spirit. All else falls into place after that. Meditate. Don't be afraid to walk your path, even if your family doesn't get it. Only you can attain your enlightenment. Develop your own practice. Be still and listen to your heart. Tell yourself the truth so that you can tell others. Tell yourself over and over, if need be, so that you may courageously speak your truth.

8. The law of balance requires us to be in right relation to our family, our community, our work, and ourselves. If all beings attain this, the world comes into balance and peace appears. Practice this daily—freely giving

and receiving love. Practice compassion. Practice forgiveness. Any unhealed feeling toward another person keeps you out of balance.

9. Great blessings are meant to be shared. Give of that which you have been given. Coins are seed energy forms. Spread some around. Seed new blessings. Let go of tension. Play some music. Relax. Let what is full empty, so that what is empty can fill.

HERU (HORUS)

From the name of the son of Isis and Osiris, the boy whom the Greeks called Horus and the ancient Egyptians called Heru, we get the word *hero*. Every living pharaoh became a Horus, wearing his white crown and depicting himself on the temple pylons as capturing Set and mastering chaos. Horus lived a life so large that it was retold over and over again. Beginning in weak infancy until finally emerging as a mighty king, the mythic life of this Heru established what we now call the hero's journey. Depicted as a hawk flying above the Earth, this Horus allows the spiritual winds to uplift him so that he can gain a greater perspective on a particular situation.

Horus leads two lives. Horus the Elder, the sibling of Isis, Osiris, Seth, and Nephthys, never took human form on Earth but remained a spiritual being in the sky, close to the belly of his mother, Nut. Horus the Younger, son of Isis, was not always a hero. The immaculately conceived child of Isis was wounded and fatherless. From birth his life was threatened. He was hunted down and haunted by the murder of his father by his greedy uncle Set. Horus grew up to fight a long battle to right the injustice of his father's death. Some say the war he waged lasted eighty years; others say eons. In one particularly brutal fight, Set blinded Horus.

He endured many hardships common to all mankind: he lost his father, he had an overly protective mother, he was bullied and suffered manipulative family members, he lost his spiritual vision, and so on. He had to grow beyond his wounding. Sometimes his own ego got in the way of his personal growth. What is the reason for one's striving? Is it important simply to be stronger and better than someone else? Or is it better to work to become a stronger and better person than one was the day before?

If something hides itself within your psyche, you can ask the wings of Spirit to uplift you so that you can see your situation more clearly. When rage overcame Horus and blinded him, it was the milk of the goddess Hathor (her compassionate love) that healed Heru's wounds.

The pharaoh embodies the great living hawk god, who is protector, husband, lover, and progenitor of the future. In wearing the Horus crown, the pharaoh declares himself a visionary leader of his people, carrying forward the divine plan that had been handed down and enacted by his ancestors. The hawk-headed human represents the heroic mind, while the human-headed hawk represents the soul of the individual. Both depict the capacity to merge human and divine worlds and to move between them with ease. The hero undertakes a journey into the depths of his psyche, into the world of duat, to understand the divine plan. Becoming a shaman, Horus listens to the voice of his father, Osiris, in the underworld and he heeds the counsel of his mother, Isis, on Earth. He is champion of the people.

Always at his back, the stars of heaven spin in the belly of Nut, the mother of the elder Horus. Called the twice-born, Horus has two incarnations. Therefore, his ba knows that he has an earthly home where he has been given a karmic task to right the wrongs that have been done, and he has a spiritual home in the sky body of his celestial mother. On Earth Horus has a communal responsibility. He must lead by example and teach others to live heroic lives. Heru was the last god to reign in Egypt before the coming of the *Shemsu Hor*. These "followers" or "companions" of Horus reigned a total of 13,400 years, according to the Turin king's list, prior to Narmer, the earliest known pharaoh. The task for which Horus came to Earth was to train the spiritual warriors to come after him.

Heru learned by intuition, by preparing himself mentally, and by laboring in the physical world. From his father, Osiris, he learned to meditate, to be still, and to listen and be taught by his dreams. Mentally, he trained his mind to envision and command the building of a great civilization. From Isis he learned discernment and natural law. Her lesson is all about karma—the law of cause and effect. From pigs you get pigs and from wheat you get wheat, he was taught. Only fools expect different results. This natural law of cause and effect suggests that we need to take care to assure that all of our actions have outcomes that benefit all. No good comes from a selfish act.

Isis also taught her son compassion. Even as he fought Set and nearly conquered him, his mother's compassion for her brother released him from certain death. It was a lesson Horus did not want to learn, and he lashed out at his mother. He had to learn that violence gained him nothing. It's not about winning or losing; it's about maintaining balance. One-winged hawks cannot fly.

In learning how to balance opposing factions, Horus acquired the red crown of the desert tribes and the white crown of the Delta and river dwellers. He equipped himself to hunt and fight as well as to build community. In this way, he is crowned the victor of both the Red Land and the Black Land. He controlled the chaos of Set, but he understood that the challenge, which Set represented, is responsible for his own ability to transform and take command. In the Pyramid Texts the two gods holding up the ladder to heaven are described. Set is on one side and Horus on the other. The law of polarity says that things are the same on opposite sides of the spectrum. It is our perception that separates them. The one cannot exist without the other.

In the town of Edfu we find the most complete temple complex in all of Egypt. It celebrates not only the battles of Horus the Younger with Seth, but also celebrates Horus the Elder. Built by Greco-Roman patriarchs to celebrate the heroic qualities of Heru, the temple complex rests atop an older temple that honors the elder hawk god. That foundational temple, it is said, was erected during early pharaonic history upon an even older, predynastic temple dedicated to the desert god Set. It often happens that sacred structures are erected over the temples of a conquered people. Throughout Egypt, Christian crosses are carved into temples of Isis, and Coptic monasteries, erected in the desert, rest on the temples of Set. In this particular Temple of Horus one feels all the complexities of conflict, resolution, and assimilation of the hero's spiritual tasks.

As the solar light of the sun, Heru illuminates the day with strength and brilliance, and by night the sun's softer, reflected light beams down upon Earth from the mirror of the moon. These are the two eyes of Horus. His right eye is the sun and his left eye the moon. The right eye brings clear vision and the left eye brings intuition or clairvoyance.

1. Stand up and lead; overcome your early doubts. Walk in confidence and stop waiting to be shown the way. Others will follow. Now is time to begin your soul's journey and succeed, to take your destiny in your hands.
2. We are all strong and weak. We all err and have the capacity to transcend our errors; in that transcendence we can rebuild so that no one suffers similarly. There is a possible way to make peace with opposition. Learn from the experience and gain support. Learn from what opposes you. What point of view do you need to see?
3. You are a divine child born under a lucky star. By meditating with Horus,

you will see your situation more clearly. Opportunities may be spied like golden seeds hidden in the grass. Things are not always easy, but differences can be resolved. Learn from your mistakes and adapt to the needs of the situation.

4. The pharaoh builds a strong foundation for his vision. From passion he creates (the fire of Spirit). With compassion he blends the needs of all. He discerns and makes new connections. He finds living, evolving forms for his work to manifest on Earth. Every Heru operates as a hero. The true heroic quest means combining spirit and matter. Seek, and ground your vision.

5. Transformation is imminent. Horus the Younger returns as Horus the Elder. What was conceived in Spirit now manifests. The king is dead; long live the king. Horus is the reborn leader in community. Always live in the middle of your life, never mourning the past nor yearning for the future. The future is assured though not fully revealed.

6. Passion fills the Horus story. The warrior god loved Hathor, the beautiful goddess who tempered him with her charms. With her breast milk she healed his eye, blinded in battle with Set. Horus and Hathor represent the pharaoh and his queen. Every king must protect what he loves—his queen and country. In your own life there is something worth fighting for.

7. Horus and Christ share kingly attributes. Both spiritual initiates became spiritual masters by overcoming their trials. Temptations of worldly acclaim mean little. True leaders lead with intellect, compassion, and vision. Trust your spirit guides and continue moving forward.

8. As a business leader many people want to be around you. Some you are grooming for future leadership positions. If you are an elder, others seek your advice. If you are younger, you may find yourself taken under Heru's wing. Listen and learn. Be inspired to become an inspiration.

9. You ride with the Ennead as one of the great souls in the boat of Ra. Victory comes after a hard battle. Powerful appointments and recognition are conferred. Your colleagues identify you as one to watch, or as one who has accomplished great things. Both an earthly and a spiritual light shine on you. Your career moves ahead. You sail through the waters of life, enjoying safe passage.

HET (KHET OR KHAT)

This hieroglyph indicates burnt offerings, crematories, or temple fire altars for burning myrrh, frankincense, and kyphi in purification rituals. Sometimes an alternate spelling of *khat* appears, but it has a different nuance. *Het* suggests a house or temple where the divine image lives. It also indicates a "fire altar" inside the sanctuary of the holy of holies. The *khat* (alternate spelling) is the physical "burnt offering" placed upon the het or the fire altar. Kundalini, the primal life force energy of the body, is the transformative fire within the living het or khat.

Sometimes when the fire in the body flares up uncontrolled, it becomes destructive. An ill-tempered passion can be a devastating, consuming flame. But fire can also transmute. It can burn away error. It may offer us radical transformation. When your house is on fire, loss is inevitable. After it, we mourn, but must return to basics again. What is it that we really need? What must be rebuilt? What do we need to let go of? At times of radical shift one must release everything—a marriage, a home, a friendship, a job we loved. Certain conifer seeds do not grow until the forest burns. The fire sparks the seed into growth. Standing before the fire altar, listening for direction from the Divine, and saying "I will to do your will" is an important prayer.

Vision quests in the desert don't and shouldn't happen too often, but they are necessary. The night fire in the quiet dark around a camp becomes a time of meditation, and sometimes an opportunity for ceromancy, or reading the flickering flames or wafting smoke from burning candles or campfires. The fire altar is also a place of ecstasy and trance. Many people can attest to the silence that descends when the woodstove is lit on a snowy winter night. It becomes a natural time and space for deep listening and meditation.

When the night fires are lit on the altar, we enter an in-between time of shift. Be ready to burn the midnight oil—that's not just a sign of hard work, but also a sign of sacrifice. If you understand the story of the Jewish Hanukkah, it is a sign of miracles. Others of us need to remember that what is burned now reduces what is available later. On the other hand, there is often a necessity for clearing. Only you know when it is necessary to sacrifice in order to accomplish what is needed and asked for.

This hieroglyph may indicate a time to clear and clean your altar. Altars need to be refreshed because each one is a living commitment to the Divine. It affirms to Spirit: I am showing up for the work that you would have me do. But when it's done and no longer needed—that is when the requested prayer is fulfilled, or the safe passage is complete— then offer your gratitude and begin a new task. You may decide to set a new intention. Especially in ritual, don't keep a lazy habit of invocation. Remember it's not a table of asking all the time. It's a table of offering. This divine relationship is a two-way street.

1. Prepare yourself and your altars for a shift in consciousness. Some new inspiration, message, or transformation is upon you. Be ready. The time is now.

2. Make a sacrifice to the Divine. Remember that everything important and lasting is accomplished through spiritual partnership. If you invoke an energy, offer your energy in turn. Really ask what Spirit needs from you as part of your loving relationship.

3. Let go of what you have carried so long. The fire will carry it from you and open a new seed. Revitalize your prayers. Craft new hymns to praise the power of Spirit. Refresh your altar.

Near the door of the aromatherapy room in the Temple of Horus there
appear many lion-headed serpents that seem to coil out of a basket.
More precisely they are wisps of flame and smoke curling out
of a brazier that burns some healing incense.

4. You have plenty to be thankful for. Yes, you've worked hard for what you've
   received, but Spirit nourishes you. In your journal make a list, numbered
   from one to one hundred. Name everything in your life that you are grateful for Spirit having granted.

5. While you are in a time of change, write a prayer of gratitude for all the
   difficult passages you have cleared. Be thankful even for what you don't
   have and contemplate why that should be so. When things in your life are
   shifting, stay open to the revelations and the reasons for the shifts.

6. A necessary sacrifice may need to be made for the family. Sacrifices now prepare the way for a future event or project. Tending to one who is ill in the family or community creates a reconciling and solidifying opportunity.

7. Kundalini energy fuels a rising flame within; a passion for living opens the seven chakras. Visualize the smoke of the altar fire as similar to the one in Edfu temple where the incense becomes a dancing serpent with a lion's head rising out of the brazier (see facing photo). Things are heating up.

8. Abundance comes. Bless the necessary sacrifices. Be nourished and thankful.

9. Amid shadow, fear, and doubt know that nothing—not even mortal death—can harm you if you are walking with Spirit. The creator of life eternal guides you through a burnt offering of your life. This end signifies a new beginning.

HET-HOR (HATHOR)

Prehistorically the Sahara Desert was a well-watered, fertile savanna. High up on the desert cliff faces, one still finds an image of the water buffalo cow goddess, Hathor, who blesses the animals brought before her. One of the oldest, most ubiquitous deities on the African continent, her petroglyph was carved in the wadis and deserts at a time when boats traversed the terrain—well before the pharaonic dynasties of Egypt existed. The Great Mother Hathor and the god Thoth appear together as horned goddess and ibis at least as early as 6000 BCE. Two thousand years later clay images of the horned goddess appear in both Amratian and Badarian cultures.

Images of Hathor appear on Narmer's palette, which celebrates the First Dynasty king's victory over his foes. Later depictions of Hathor show her as a beautiful cow goddess with the full face of a woman and wearing upon her head a diadem of cow horns cradling an orb. The only thing that betrays her bovine qualities are little cow's ears protruding from her stylish hair.

Nearly all Egyptian goddesses connect to Hathor in some way. Identified with the Milky Way galaxy and its abundant stars—the *gala* (for which *galaxy* is named) was the milk of the udders of the cow goddess. Isis and she appear indistinguishable on temple walls except by name; both wore cow horns as emblems of the bovine qualities of abundance, fertility, patience, and nurturance. Her diadem held the sun, not the moon as is often believed. As a solar goddess one of her epithets was the "Golden One." Most likely Hathor was the idolatrous golden calf that was worshipped in the Hebrew scriptures as the Israelites came out of Egypt.

Honored alike by miners and workers in the necropolis as "Lady of the Western Lands," her desert temples were adorned with gold and malachite, gilded and painted in beautiful crushed gemstone colors. She found honor among healers and desert dwellers as "Lady of the Sycamore." The sap of her tree, the sycamore fig, removed warts and healed wounds and ulcers. Scenes depict her healing the blind Eye of Horus with her breast milk as she emerges from the branches of a sycamore. Wherever a sycamore fig tree grows, a source of water is nearby. The tree's appearance in the desert was a welcome sight to those in a dry climate for it offered rest, shade, and water. Such a desert tree expressed the miracle of life over death. In the Book of the Dead, Het-Hor's sycamore offered magical elixirs for eternal life.

Perhaps, as feminist author Merlin Stone suggested, Hathor's was the forbidden fruit.[23] Her sycamore fig may have been ingested as an aphrodisiac or even offered up for its mind-altering properties. Often called the Lady of Drunkenness, Hathor's epithet may refer to the story of appeasing the lion goddess Sekhmet, her sister goddess. Sekhmet's voracious bloodthirst was quenched by drinking a magic potion of pomegranate juice, intoxicants, and beer that had been concocted by Thoth.

Whatever was beautiful was Hathor's domain, from the gold, turquoise, malachite, and lapis lazuli of the mines to the glittering stars of the night sky. Her priestesses in Dendera were well-known astrologers. The temple houses famous astrological scenes, including a side chapel depicting the sky goddess Nut who illuminates and blesses the Temple of Hathor at sunrise. The ceiling of the temple's hypostyle hall depicts the hours of the day and night in a linear catalog of constellations that signify the thirty-six decans of the Egyptian calendar (see photo on page 118). Possibly her name *Het-Hor* refers to the temple itself—*het* being the temple as a repository of the constellations, and *hor* being another word for the hours. The zodiacal ceiling appears upstairs in the enclosed pronaos of the Osiris chapel located on the temple roof. It shows the progression of the constellations throughout the year. Intriguingly, however, the polestar Draco depicted in this zodiac suggests that the temple had its origins as far back as 3942 BCE.

Dancers, singers, musicians, and courtesans appear in the stairwells leading up to the open-air rooftop at Dendera. These seven sisters dance, tap frame drums, shake sistra, play flutes, and strum lyres in celebratory procession. Like the Hathor columns of Philae, the Greek caryatid depicted strong women standing upon a firm foundation and holding up the roof of the Temple of Athena. The Seven Hathors, seen as the Pleiades, appear in the night sky near the constellation Taurus. The origin of Egyptian history begins during the Age of Taurus, approximately the period between 4400 and 2200 BCE, when the sun rose at the spring equinox in that constellation. This era coincides with the making of predynastic clay statues of cow goddesses in Egypt.

Every pharaoh celebrated Hathor as his beloved consort, and he was her Horus. Her Egyptian name, House of Horus, implied that as lover of the pharaoh, her womb housed his spirit while she conceived a future pharaoh. Whereas Isis births the child and becomes its mother, Hathor depicts a woman's sensuality, fertility, joy, and ecstasy prior to motherhood.

The hypostyle hall at Hathor's Temple in Dendera depicts the yearly calendar in thirty-six decans, showing the prominent constellations and the deities that rule them. By knowing where to look when glancing at the ceiling, one could tell which festivals were upcoming for the month.

It may seem confusing to the reader to have heard so much about Hathor's cow form, only to find that her hieroglyph actually resembles the image of a caged bird. That is a misunderstanding of an image that celebrates her sexual mysteries. The enclosure that is often used for the hieroglyph of a house is, in this case, more precisely her womb, which wraps around the essence of her lover, the hawk god Horus. We can see this reflected in the images of this hieroglyph (Het-Hor) on page 115.

Her name, literally translated as "House of Horus," refers to their sexual union, and to their progeny. The presence of the divine feminine in what began as a matriarchal society predating Horus essentially makes a king of the masculine energy of the Horus god-man. Like Ast who predates Het-Hor, the divine female who conceives the next pharaoh, or Horus, marks the mystery of a woman's progress from lover to mother.

The first syllable of her name, *het,* also meant "to rejoice." When Horus is in the house, all rejoice, alluding to the orgasmic quality of each lover's experience. The Greeks compared her to Aphrodite, the beloved of many gods. At the marriage festival that celebrated her conjugal visits with Horus, a hymn was sung, which contained these words: "The pharaoh comes to dance. He comes to sing for thee. O, mistress, see how he dances! O, bride of Horus, see how he skips!"[24] Play and fun exemplify Hathor's domain, and so it is fitting that the cow, as depicted in an Opet Festival scene from the Temple of Luxor, is one of my favorite hieroglyphic puns. In the festival procession, the priests and sons of Ramses II lead lavishly festooned cattle to the temple. One cow's curved uplifted horns are drawn in the shape of a ka; the horns becoming human arms and its diadem a human head singing. *Kau* (which sounds like *cow*) means "multiple spirits" and so, in the spirit of Hathor's jubilation, this particular cow appears.

Hieroglyphic puns and double entendres show the use of visual and auditory poetic devices that the Egyptian scribes used with frequency. In this scene of the Opet Festival at Luxor Temple, the diadem between the cow's horns becomes a human head singing. The bleating cow makes a joyful sound and its cow horns are cleverly carved into the shape of a jubilant singer holding his swaying arms extended like the hieroglyph for the ka, or spirit.

1. Stars influence earthly activities. Even cave dwellers used the night sky to determine the coming seasons. A brilliant star led the magi to a holy child. The streaming galaxy of stars formed the body of our great sky mother overhead. Your own body is composed of stardust. Look more closely at how some of the planets, fixed stars, and constellations may be affecting you now. This is a great time for an astrological reading; an even better time to learn astrology.

2. Get in touch with your feminine energy. If you are male, access your inner feminine by soliciting uniquely female perspectives on life. Celebrate the women in your life. If you are female, see all women as your sisters who need your support, your friendship, and your love. Do not fall into competition for the affections of others.

3. Create something beautiful: music, poetry, theatre, or dance. Learn to belly dance, which can improve the agility of your mind as well as your body. Or begin to paint or take some classes in poetry or music. The rhythms of the universe heal us and harmonize us with ourselves. The Goddess calls you to make something beautiful.

4. Hathor became the prototype of all mother goddesses. Have you considered becoming a role model for younger women in your community? What skills do you possess—art? gardening? public speaking? writing? bookkeeping? engineering? astrology? Teach them to a young woman and watch her grow.

5. Hathor's image proudly sailed from one end of the Nile to the other as the masthead on the boats of her flotilla. So many were her festivals that her boats often went sailing up and down the river carrying statues of the goddess, accompanied by singers, dancers, and festivalgoers. Be your own traveling feast. Take a trip for pleasure or add some pleasure to any business trips you embark upon. Sponsor a workshop for women in your community.

6. Be a loving partner. There is nothing that love cannot heal. Respect heals. True presence heals. A beloved companion listens deeply, touches deeply, celebrates deeply, and feels deeply another person's story. This is a time of healing and true spiritual communion.

7. Work on self-fulfillment. Identified as daughters of an Amazon queen in

Greece, the Seven Hathors (Pleiades) in Egypt were singers, dancers, and musicians. They attended the birth of every child, bestowing its fate like fairy godmothers. Spend time writing, playing music, dancing, researching genealogy, or studying the stars. Taking time for ourselves offers us a deeper peace and, as a result, more willingness to give time to others.

8. Other powerful forms of Hathor were Sekhmet and Bast. More than a playful courtesan, Hathor was also a strategist. As Bast she cares for the young. As Sekhmet she safeguards the king's plans from his enemies. Let Hathor help you craft your best plan for fulfillment. Let her help you separate the wheat from the chaff in your life.

9. A time of waiting has ended. Bring your dream to fruition. When something dies, bless it, and with the eyes of Hathor, turn toward the future sunrise. A new dawn follows a dark night. The Golden One, Lady of the Western Lands, Goddess of Renewal, blesses what is passing away. Love it, let it go, and know it is transforming anew.

HOTEP

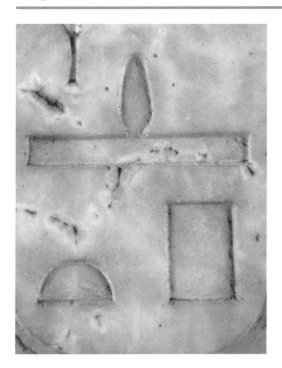

In its original sense the word *hotep* meant "the peace that passes understanding"—the kind of peace that comes when we realize that Spirit will supply us with whatever we need. There is no restless reaching for what exists already. Hotep releases us from fear and worry. I often quote actor Robert Downey, Jr. who says, "Worry is like praying for something you don't want." There is joy simply in living. The first precept of the trestle board of the Builders of the Adytum reads: "This is the Truth about the Self. All the Power that ever was, or will be, is here now."[25]

Hotep exemplifies the perfect communion of saints in forgiveness. When feelings are hurt, peace comes by breaking bread together. An important part of any community, shared food passes on to others the abundance of our gardens and kitchens, made with loving hands. The spiritual bread we share is peace, truth, and the reconciliation of opposites. King Arthur's round table symbolizes the circle of friendship and meals that all partake of together. In the sands at Abu Gorab, the Fifth Dynasty sun temple of Nyuserre near Abusir, a large crystalline alabaster altar stone lies open to the four cardinal directions. In all four cardinal directions, the sides of the altar offer peace, shaped in the hieroglyph for hotep.

Hotep is the practice of saying grace before eating, of laying down our differences, and sharing food. The community feast and family table join us as a unit, keeping us in sync with each other so that Spirit sees we are of one mind, stronger together, with our wills aligned. A family that dines together, sharing their stories and speaking their thoughts, is more unified than families who do not share a meal, or even those who bring cell phones to the table.

Obviously simply holding one's tongue does not constitute creating peace. A synonym for *hotep* would be *ma'at,* the concept of resting on one's truth. A peace offering is not something that happens as a compromise or as a bargaining chip. True hotep is the consistent and daily practice of truthfulness.

The idea of Communion—that is, the Communion rite of Christian tradition—derives from an understanding of this hieroglyph. In the modern Eucharist, we find an altar cloth spread upon the table. In the ancient Egyptian tradition, we see a reed mat rolled out upon an altar stone outside the pyramid. In the modern Eucharist we find a chalice that contains a sacred libation, often red wine. In the ancient world we see a clay libation vessel that will soon be filled with beer. In the modern Eucharist we see unleavened bread that will be broken and shared with the community members. In the ancient tradition a loaf of risen bread heaped in the bowl will be broken and shared by the community.

The idea of breaking bread with our community, even with those whose ideas and values differ from ours, is what solidifies community. In this we share a common caring for each other. We see the value of those who differ from us in some respects, but who belong to our human family, who love, cry, suffer, and are in need of healing and who require understanding, just as we all do.

Creating goodwill does not stop in the physical world, but continues into the spirit world. The kas of our ancestors prepare a place for us at the table when we pass into Spirit. They feed us with their love and welcoming thoughts—a spiritual food as delicious as my Grandmother Maude's angel biscuits. A religious sharing of bread and drink placed upon the altar symbolizes a mutual nurturance of our family members in Spirit.

Bread became the symbol of sacred shared love. Osiris, like Christ, was the wheat, the sacrifice turned into sustenance. "Take. Eat. This is my body. Do this in remembrance," Jesus said in Matthew 26:26, a statement that refers back to Egyptian myth. Thus is Hotep, the breaking and eating of bread, a sacred remembering—a reconstitution of energies and a putting back together of what may have been torn asunder. Osiris was re-membered by his wife and sister after he was murdered a second time and his body parts cast into the river; he had to be gathered and put back together again. Subsequently, Osiris, the god of grain, was re-membered by every person who was given their daily bread. The wheat kernels that were the body of Osiris were broken down into flour, mixed with water, and reassembled into bread—something new and newly risen. The eating of divine food equals an acquiescence to divine will. Hotep is a memory of every abundance that Spirit has given us over and over on a daily basis for a lifetime, whether we deserve it or not. That truly is the peace that passes understanding.

Near the grave sites at the Saqqara necropolis in Egypt the word *hotep* is inscribed to indicate the place where families came to make their offerings to the ka spirit of the deceased. To this day many of our gravestones repeat the refrain "Rest in peace." Our souls and spirits are fed with shared memories. An actual graveside picnic with our ancestors is a tangible symbol that even after death we continue to feast upon the presence of those people whose lives came together and created ours. I feel close to my father when I attend his grave with a drink in one hand and bleu cheese dip and crackers in the other—his favorite midnight snack while we sat watching Johnny Carson together. My modernized hotep offering may differ from that of the Egyptians, but the feeling of communion remains the same.

1. Enact pure and simple peace. Open yourself to a moment of relaxation, knowing that life is as it should be and your needs will be met. Your peace of mind is your own doing.
2. Sharing ourselves with others, speaking from the heart, and listening from the heart without judgment is true communication. Sharing our thoughts and lives moves us into wholeness.
3. Create a space for peace in your life. Create an altar room or find a corner where you can feed and honor the Divine daily with candles, flowers, and/ or prayer. Gratitude should be the first attitude.
4. Focus creates peace. Peace does not happen when our energies are scattered. Plan to create peace in your life. Complete the hectic little details on your list. Set aside a day for nothing but peace, pleasure, and self-care.
5. Attend a small church that differs from your regular denomination or faith. Listen with an open heart. Be still and without judgment. Express your appreciation for another's spiritual life.
6. Many opportunities appear in your community to work with the hungry, poor, and homeless. Give your time at a shelter, or food bank, or donate a few items. If you can, invite someone in your community to lunch; make

it a beautiful occasion to get to know them and learn about their lives.

7. Invest in an altruistic organization that helps communities around the world and at home. Consider humanitarian service organizations that offer educational scholarships. Adopt a pet. Promote peace, love, and joy.

8. Egypt's most famous architect-scribe was named Imhotep, which meant "I come in peace." It was not the name of a horror movie antihero. Make amends to one from whom you have become estranged. Become the instrument of peace for someone else by getting them to a doctor, helping to paint a house, weed a garden, or organize a checkbook. It's no big deal.

9. Plant flowers on a relative's grave. Take a picnic basket to a parent or grandparent's grave, or plan a birthday party for one in Spirit. As you walk around the graveyard, pause at each headstone to say the names of those in Spirit. Pray for their peace. Gather with family and tell family stories.

HU

We enter and we exit life on a breath. Breath is a powerful spiritual tool. God's breath inspired us into being as Atum or Ptah exhaled.

Inspiration means "breath of God." In the beginning, Hu, the authoritative utterance of God, accompanied Sia, the wisdom of God, and Heka, God's magical expression. In his book *The Spiritual Laws of Life,* Sri Harold Klemp of Eckankar stated that he believed chanting the name of the god Hu reenacted the sound and light of Creation, connecting us with the heart of God.[26]

Because we, too, possess that divine creative spark, our breath is powerful as well. In our breathy vocalization we craft, weave, and speak our understandings of reality. We create reality itself through our thoughts and speech. To speak with immediacy and conviction offers strength and weight to our daily life. Hu, Heka, and Sia operate in Heaven and on Earth to provide us wisdom and authority. The pharaoh and the magi understand the phrase *My word is my bond, my power, and my command.*

"In the beginning was the Word," says John 1:1, and *Hu* was that word. Considered the soul of Osiris, Hu offers the consciousness of the Creator breathed into his first Hu-Man. The Sphinx, resting on its plateau and facing the darkened sky of the eastern horizon, awaits the energy of the rising sun. This image depicts the energy of Hu when the dawn comes and the breath of God reaches its nostrils. At dawn all the world inhales the fragrance of light.

One might envision this powerful Hu as an explosive utterance, an orgasmic gasp of air released by the god Atum at the moment of Creation. Darkness cloaks everything, all is still; then in one breath there is light. The name of this deity is an imitative word that sounds like a long sigh or exhalation after a deep inhalation. In moments of stress, confusion, panic, and darkness (similar to what Osiris experienced in the underworld after death), we suspend our breath. The most important thing to remember, of course, is to breathe.

Similarly, one moves from unconsciousness into consciousness through the breath. A woman giving birth to her child through Lamaze breathing techniques uses belly breathing. The focus on the breath pushes one's labor pains to the edge of one's awareness. Such breathing techniques are depicted on the back wall of the healing temple at Kom

Ombo. Bes, Hathor's assistant, breathes with the laboring mother. He sticks his tongue out between his teeth, as if encouraging her to breathe in the pattern: *he, he, he . . .* or *hu, hu, hu.* Another way that Sia (wisdom) accompanies Hu (the breath) is through meditation. Many meditative breathwork techniques take us into altered states—holotropic breathing, shamanic breathing, kundalini breathing to name a few. (There are too many to enumerate here and they are beyond the scope of this work at this time. I recommend reading and practicing Stephanie Clement's *Meditation for Beginners* for more on this topic.)

1. The breath of God is upon you. Be inspired; be the best you can be. God is the wind in your sails. Begin your day before dawn, sitting quietly and breathing in the early morning light, inhaling deeply the moist night air as the Earth exhales and wakes from its sleep. In meditation allow your breath to call to your higher wisdom and consciousness. Gather your energy for beginning anew.

2. Spend quality time (not virtual time) with a friend or partner. Say what is in your heart. Practice taking a deep breath when you speak. Breathe in the words of your conversation partner, so that you really understand. If difficulty lies between you, repeat their words in their breath pattern so that you feel what they said and how they said it, so that you may better understand what they mean.

3. Begin a work of conscious creation. Speak your heart's desires—the heart and lungs are partners. Affirmation makes magic of our lives. When you come to a stopping place at work but the day is not yet finished, close your eyes and blow your breath upon your work to bless it.

4. Sing and chant in all four directions around an open fire, or call the archangels to assist and support you throughout your sacred work. Use your breath and intention to create a strong foundation for your life.

5. Transformation comes through ritual. Write a prayer on a piece of paper, center your intention, and know it is done. Read your affirmation aloud. Roll it up and tie it with a red string. Blow your breath into it, transmitting the breath of God. Place it on your altar or burn it as an offering, then use the ashes to fertilize the roses in your garden.

6. Open the windows and doors. Bring in the breath of God. Make a clean sweep. Blow the dust off your life. Take care of your body using your breath by practicing yoga, dancing, or engaging in aerobic exercise by walking or running.

7. Buy a book on meditation and breath. Practice some new techniques to improve your clarity, intuition, and spiritual connection. Try Kirtan chanting, the healing mantras and sounds of the Hindu tradition, which are similar to ancient Egyptian song. The work of sound healer Jill Mattson may provide a breakthrough into your understanding of the emotional resonances of ancient Egyptian sound healing.

8. Breathe some life into your day with Tai Chi. Move breath energy through your body. Anytime you feel as if you are losing focus do some Tai Chi. See breath moving through you as if you were observing wind filling the sails of a ship.

9. Catch a breath of fresh air by walking in nature to gather inspiration and release stale ideas. Nature, the divine body of God, has a powerful capacity to heal. Explore the Shinto practice of *shinrin yoku,* in which one regularly walks and lies down in nature, breathing purified forest air filled with oxygen and birdsong.

IB (AB)

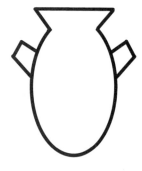

The heart, the central chakra, circulates life blood throughout the body. It connects the upper mental and spiritual chakra with the lower sexual and emotional bodies. The heart symbolizes the life force itself, the rhythmic pulse of the universe. Ib is the intermediary between the realm of humankind and the realm of the neteru. Here the sanctuary of the temple of life exists for all beings, spiritual or physical. The first sound that a child in the womb hears is the beating of its mother's heart, like the drumbeat of the universe.

The tombs of the ancients depict many feasts with pomegranates, sweet cakes, and all manner of meats, vegetables, and fruit. The scenes on the walls depict happy life, holding hands with a friend or lover, dancing girls, standing before the shrine of one's god or goddess making an offering and/or reciting a hymn. The tombs depict the many desires of the heart. The heart wants what it wants. Sometimes this manifests as earthly desires, but what the heart really wants is love. Love may be spiritual (agape), brotherly (philae), or erotic (eros). All love fuels transformation. And transformation is the point of all of these books about living and dying.

Ib suggests two states of being: a thirst for or a satisfaction of the heart's desire. We are social creatures who demonstrate compassion and love through relationships. No one needs to feel lonely or isolated. Intimate connections in the physical plane demonstrate how to operate in the higher realms. Transformative love in action and thought is the ultimate goal and the means to attain higher consciousness.

Called the seat of intelligence, the heart contains our life record. So important was it that Egyptian mummies were buried with the heart intact, while the brain was discarded. To them the heart held our higher consciousness, but the brain operated simply as a control panel. The heart was the repository of memory—a lifetime of thoughts, feelings, actions, words, and intentions.

In the afterlife, the heart was weighed on the scales of truth. One's karma was measured by the weight of the heart. To be lighthearted meant to have your consciousness so exhilarated that not even the sorrow over a loss could cloud it or weigh it down. The heart soul was one of the most important spiritual bodies in the Egyptian tradition. Weighed upon the scales of Ma'at, one's heart needed to be as light as a feather. If you can visualize the Judgment card in the tarot, you see that the successful heart attains a feeling similar to having one's coffin lid thrown open and the weight of the world lifted off. We are open to receive Spirit at last.

This card speaks volumes about consciousness, compassion, and karma as heart issues. Every religious tradition offers its list of core values such as the Ten Commandments, the Buddhist Eightfold Path, the Hindu Ten Disciplines. The forty-two Negative Confessions of the ancient Egyptians offers an ethical code that includes social, personal, and planetary prohibitions. Karma is more than following a prescribed book of law; it underscores an all-inclusive respect, compassion, and understanding of the intimate connection between all beings on the planet. It understands that even the animals, plants, and the planet itself have sentience, or consciousness. All is God. A heart circulates its flow of energy to nourish every part of the whole. Think on this fact as you consider social issues as they pertain to economics, education, social justice, and natural resources.

1. In the Land of Oz, the Cowardly Lion prized courage. Openhearted leadership comes from those who hold compassion for all. Rewards and responsibilities are shared values. People follow you because they trust you. As a leader, be clear about the need to demonstrate compassion.

2. When two hearts entwine in deep relationship, giving and receiving love transcends the physical realm. This love might begin on Earth, but it continues beyond death. Deep love offers an understanding of the flow of give-and-take and embodies true spiritual commitment.

3. Follow your bliss, follow your heart, become a co-creator with God. Ask yourself: "Is what I am doing bringing joy to others, to myself, and to God?" True co-creativity serves all three. Be inspired to inspire others. Become as light as a feather.

4. Order is not the opposite of passion. Put heart in your daily life by taking care of your body, your home, and your relationships. Putting more heart into your life may include praying over your food, for instance, or thanking God for a sunny day. Thoughts manifest in the physical; the soul records them in the astral. Pay close attention to what you eat and what you say. Honor your life for its healing capacities.

5. Speak from the heart—write and tell the truth. Engage in truthful dialogue with loved ones. Treat yourself as you would treat others. My friend Deborah Jones of Nine Gates Mystery School taught me a powerful mantra for all communications: "I vow to you conscious speech, compassionate action, and purity of heart."

6. Love your fellow man, your community, your planet, and yourself. Love is never going against the common good. It is a distribution of energies that uplifts everyone and everything. Joy will alleviate anxiety.

7. The love wisdom of the Christ/Buddhic consciousness raises our human consciousness to a higher level. Anger-provoking stories that appear in the news create depression and sadness about which we do nothing. Read instead the biographies of people like Gandhi, Mother Teresa, or the young Pakistani woman, Malala. These teach us how to change the situations that we face with love.

8. Practice gratitude. Be grateful for everything you experience. Do everything with love, even if it's washing dishes or changing a tire. Love is the reason for being alive; therefore, manifest love in all things. Be grateful for sorrow because even loss draws us closer to Spirit. Keep a gratitude journal.

9. As you live love, act with love and grow more completely through love. Contemplate how adhering to a set of spiritual precepts has played out in your life. If you don't like what you have reaped, lovingly sow some new seeds. This is a time of putting things behind you. It's not about what we have done or left undone, it's about how we can do more, love more, and live in unity.

IR-MA'A

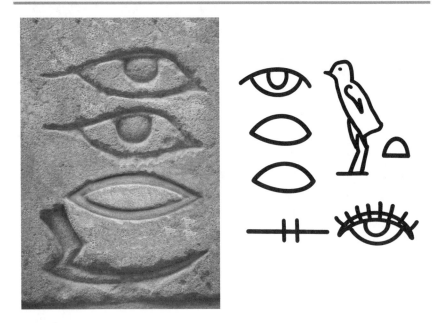

Many kinds of making and creating exist. Envisioning is one of them. Ir-ma'a shows the way of the artist, metaphysician, magician, shaman, and visionary. We often hear the phrase *Seeing is believing,* but the question really is: Is seeing reality? This *ir* or "Eye of God" means creating something through ritual, prayer, or a specific action, for example, making peace. The action undertaken creates enlightenment.

The second hieroglyph ma'a refers to the "truth" as we understand it, which is the foundation of experience. Thus *ir-ma'a* means "seeing true." It refers to the experience that we would most commonly call clairvoyance. This highly prized quality of the shaman-priestess endeared her to the royal household. Perhaps it referred not simply to offering good advice in a rather Solomon-like way, but entering into a trance state wherein through a kind of soul flight one could attain a visionary experience, replete with deep insights. Ir-ma'a may be akin also to the concept of lucid dreaming. Awake or asleep the intention was the same: to see truth through a vision quest. Accordingly, this hieroglyph features two eyes with which to see and discern the truth.

A related hieroglyph, *ir-rswt,* shown in the line drawing above, might be interpreted as "waking up" from a dream. The half-opened, heavy-lidded eye indicates that one hovers between worlds in a hypnogogic state. This particular hieroglyph indicates a kind of envisioning or dreaming. Although it implies taking action while awake, it also indicates those beings, called night watchers, in the halls of duat.

Take a look at the work of active dreamworker Robert Moss. In particular, his book *The Dreamer's Book of the Dead* explores the ways in which ancient Egyptians viewed the intersections of the dream world, the realm of the neteru, and our "awakened" daily lives. This dream state transcends time and space. *Rswt* also means "tomorrow" and may indicate precognition. Precognition may be possible because, as physicists are discovering, time and space are mental constructions from a mind much larger than our own. We may be living in a virtual reality, a holographic universe.[27]

Restau is another name for the astral realm. The imaginal world is as real as the "reality" out our window. Nowhere is it clearer than in the hieroglyphs that dreaming is really more akin to waking up. If you can see and imagine something completely, it exists in the mind of God. Both the dream world and our daily life are held inside the god-field. Reality is primarily a mental construction. Gautama Buddha's enlightenment beneath the bodhi tree resulted in his becoming a radiant being, a sahu in other words. Asked by one who met him walking on the road how this was possible, he answered, "I Am Awake."

Moss suggests to us that a dream is a wake-up call that takes us beyond what we already know.[28] The conscious sojourner who has actively awakened in a lucid dream becomes a shaman. The ancient Egyptian shaman understood that alternate realities held instructive truths, and he went in search of them. These are not imaginings. These are parallel realities. Flashbacks, déjà vu experiences, and dreams become accessible to those who can see clearly that time and space comprise a field of possibilities. Travel in alternate dimensions can be fluid, the equivalent of dipping a toe in the Nile, knowing that you have touched ancient, modern, and future Niles in so doing.

In Pyramid Text Utterance 260 Unas proclaims himself as a master visionary, saying, "I am the one who went and came back."[29] The biblical Jacob dreamed of angels ascending and descending the ladder of heaven to confirm the prophecy of his ancestor Abraham. Like Jacob, Unas traveled to the land of his ancestors who lived in Restau in order to receive and bring back his part of the great vision, and thus transform a future divine plan into a local, living reality.

Dreams operate in similar ways to hieroglyphs, often containing double meanings and puns. They may also operate on multiple levels, making them open to messages that pertain to more than one aspect of life. Those lector-priests who crafted the texts for the tombs of the pharaohs were magnificent dream interpreters because they had steeped themselves in the knowledge and power of the hieroglyphic symbol. The New Kingdom scribe Kenhirkhopeshef, who lived in the workers' village at Deir el Medina, compiled the first known book of dream interpretations with 108 symbols. The priests of Amen in Siwa Oasis foresaw the rise of Alexander the Great when they interpreted his dream in their oracular temple.[30]

The hieroglyphic eye indicates enlightenment and seeing, as well as envisioning and creating. We create our reality; we create our truth; we create our entrances and exits. We envision a world and manifest it by how we look at it. If you can see something clearly in your mind's eye, you can bring it to fruition.

Another possible meaning for the hieroglyph of the eye, ir, is the conjunction if. Our if only thoughts fuel our creative vision. Again, Robert Moss in The Three "Only" Things suggests that there is no such thing as "it's only a dream," "it's only a coincidence," or "it's only my imagination." Before we experience a reality, it must exist as a possibility. For this reason, crafting vision boards has become a frequent metaphysical practice, but often we don't envision all possible outcomes in full detail. Or else we partially see it and can't hold its fullness, so it becomes distorted. Reality likewise distorts. We live partial lives because we lack the capacity to fully envision a life and inhabit it.

When we sleep, the rational mind sleeps. Without the distractions of daily life, we step fully into the timeless imaginal landscape. Learning to see clearly in both sleep and wakefulness becomes a dreamer's gift. Sometimes the gift upon waking tumbles out in a well-crafted, inspired, and beautiful poem. When we are not "awake" in either world, however, we experience nightmares. This hieroglyph ir encourages us to check in with our dream life, with our clairvoyance or clairsentience, with our creative life, and especially with our shamanic questing.

One more thought: Our ancestors and those in the spirit world are also dreaming us. They walk into our living rooms, call us on the phone, or have dinner with us. Our encounters with them in the astral world are as real as encounters with the neighbors across the street. The dead are not departed. The ancient Egyptian spirit door drawn with a pair of eyes appeared in every tomb so that the ancestor could look out from Restau into our world, call us, communicate with us—even dine with us.

If you work with your dreams, practice clairvoyance, write poetry, or paint, this hieroglyph portends an open channel. Your commanding vision makes things happen. If you meditate or enter into trance work as part of a spiritual practice, this hieroglyph symbolizes the taking on of more responsibility. Having made it a reality, become a guardian of it, a night watchman, and a protector of the ways to move through this envisioned, magical world.

1. Create your own reality. Begin anew—a habit, a way of being, an artistic process. It's time to live a dream that you've held for some time. See all of the pieces of this life working together.

2. You and another hold a common dream. Talk it through so that you see it in the same ways. Nurture the dream you share. Shared dream space is sacred. Work with a group to share dreams.

3. We make with our hands, but first we envision. One of your dreams becomes a reality. As your third eye opens it increases responsibility for what you say, do, and create.

4. Be responsible for your creations. It's time to do the work your vision requires. Do not expect your project, or your life, to create itself. Hold on

to your dream and its specific actions to bring it to fruition. Lovingly apply your will to the process at hand.

5. You've been astrally traveling at night, living inside alternate realities. Develop your strong precognitive abilities. Many people that you meet in dreams will be drawn to you in waking life.

6. The most important creative act is the enactment of divine love. Follow your passion, love what you do, and see your part in the divine plan. The departed loved ones you meet in a dream bring messages of encouragement. You are not imagining them. Pay attention to intuition and dreams.

7. Gain mastery over your dreams, whether you dream lucidly or dream precognitively. A dream figure guides you like the dream avatar Philemon who worked with Carl Jung. *The Red Book* by Jung shows you a possible intersection between intuition, dream, and artistic endeavor.

8. What you have created on a spiritual level will soon manifest. Your thoughts have evolved it, developed it, and made it happen. Continue to work its details to bring your vision to fruition.

9. Forgive. Understand. Accept and work on your part as a co-creator of Spirit's divine plan on Earth. Turn your passion into creativity for spiritual purpose and the good of many.

KA

In ka, the arms are extended at right angles from the chest to open the heart and to draw another's essence close. The palms of these uplifted arms reach toward heaven, symbolizing spiritual surrender. See all of this reflected in the image of ka above. Stand this way and feel the stretch inside your chest cavity to receive the energy of Spirit. Doing so, you receive the courage necessary to live a full and abundant life. Open your heart as you open your arms. Be penetrated by the light. This ultimate creative spiritual impulse offers a partnership between human and divine beings. This is da Vinci's perfected man, wide open with arms extended toward Heaven and legs touching Earth. Receiving and giving life force energy, this is the stance of chi. On the cross Jesus prayed with open arms, saying, "Into thy hands I commend my spirit."

Both *ka* and *chi* refer to the animating life force principle of spirit infusing matter. The horns of the cow, long a symbol of the goddesses Isis, Hathor, and Nut, suggest a life-giving sustenance. The Greek god Zeus appeared as the bull in the Taurus constellation; the Apis bull of Egypt was sacred to Osiris. Some Latinate versions of Exodus (the Catholic Douay-Rheims Bible, for instance) even describe Moses (Exodus 34:29) with two horns of light (a radiant aura perhaps) when he descended from Mount Sinai with his two tablets after speaking with God.

Ka energy functions like the energy of an electrical cord. Imagine the two horns of ka as the two prongs of an electrical plug. These plug into Source to create a connection that can receive and transmit energy. Thus our two arms and two hands are designed to both give and receive. To stretch this metaphor a bit further, let's say that the synapses between the two poles contain the life of the electrical current. Ka, the animating principle, runs its current between these two poles. Some suggest that ka operates as the personality, but I see it as an understanding of individual life, given the work we do in this lifetime. Ba, on the other hand, represents our accumulated lifetimes of work or karma.

Imagine Spirit as the source of all energy, and you (as energized form) being plugged into Spirit by virtue of the fact that you were born. Unplugged—that is, when the cord is cut—your spirit goes back to Spirit. Without the energy of a living spirit, we are just a piece of meat. So ka is the life force energy, but it is also the life that once sustained the being of an animal or plant.

Ka is another word for bread and for meat. Prayer is one of the ways in which to honor the ka spirit that animates all life. When we eat meat, vegetables, and fruit, or drink water, praying over our food before we partake of it honors the life force of the living being to which we are forever connected. Its spirit merges with ours. One of the higher bodies on the plane of spirit, ka is life force energy that animates, but it is not permanent. It needs to be plugged into the divine Source. The living energy of ka is maintained as it circulates from above to below, and from below to above. When we open our arms in prayer, we are as much feeding the divine Source energy through our attention as we are feeding our desire nature through our intention.

1. Reach up. Draw down Spirit. It's the magic part of your life—a field of possibility that you can tap into. Put your faith in the fact that spiritual energy is as real, tactile, and important as electricity. You can't see ka in the air, but you know when the switch is on or off by whether or not you feel light and liveliness or ennui.

2. Arms are meant for hugging and receiving love energy. Maintain the spirit connection to God through loving. Every time you hold a child, a beloved, or a pet, you exchange life force energy. Sexual love transmits and exchanges life force energy, prompting a desire for life beyond sensual pleasure. Be willing to receive love, to receive the gifts of Spirit, and do not worry.

3. Ka supports making mental and spiritual connections with others, recognizing a divine kinship. The two are made one. (Sometimes the two make another one.) Words also exchange energy and love. Sharing ideas and accepting another person's point of view becomes a form of love. That is a true co-creative process. You do that with people and you do that with God.

4. Get busy. Get your hands in the dirt—moving, building, creating patterns, following the steps of a project that you're creating. In all you do, love it to the maximum potential. The ways we do something, such as combing a child's hair, express our love for the creative process.

5. Be open to change and divine influence in your life. Embrace a new

activity, a new friend, an inspiring message. Let your emotional baggage go. Enact some magical work. Pray.

6. Ka is the energy of the ancestors. Telling the life stories of those who have passed shows us where they put their energy. Think about how they did what they did with what they had for the future (that is, you). Tend a grave, show your gratitude, and receive their blessing.

7. Invoke the power of God, the ancestors, and the masters. When you feel a spirit arm around your back or shoulder, know you are connected with a powerful spirit life force. Investigate what this phrase means to you: *zeitgeist* or "spirit of the times."

8. Meditation maintains your daily spiritual connection. Remember to take your spirit guides off the shelf. Walk around with them, put them in your car when you drive, sit them down when you read, talk to them. In all things, communicate with Spirit.

9. Maintain a spiritual connection to the Divine by relinquishing a dysfunction. Abandon an irresponsible connection to food, work, television, or money. Trim your possessions. Take books off the shelf and either read them or give them to others to read. Clear out the old so the new may enter. Be generous, but don't push discarded possessions onto others. If no one needs it, bless it and get rid of it.

KHAIBIT

The khaibit is a shadow figure—some say ghost or double; others say a hologram, a bilocated individual, or the remnant of a memory. Of all of the mental or astral bodies, it may have the densest appearance given its hazy, etheric, earth-bound shape. Its psychic impressions primarily adhere to the personality of the individual rather than to the individual's soul purpose. Two hieroglyphs depict the Khaibit. First, we see a sunshade, the feathered fan upon a long pole, which shaded the pharaoh from the intense sun in a treeless climate. The fan-bearer had to stand close to the pharaoh, as if he were his shadow. Second, the ancient Egyptians depicted the khaibit as a completely dark human figure—not dark as in malevolent, but dark as in unaware, perhaps still a little uncertain as to its status as an entity. I have often said that understanding the disincarnate khaibit (dark shadow) and the sahu (bright shadow) may be equated with the similarity and differences between clouds. At night, clouds passing over the dark sky sometimes look luminous, while denser clouds in the sunlight appear gray or black. Both are simply clouds. One cloud is not necessarily better than the other.

Negative associations with the shadow were not common in Egypt. In a land that craves a bit of shade in the middle of the blazing hot desert sun, the pharaoh needed his ostrich-feather fan to keep him cool and covered. The fanbearer's job must have been one that required stamina and patience. This was a job given not to the lowliest of servants, but to the king's eldest son and chosen heir. He literally shadowed his father every hour of the day, listening to his conversations with viziers, priests, judges, and ambassadors. Whatever was on the king's mind, his fanbearer overheard. Wherever the king traveled by boat or chariot through the fields, or through the temple, his fanbearer followed. Thus the king's son traveled the entire country and outposts of Egypt. He learned to think, speak, and act like the Horus-inspired ruler that he would later become. He learned his father's prayers, invocations, commands, and he also knew his wishes.

Egyptologist Jimmy Dunn explains that even the gods had their shadows. "Like other components making up an individual, the shadow was both viewed as a component of its owner, and as a separate mode of existence. Furthermore, the image of a god that was carved on a temple wall could at times be referred to as the god's shadow, and even the temple itself was sometimes known as the shadow of its deity."[31] It was understood that Nekhbet, the vulture goddess on the lintels above the doorways of the temples, was showing a mother's love by shadowing the individuals in her temple with outstretched wing.

When an individual passed into the next life, he wanted to take his shadow with him and not leave it hanging around, uncertain of its purpose. Soul fragments or splinters of the individual sometimes remain in places where there has been unfinished business, where emotions were keen or regrets laid bare, or where an attachment to people or things kept the soul earthbound. Unconsciously hanging around was not a good thing. Said the Book of the Dead, "Let not my soul be shut up. Let my shadow not be bound. Open the pathway for my soul and shadow that they may see the great god."[32]

1. Someone has left your life but their influence can still be felt. This person may have passed into Spirit. It is possible the bond is not broken and the connection continues, but it may continue in a different way than it did previously.
2. Darkness and light are partners. Stillness precedes action. Sometimes quiet helps us consider outcomes before moving ahead. Consider the polarity of the ebb and flow of life.
3. Something waits in the wings for the right time to manifest, the way baby souls wait on the periphery, watching their parents until they see the right time to dive in. Or a creative idea may be forming in the dark and empty space before fruition.
4. Four spirits, either ancestors or angels, gather around you now. They protect you, guide you, and place before you the tools that you need to accomplish your next life task.
5. Expect an upcoming shift in energy. It may be disguised as a loss of clarity, a misstep on the path, or a sudden whirlwind, however, it is necessary and something new. After the confusion clears, it will be very good.
6. The spirit of a beloved one contacts you. Find them in your dreams,

through messages, or out of the corner of your eye. You can create a stronger connection if you ask your beloved in Spirit a question, or ask them to simply make his or her presence known.

7. The Lord giveth and taketh away. A space was made that Spirit will fill with something important and vital. Accept the emptiness with gratitude, for a powerful healing follows.

8. A long line of ancestors stand with you. Their story is a part of your story. You can gain some understanding about your life by researching your ancestors. You may discover a key to a question or a key to something that you've always wondered about.

9. The darkness will come to an end when the understanding of it is clear.

KHAT

Khat is the empty vessel waiting to fill prior to conception, and it is the vacant body shell after the soul takes flight. While some hieroglyphs are purely phonetic, others work as both images and sound. In one instance, the striped circular glyph in the photo denotes the sound *kh* and the image of that sound is the darkened circle of the new moon. One might think of how a new moon in the sky is a form, a circle that contains no light but once held the reflected light of the sun. The body on its bier demonstrates that the light has gone out of this form. It is an empty shell. The khat is a form that once contained spiritual vitality but is now devoid of spiritual light.

The line drawing represents a second way of writing the word for khat. It depicts a fish, expressing the idea of the smell of a decaying life-form. The fish hieroglyph is sometimes accompanied by a hieroglyph of a pustule, again suggesting putrefaction. Whereas birds are life-forms that live high above us, fish live far beneath the ground.

The word *khat,* the hieroglyph for the body, is an anagram for the hieroglyph for Spirit, akh. At death, akh is the spiritual body bound for Heaven; the physical khat is bound for Earth. For the physical body, modern priests commend the body to Earth with the phrase "Ashes to ashes." Although the Egyptians mummified the body, their comparable phrase would have been *Body to earth; Soul to sky* (Pyramid Text 305).[33]

Since the khat had been a receptacle for the Spirit of the Divine and contained a living energy field, it retains remnants of Spirit's energy. The living vibrations of an individual leave "fingerprints" upon the object it touches or inhabits. Having a long history of attachment to a particular body, or inanimate form for that matter, enlivens the form. The khat retains the memory. In such a way a medium may pick up impressions from objects worn by an individual, whether that individual is still among the living or not. A holy relic on an altar in a church, or worn by an individual, contains the sanctified vibrations that it has acquired through ritual, prayer, or daily conscious attention.

The basalt statue of the lion goddess Sekhmet in Karnak (see page 144) has been a living entity for thousands of years, beginning with the enlivening rituals of the ancients and continuing through the spiritual attention of those modern-day priests and priestesses who travel to speak with her. Lyall Watson, in his book *The Nature of Things: The Secret Life of Inanimate Objects,* discusses the way reanimated statues, in particular a Virgin Mary statue in a Southern California mission, seems to come alive, weep, and wander about the sanctuary of the church despite the fact that it weighs sixty pounds and is anchored to the floor by an iron chain.[34]

The word *khat* also means the "fire altar" within the sacred temple, where wafting incense, or *kapet,* and earthly offerings were burnt and made sacred. (See het.) Imagine the khat form as an enclosed container for light. Within the temple or within the physical self, khat defines

Often spirit orbs, eyes of fire, or apparent energetic arms and hands
have been photographed around the living black basalt statue Sekhmet in
her adytum at the Temple of Ptah near Karnak. Iron gates that secure her
chapel have been known to be shut and locked by unseen hands.
Lore has it that the gates will remain locked until Sekhmet is ready to
release her priestesses following their convocation.

the space where transformation occurs. In Egyptian religious rites, the
naos, which contained the sacred statute, could only be approached by
the pharaoh or his high priest.

In a similar way the now vanished Ark of the Covenant contained the holiest relics of the Jewish faith. Only the pure could approach the ark or the naos, but none might open it except the most holy man. Otherwise, once released, the intensity of the light contained within would sear whomever opened it as the pure energy returned to its source.

Khat signifies a sacred relationship to God given that those embalmers of the ancient world were high priests of Anubis. One who assists souls in transition, hospice workers, undertakers, and Reiki masters all work with khat energies. They know how to roll up the Akashic Records, bundle them, and send them with the deceased into the next realm, for our Akashic Records go with us when we depart the physical plane.

Both the corpse and fetus may appear as khat bodies, represented by the fish as depicted in the illustration. The Oxyrhynchus fish was often used as the hieroglyph for khat because in certain versions of the Osirian myth it was this fish that ate the phallus of the dismembered Osiris. For that reason, the generative part was never found, thus Osiris couldn't complete his physical resurrection. The fish later became a symbol in the Christian tradition for the god resurrected in Spirit. Alive and thrashing in the subterranean waters, swimming in the flow of psychic unconscious, the fish connotes the profound life of Spirit that underlies the world of appearances, said the late mythologist and poet J. E. Cirlot.[35] All life, whether mammalian, avian, or amphibian, begins life as a similar looking bean-shaped, big-eyed fishlike fetus. The word *khat* is also written hieroglyphically, with the emblem of a cow's belly and teats signifying the womb of the Great Goddess.

Sometimes the word *khat* contains an image of the lion bed, similar to the one that appeared in the treasures of Tutankhamun that contains a swaddled human. This lion bed was used as one of three gilded funerary biers in the mummification process. This lion bed represents the energy of Sekhmet, the goddess who is both devourer and protector. That swaddled being on the lion bed may indicate that at death, or in a trance that induces a near-death experience, the Egyptian initiate was devoured psychically by Sekhmet. When he awakened reborn, he was said to have "passed through the skin of a lion." Surviving the experience of having died and being reborn was the hallmark of the shaman or high priest.[36] A shaman returns to the body with renewed spiritual vision and the information he or she seeks, but at death the soul is released and we are consumed by the light and the fire.

1. Incarnation is the soul's way of experiencing human life and spiritual life inside a biological container. The shell is not the experience. The ego is not the point.

2. Here are two fish—the *an-t* and the *abtu* fishes. The abtu fish is the brother of Horus and represents the innate wisdom of God that pulls us through life. We are not always aware that God directs all physical life, but it is so. The an-t fish, as Isis, is light itself. Isis arranges the ways of our lives so that light shines through us. This is the light that is born of our wounds.

3. We rise up out of death. Body, mind, and spirit create a trinity of being. The body leaves first, then thought, then the soul returns to Light Land. Now the light comes and inspires the mind, it stills the emotions. The body reacts to this palpable experience of light.

4. A physical object like a statue, a photograph, or a candle may be enlivened through the power of thought and love. Know that Spirit forms the foundation and formula of all matter.

5. Ichthys is the fish that often symbolizes Christ. The fish does not mean death; it means transformation. Khat is creation in its cycle of life-death, life-death, and so on, moving and spinning end over end like the wheels of fire. We are God's kindling for his great fire. Do not be attached to the form, instead be the light.

6. Here is the fire altar. Your life itself is the incense burned within the body. The incense burns with the light of God. As we age, our understanding deepens. The light creates the essence, the body does not, the personality does not. Love is the fire within.

7. Whether you know it or not, you may be astrally traveling. Your physical form houses your astral light body. Learning to leave the body at rest and

return to it requires some practice. If you are not already dreaming and meditating on this possibility, begin to do so now.

8. The fish, like the number eight on its side, swims through all the layers of consciousness—the waters of Spirit and mental vibration. It rises up; it sinks to the depths. Osiris is that fish, floating inside our bodies. We can get stuck in the seaweed at times or we can rise above it.

9. Light flows into the body at birth, preparing a place for life experiences of transformation. As the light leaves the body it takes with it its experiences and wisdom. Someone in your community or family is completing their karma now, preparing to leave. Or it may simply be that he or she is leaving behind a matter that is over and done with. It's time to close the book and move on.

KHEPER

One of the major symbols of transformation that nearly everyone knows from Egyptian lore is the *Scarabeus sacre,* or dung beetle. This incredibly versatile hieroglyph symbolizes all kinds of states of being: becoming, existing, transforming, making, doing, creating, beginning, returning, and so on. Kheper denotes all of the surprising ways that form arises. In the Book of Knowing the Creation of Re (also called the Bremner-Rhind Papyrus) one poetic chant line appears to be little more than a string of dung beetles. When chanted it reads something like: *Nuk pu em Khepera khepery khepru. Nuk pu em Re.* Its equivalent meaning is: "In the beginning, I became the becoming, being what I created."[37]

After the beetle laid its eggs inside a ball of cow manure, it pushed the dung ball across the sand until it was buried in the earth. Dung beetles feed their young manure until they are grown. (Sounds like some families I've known!) When their transformation is complete the hatchling beetles emerge from their dung balls to wing their way upward toward the sky.

In Egyptian myth the dung beetle pushed the golden globe of the sun over the horizon every morning. The morning sun was called Kheper, the light of the midday sun was Ra, and the diminishing light of dusk was attributed to the sun god Atum. Thus this kind of creating in a specific time and place has a beginning, middle, and end. The riddle of the sphinx asks, "What walks on four legs at dawn, two legs at midday, and three legs in the evening?" The Greeks told us that the answer was the lifespan of man, saying he crawls on four legs as an infant, walks upright in midlife, and uses a cane in his old age. Clearly though, this riddle also referred to the three names of the sun god and the three aspects of light. It also relates to spiritual progress demonstrated on the physical and mental planes.

Despite this association with light, recent evidence indicates that dung beetles are nocturnal creatures that navigate and orient themselves to the light of the moon and particular stars in the Milky Way. Perhaps we might see this nocturnal creature as teaching us how to maneuver through our dark nights of the soul by following the light reflected to Earth by the moon and stars. This idea may be similar to the meaning implied by the tarot card the Moon in which the crab emerges from a sacred pool and crawls toward the light. The path in the moon card goes up and down the hills, leading us to places high and low. The dung ball rolls over and over on itself, following a single path. One message is to keep going. A change is coming. You just have to keep on keeping on.

Carved at the heart level in every temple behind the naos or shrine containing the statue of the god, one finds the winged scarab. The dung beetle works its magic on both inner and outer walls. That hieroglyph represents the life force energy of the cosmos. Its presence signifies that not only is the statue contained within the sanctuary—the actual, living deity—but the entire *temple* is a living entity. The transformation of inert matter into life became the foundation for understanding consciousness.

A dung beetle talisman, placed over the heart inside the mummy wrappings, contained an inscription of the individual's sacred name. It conferred upon the deceased the power to make life-asserting affirmations of spiritual truth during his or her judgment before Osiris in the after-life. The Book of the Dead centers around the transformation of death consciousness into life consciousness. In psychological terms we might think of it as how to turn the dung of our experience into enlightenment. My father would have called that "learning the difference between shit and Shinola." The dung beetle is the symbol par excellence of alchemy; *Al-Khem* referred to the wisdom of the ancient Egyptian magi, the high priest living in the Land of Egypt, which was known as Khem.

Pushing a dung ball for this beetle is the equivalent of a person who weighs one hundred and fifty pounds pushing an eighty-ton sphere. This process of becoming takes quite a bit of elbow grease and commitment. Kheper is brimming with potential future lives and promises the emergence of a new life, which differs from a life already in progress at full strength. The carved granite dung beetle near the sacred temple at the lake of Karnak retains a magical power to grant wishes. According to the local guides, if one circumambulates the temple three times, it confers luck, strength, and power; seven times and it brings about love or pregnancy; nine times, victory, and the completion of one's desires.

The red granite scarab in the courtyard by the sacred lake at Amen's temple in Karnak represents the rising sun aspect of Amen.

1. Start something. Begin. Hatch a plan. There is no time like the present. Even if you are not sure how the plan will turn out, begin. Kheper rolls it along nicely into a workable outcome. Enthusiasm for the process of creating sustains you.

2. Kick things up a notch. When faced with dilemma, keep pushing toward the light, seeking truth to illuminate the outcome. Someone you know will give you the boost you need.

3. Everything happens in stages. Transformative power begins with a creative idea, continues through elbow grease, and comes to fruition in its right time. Luck depends on how you use the opportunities at hand.

4. Build your foundation from idea to conclusion through the use of the will. Listen for the input of the universe. Intuition—that still, small voice—activates as we lie fallow (or what appears to be so), waiting for the right time. Deep development continues unseen.

5. Keep moving and following the light. Sometimes it's darkest before the dawn, but do not let fear, doubt, or anxiety keep you from this depth process that will ultimately shine a light on your life. Do not resist your own process.

6. Love fuels every transformative act. The heart is the engine of life force

energy. Imagine standing before the image of the scarab, feeling your heart beat with life. Breath and hold the truth that lies between the spaces of each beat. You are a living vessel of the Divine.

7. The time approaches. How will you welcome this creature of your mind or body into the physical realm? The birth of any book, project, home, whatever . . . needs a plan to sustain it. What supports its continued unfoldment? What is no longer needed? Pause if you need to; even Yahweh rested on the seventh day.

8. Your desire to bring a project or idea into fruition manifests precisely because you dream big and are willing to work on it. Continue being both visionary and specific about your desires to create the life you want to live. Also be specific about envisioning the world you want to live in, which will live on after you. Continue to make progress through your insights. Beware of exhaustion.

9. Cast off the husk of a former life. With a completion comes a beginning. Satisfaction leads to renewal. There is no end of becoming, no end of things of the heart. All is process. Nine, the number, is a spiral, the last revolution of the current evolution. A revelation helps you break free.

MA'AT (MA'ATY)

Aside from the ostrich feather, the primary symbol of the goddess Ma'at or the concept of ma'at is the plinth. It represents the contact point between Heaven and Earth, that is, the Earth emerging from the watery chaos of Creation. The plinth of ma'at is the foundation of existence upon which all temples are built. All of the columns within the temple, and all of the statues of the neteru stand upon the plinth that represents the stability of the goddess Ma'at. She was called the heart and tongue of the creator god Ptah. We share in that divine capacity to use the heart and tongue to create a legacy by our thoughts and actions.

The goddess Ma'at most often appears wearing a single white feather on her head. When depicted by itself, the feather represents the concept of ma'at: cosmic justice and truth. The feather may be an ostrich plume or an ibis feather from the crest of the sacred ibis that's associated with her companion Thoth. The ibis feather represents high consciousness, while the lower consciousness might be represented by the ostrich feather used in the pharaoh's sunshade fan, which was a symbol for the shadow astral self.

The natural laws that govern our world come under the purview of ma'at. Although we don't normally see these laws with our physical senses unless we are looking for them, they exist on the spiritual, mental, and astral planes. We could not exist without them. The three immutable laws are these: the law of mind, the law of correspondence, and the law of vibration. Ma'at reminds us that we are a divine thought rippling through a universal "mind-field," entering physical manifestation. From this point all other mutable natural laws flow. Thoth is the scribe and architect of every natural law, Seshet records it, and Ma'at finds its balance point. Our work is to develop our understanding of these laws, for the plinth of ma'at is "under-standing."

The primary tool of ma'at is the heart, the central point of being that represents the interplay of mind and love—the knowledge that everything is holy, everything is sacred, everything is God. It was said that every god and goddess (every neter in the natural world) stood upon ma'at and was governed by Ma'at. Even Ra, the light principle of the cosmos, obeys her inalterable laws of ebb and flow.

Every Egyptian child grew up knowing his or her purpose was to serve ma'at—cosmic truth and justice—and to maintain the harmonic balance of the universe that Ma'at represented. The ancient author of the manuscript *The Eloquent Peasant* says, "Speak Ma'at. Do Ma'at. For she is mighty. She is great and endures. Her value rests in the hands of those who use her. Ma'at leads one to sacredness."[38] On the temple wall at Abydos, Pharaoh Seti I makes an offering of the goddess Ma'at, who embodies divine order, balance, morality, truth, and justice. In his cupped hand he offers to the gods an image of Ma'at, saying, "This is the order and balance you gave to me as pharaoh, and now I offer it back to you, having changed it not one bit."

In Abydos, Pharaoh Seti I tenderly holds in his cupped hand the beautiful, delicate image of the goddess Ma'at. Her truth, balance, and love he offers to the gods. The uraeus serpent coiled at his brow indicates that he is a true initiate with amplified and activated spiritual vision.

Ma'at represents consciousness, self-awareness, and an understanding of how the principles of the material world are put together.

Therefore, she is called cosmic order, or truth. By demonstrating an understanding of the principles of natural law, we come into an awareness of our place in the cosmos. We can try to bend a natural law, such as believing that our selfish actions will have no consequences, but the law of cause and effect, or karma, cannot be broken. Eventually, karma springs back on you. Thus we develop a sense of conscience and a code of ethics that make living in the natural world more manageable, more conscious, and more blessed.

Ma'at can be thought of as the Eightfold Path of the Buddhists, or the Ten Commandments of the Jews, the Ten Disciplines of the Hindus, or the Golden Rule of the Christians. The forty-two Negative Confessions of the ancient Egyptians listed those things that one must not do and for which one might be judged in the next life. These were the laws of ma'at. They included commonsense prohibitions against killing, stealing, lying, adultery, blasphemy, and so on; and went on to include such other more specific declarations forbidding the mistreatment of children and animals, the desecration of tombs and temples, gossiping, or talking too much. Even environmental laws were included, such as not polluting or damming the river. If one saw all the world as holy as the Egyptians did, it would make sense not to mess with the gods. At death, when the Negative Confession was read before Osiris and his assessors, each of the forty-two minor neteru was responsible for seeing that the particular ethical statement that was part of his purview was correct in truth; for example, one assessor assured that the individual had not decimated the land, while another ascertained whether the individual had stolen from his neighbor. Afterward, the feather of ma'at was placed upon the scales in the Hall of Judgment. That feather represented the well-developed, highest consciousness of that which was being weighed. The record of our lifetime of thoughts, words, and deeds are recorded on the heart and that heart must be equal to or lighter than the feather. Now more than ever we need to practice ma'at in order to regain a state of grace and improve the quality of our lives. The outer world will mirror back to us our inner alignment with ma'at.

1. God-thought is ma'at—pure and written in the heart. You can do nothing in opposition to that pure spark of God without harming yourself. Remember that when you say the phrase *I am . . .* , what follows is God speaking.

2. The law of polarity exists. *Ma'aty* expressed the duality of truth with a *y* sound written with two plinths or two feathers. This demonstrates that truth is more than one thing. Hot and cold are not opposites but polarities of temperature. Love and fear are polarities of emotional attraction. A situation in your life needs balance. Examine where each conflicting thought lands on the barometer of thought and emotion. Work to even out the mind.

3. Ma'at offers a path of creativity. Fiction is meaningful, for example, because there are kernels of truth in everything. Many fiction writers find that their muses have actually been working in cahoots with Spirit. Let ma'at help you discover new poetic ways to express reality.

4. The foundation of all life is ma'at. Whatever you are building—whether it's a physical or mental construction—you must lay every brick in it on a straight and true line. Be in truth. See that your foundation is firm, and set your intention according to the highest ethical principles. Your building is meant to last. Meditate and invoke what sustains this project in every step.

5. There is always a midpoint, or a brief period of stasis. Any forward movement in life involves a bit of swing. We can't walk if we don't allow the body to swing its weight from one foot to the other. The true test of ma'at lies in the rectification of mistakes.

6. Families can be fraught with secrets. Some truths have yet to be discovered. If it comes to you to know something, then hear it with compassion and nonjudgment. If you feel a need to tell another person's business, don't; that goes against ma'at. If someone divulges a secret, weigh the value of the speaker, not the secret.

7. Where you find feathers, you find protection, truth, and balance. Spirit is a delicate feather that catches the breath of God and moves in subtle ways. Look for signs from the Divine. When you find feathers, see that as a sign of truth and protection as well as portents of things to come.

8. The lemniscate that appears in the Magician and Strength cards of the

tarot shows us the balance of personal and divine wills. Truth is the will of God. Hold a vision of the highest and best for all of your endeavors and in all difficult situations. Apply compassion to your work.

9. If you start something, finish it. Work with the highest integrity. In the end your heart will speak to answer these questions: How well did I do? What might I have done differently? Love everything that you can. Bless the things that can't support you, then release them with gratitude for the lessons.

MANU

This hieroglyph represents a difficult passage, what some might call being caught between hell and high water. To the ancients, manu was that high hill that arose from a lake of outer darkness in the western lands. The dead made their passage across the dark waters of the night sky in a boat similar to the hieroglyph depicted in manu. Passage to the western lands was not easy. It was possible to fall into these waters and drown. Even when one reached the western lands, the journey still contained danger. In the photo above we see a Saharan horned viper, the deadly *Cerastes cerastes*. The journey needed the assistance of an able ferryman to carry one across. Three gods supported the dark-night passage across these waters—Upuat (or Anubis), Ra (the sun), and Horus (appearing as the moon).

To the modern mind an equivalent passage in life would be experiencing a dark night of the soul. This may be a long journey, more than a simple day trip into depression. The idea is not to replace the darkness with artificial light, but to incorporate darkness into your essence. Try living a winter without an electric lamp to read by. It alters your appreciation of light and the cycles of time. Learn to use the dark to release, relax, and rest. This dark water represents the body of the night sky goddess Nut, the darkness in the womb that we must experience, and which ultimately nourishes us until we are able to be reborn.

In Egypt the souls of the departed followed the path of the sun from the eastern side of the river into the western lands, or into the neterworld. This boat sailed across the deep water to the Field of Reeds in a fashion that was reminiscent of the sailing of Charon's ferry, which carries souls across the River Styx in the Greek tradition. The boat is a funerary barge indicative of completion—either of a life or a project.

1. Something has ended. It's time to begin a new life. Give thanks for a safe passage.
2. An upsetting situation can finally be put to rest.
3. A sprite, or a young person in spirit, wishes to contact you to establish or maintain a relationship. Meditate in a dark room and be open to surprises from the world of Spirit.
4. All the air seems to have gone out of the room and depression has taken over. This is a process you are going through. Attend to details you'd rather ignore. You will get through this by going through it and reaching a safe space on the other side.
5. You travel into the spirit world on a voyage that changes your life. A shamanic journey or an illness brings a healing vision.
6. Look after your health or the health of one you love. Stay alert to unexpected slips of attention. Sometimes a rough passage makes us want to jump ship. Stay the course.
7. Meditate with your guides to gain insights. Dreams, visions, and altered states radically shift realities. Do not take any feelings of melancholia too seriously.

8. Do not attach to outcomes in the material world. The spirit world greatly interests you now.

9. A life cycle completes or a project comes to an end. Experience a respite. Celebrate work well done.

MERI

The Divine Beloved whom the Christians called Mary the ancient Egyptians called Meri. Many kings, queens, mothers, and even nobles were named Meri in the ancient world: Meriaten (Beloved of Aten, daughter of Nefertiti and Akhenaten), Meritamen (Beloved of Amen, daughter of Ramses II), and Merenptah (He who loves Ptah, a son of Ramses II and a reigning pharaoh). The hieroglyph *mer* is also the root word of *to marry,* meaning "to bind together." The *y* sound in Meri is denoted by a hieroglyphic feather. Sometimes the hieroglyph contains an image of two feathers, moved in unison by the vibration of air between them. The image could connote two people becoming one, and in the process creating a third being or a blessing. Beautiful, delicately carved depictions of the immaculate conception of Hatshepsut appear in her temple at Deir el Bahari where we see her mother, Ahmose, sitting with the god Amen, their knees interlocked and their feet held up by goddesses as they consummate the conception of Hatshepsut in heaven. Similarly, divine conceptions appear as a metaphysical and metaphorical truth when used by Eighteenth Dynasty rulers, as in the image below.

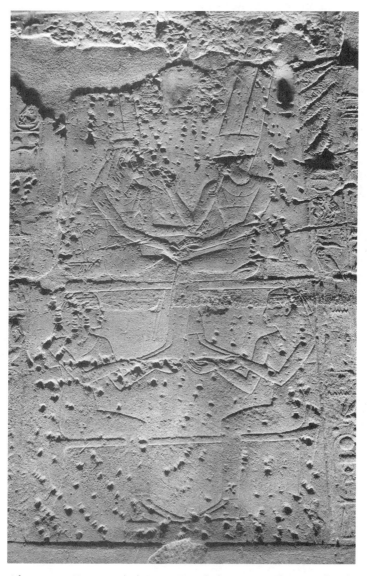

After pagan Egypt ended, Luxor Temple became a Christian church. To accommodate Christian beliefs, carved reliefs were either painted over or covered with curtains. This badly damaged image, however, still holds the delicate detail of Queen Mutemuia consorting with the god Amen who fathers Pharaoh Amenhotep III. This image of an immaculate conception dates to around 1390 BCE.

Additionally, the hieroglyph is drawn with a rudimentary hand plow, which refers to a farmer opening a furrow and planting seed. One relied not upon the strength of an animal to plow the earth but one's own personal power, wielding a long-handled, two-pronged trowel. As an image, meri symbolizes the relationship between husband and wife, and the duties of the farmer, who is a husband of the Earth. There is no go-between such as oxen or ass. The husband himself sows and makes fertile the field, tends to the needs of the land (his wife), and prepares it for new growth. Not only was the relationship to the Earth and to his wife about fertilizing but also keeping, caring, supporting, and tending to the beloved. He cultivates both so that his wife and the Earth are well-tended.

We seem to have forgotten the idea of being good stewards of the Earth. We seem to have forgotten our responsibility to the Earth that sustains us, the fertility of its fields, and keeping them blossoming by treating them well.

Meri refers to what one desires, wishes for, and uses one's sense of purpose to attain and to keep. It is a quality of the heart related to ib. Just as there can be too much of a good thing, we must return to the idea that meri also means to care for and tend to that which we desire. The heart hieroglyph connected to the ma'at hieroglyph reminds us that balance in all things is to be desired.

1. Whether you are male or female, follow the call of the divine feminine. You are beloved of the gods and goddesses. Open yourself to be loved.
2. Partnership is in the offing. Be the kind of spiritual companion your beloved would love to be with in a relationship. Nurture your partner and the partnership.
3. Welcome a young person coming into your life who will bring great love.
4. Take care of and tend to the Earth. Plant flowers, keep track of details, and prepare for a future harvest. A well-kept home is a sign of a well-kept family.
5. A spiritual desire always trumps a physical desire. A change heads your way.

6. Family is the core of the loving relationship. Father and mother pull together as equal partners and the whole family succeeds. Remember, too, that your physical and spiritual selves partner each other, working together to keep you balanced.

7. A spiritual and emotionally fulfilling relationship means that you are able to love yourself unconditionally all the while making yourself a better, more balanced person.

8. If there is something you wish to attain that your passion moves you toward—say, the creation of an art form, building the home of your dreams, or the trip of a lifetime—know that you need to align and focus on eight details that bring what you desire toward you. Meditate on this, then take action.

9. Reach out. What you desire is right there, but once you have attained it, do you know what to do with it? Do you know how to preserve it? Do you know how to make its abundance grow?

NEBHET (NEPHTHYS)

Nephthys was the last of Nut's five children to be born. She knew the loneliness—and the sanctity—of belonging to a space and time that others had left. The hieroglyphic name for Nephthys, the sister of Isis, literally means "Lady of the House." The hieroglyph of the home or temple appears here; the offering of bread within it indicates the feminine presence within the home or temple. Above the temple is the hieroglyph of the basket, perhaps indicating the nurturing qualities of the woman depicted—rather like the native Egyptian woman often seen carrying the basket on her head to market, to the river, and so on. Egyptian miners can often be seen carrying baskets of rock or gold nuggets upon their heads as well. *Nebhet* can also be translated as "the golden enclosure or shrine." It may refer to the mystery of her sexuality as well as to the naos of the Divine.

In a case of mistaken identity Nephthys bore the first child of Osiris, the jackal god Anubis who works with his father in the burial rites linked to the neterworld. He was conceived in the illusory moonlight of Osiris's garden one night. The god mistakenly thought Nephthys was her twin sister, Isis, and Nephthys did not correct him. She tried to hide her pregnancy from her husband, Set. She gave birth to her child in secret, leaving him in the desert to be found by the handmaiden of Isis. Her sister Isis raised the child.

Rather than being rivals, however, the sisters were dearest companions. Nephthys helped Isis to mourn the death of Osiris, to find his missing pieces, to give him his burial rites, and to help to raise the dead into the spirit world. She guarded the western gate where the sun set; Isis guarded the eastern gate. Nephthys stood opposite her sister in guarding the shrine of Tutankhamen. As Isis saved Anubis from death in the desert and raised him as her own, so Nephthys became the nursemaid of Horus in the swamps where Isis hid him from Set.

Often we see Nephthys and Isis standing together, with Nephthys appearing behind Isis—almost as if she were a shadow figure. She is the hidden side of the goddess energy. Isis is the face of Egypt's most prominent goddess, the one most of us see; but Nephthys is the face of the mystery of life and death itself. At the entrances to the tombs in the Valley of the Kings she stands at the doorway, facing her sister. Both of them lift their palms in blessing as the soul passes into the underworld. Sometimes the sisters are winged, sitting facing each other in the same fashion as the angels who later graced the Ark of the Covenant. They guard the greatest mystery of all: the death and resurrection of the soul.

Like Isis, Nephthys may also be linked to Sirius, the brightest star in the Canis Major constellation. Most of us once thought that the Sirius solar system had but one star, which the ancient Egyptians linked to Isis. Scientists later revealed that there were two "Dog Stars" (Sirius A and B), yet the African Dogon tribe was long aware of the mysteries of Sirius and had already equated that second star to Anubis. Then, in 1995, astronomers suspected that yet a third star, Sirius C, existed in the same solar system. Almost invisible, this hidden star contributes to the overall radiance of the Sirius solar system. That star may be Nephthys, the hidden twin of Isis. (See Sopdet for more information on Sirius.)

1. Nephthys accomplishes little on her own, willingly giving her sister the limelight. Your power is behind the scenes, working with your altar and talking with your spirit guides. Through meditation you gain incredible insight.

2. Your sister has your back and you have hers. Keep this connection strong. Whether your sister is in the spirit world or in the flesh, the two of you share a karmic link.

3. At times you feel your presence is unnoticed in a crowd. Know that your love, compassion, and even your simple presence is a battery for others. They look to you for grounding. You serve a higher purpose than you know. Through you much spiritual work is accomplished.

4. Stand your ground on an issue. Protect what your heart cherishes. Release what does not heal you or heal another.

5. When you hold your tongue, you gather energy for the next time you speak. Make it count. Called true of voice, those priestesses of Nebhet's mysteries were seen as oracles. You have a natural affinity for working as a channel for information from Spirit. If you have not done so already, begin this study.

6. If your actions arise from love, there is no mistake. Love and compassion are the highest service of all. Continue to love and tend to the needs of others.

7. If you have not already begun to work as a trance channel, you might engage a trance teacher to work with you. If you already work as a trance channel, you are called to offer yourself in service to a master teacher on the other side.

8. Building a spiritual community takes many hands. You may be traveling to various places to work. Your presence helps others create a holy place to commune with Spirit and the ancestors.

9. Many across the spirit divide reach out to you. You can be their voice. While your friendships on Earth may not be plentiful, celebrate those that are deep and abiding. Always remember to be a help to your community of sisters, saying "What can I do?"

NEFER

All that is happy, peaceful, and content, all that is beautiful, perfect, and good—that is the essence of nefer. The word appears as an appellation of many gods and goddesses in the Book of the Dead. Osiris becomes Unnefer, "the Beautiful Being," in the underworld; he is equivalent to the Green Man. His name uses the desert hare as a hieroglyphic determinative to connote his fertility. Most often nefer becomes attached to a human being, such as the wife of Akhenaten, Nefertiti (meaning "the Beautiful One has come"); the wife of Ramses the Great, Nefertari (meaning "the Beautiful Companion"); and the Fourth Dynasty princess Neferet (meaning simply, "beautiful").

The hieroglyphic symbol is a mysterious one. What could be so beautiful about what some Egyptologists explain away as an image of the heart and trachea, other than that the word derives from the Unnefer hieroglyph of the Good Being? Certainly, goodness and beauty may be equally represented by the heart and voice. The cantors of Egyptian rites were priests; but its priestess-singers were called true of voice. Other Egyptologists equate this hieroglyph with a lute or banjo, the music of which is also good and beautiful, making one feel happy and content. In the Land of the Dead, scenes depict memories of happy concerts, dances, and parties in which priestesses play the lute. I know a number of Appalachian musicians who play the banjo, which is essentially an African instrument that migrated to America. Some see it as a "play-party" instrument. There may be something to that idea. Some moments in life just need music. Hieroglyphically, ben-dja would mean "beautiful speech," sound, or voice.

Nefertum, the child of Ptah and Sekhmet, appears as a blue lotus. He is the child of expression and power. His name means "Beautiful Completion." Art is also a child of beauty, expression, and power. In the natural world, music, visual art, and poetry are nefer. Even saying that sibilant word creates the soft stirring of breath, evoking a breeze among the reeds and flowers. Related to the invisible, nefer is the palpable vibration of life and emotion.

1. Something beautiful approaches—a person, a blessed event, a moment of joy. Savor it.
2. Happiness oozes out of us when we enter a new relationship. That satisfied

feeling between lovers is the same as the satisfying relationship between an artist and his or her muse.

3. Friends gather to share interests in art or food. Nothing matters more than being in the presence of good friends, accompanied by music and conversation, amid the beauty of the natural world.

4. When things are in order, peace comes. Work on organizing your possessions, your projects, your home, then rest. Create a sure foundation and be at peace.

5. A surprise awaits. Good news or a happy visit comes out of the blue. You hear something said that is music to your ears.

6. Let the beauty of the Earth heal you and your family. Go on a picnic in nature. Feed each other with laughter and love.

7. You can't set the world aside in order to see spiritual things. The world itself is spiritual, with its wind, rain, snow, sunlight, midnight falling leaves, and ebullient buds of flowers.

8. God has a plan. God knows what happens next. Let it unfold. Let it flow. Be in its music.

9. Do not try to hold on to what is passing away. Something more beautiful comes to replace it.

NEFERTUM

The name of the child of Sekhmet and Ptah, Nefertum, means "beautiful completion." His name as it appears on the walls (see photo) is a combination of trilateral sounds that become the *nefer* hieroglyph and the final *tem* sounds. In some texts Nefertum was simply drawn as a boy wearing a lotus crown (see line drawing). Nefertum meant the "completed one," the "beautiful child," the sanctified and perfected human being. It was a designation of perfection. The first hieroglyph in the photo above, the image of the lyre, obliquely refers to the beautiful music that emanates from such an instrument. The final hieroglyph is the sledge used to carry the mummy and its grave goods over the sands toward the tomb, during its last transport on Earth. Together the two hieroglyphs symbolize a beautiful life in the end. The perfected spiritual child of Ptah and Sekhmet often referred to the high priest Imhotep. This common man was the Leonardo da Vinci of ancient Egypt, a chief vizier, architect, doctor, high priest, magician, scribe, and so on, who built the first magnificent pyramid of Egypt for his pharaoh Djoser during the Third Dynasty.

We are all children of a Divine Creator. Our task is to ascend to mastery over the flesh, to transcend humanness, and to let the god spark grow into the full light of divinity. We are but closed buds of god essence sent here into a base material world. Let us use the muck of the riverbed in order to grow. Use that base matter and transform it into light, into perfume, into beauty, opening up like a lotus emerging from the pond. We must rise above the waters of the unconscious mind into full awareness of Spirit. There is a reason for all things that happen. It is our own muck from which we arise. Even as the old life decays, we know we have drawn sustenance from it, learning its lessons.

Nefertum opens to the sunlight, to the warmth and energy of his mother, Sekhmet, who protects the child and the world. Nefertum is inspired into being by the divine mind of his father, Ptah. His father's warm words of encouragement curl around Nefertum's ear. This child and you are their beautiful golden dream, the perfected cosmos. This is the golden child of the Sun card in the tarot, with a red flame of feather in his hair and a laughing smile as he rides bareback on a white horse. In some Greco-Roman images of him, Nefertum rides on the back of a lion. This may indicate his powerful mother, Sekhmet, carrying him.

The blue lotus that opens at Nefertum's crown chakra embodies spiritual awakening. In ancient times the scent of blue lotus—even eating its leaves—produced visions of meetings with ancestors, as well as the gods and goddesses themselves. If we were able to see that all of the things of the world are maya, that they are sprung from the mind or ma'at of the Divine, we would no longer struggle to survive the lot we are given. The lotus-eaters of Homer's myth are not lost in a dream. It is we who are lost in the dream, dreaming that we are awake. Inside the flower, seated in the center of the lotus that is the mind of God, we would see that we already exist in the center of heaven, and everything is okay.

"Be," Nefertum says. Be jubilant. Be happy. Be guileless and innocent. Be the beauty that is within you and all around. Whether it is in its beginning or in its ending, it does not matter. This is wholeness. The vibrant fire of life is joyful ecstasy. Offer gratitude for all.

1. See your place in things. A sudden insight comes: I am where I am meant to be.

2. We live in two worlds simultaneously—the material and the spiritual. Stay open in the midst of difficulties to receive divine wisdom, assurance, and grace.

3. Pleasure and protection are yours. You are held in the light. Dance in the light. Bask in it, knowing you are a child of God. It is your birthright to be happy.

4. The noble attributes of Nefertum are happiness, beauty, a kind disposition, and sharing one's good fortune and success. Here, Nefertum represents prosperity for one and all.

5. You've seen many changes of late; some have rocked you. Think of the flower floating in perfect peace as the wake of a passing boat rocks it. You are that beautiful lotus riding the waves.

6. In this happy family, emphasis is placed on the protection of children—

see to their physical safety, their education, and teach them to overcome adversity. One of life's greatest lessons is this: Keep loving anyway.

7. In sleep and deep meditation, astral travel enhances teaching or learning in the spirit world. There is powerful magic available to you.

8. Nefertum possesses a kind of charioteer energy. By learning the answer to the riddle of the sphinx, one learns how to harness one's own life force energy. Live your life in abundance and in harmony with the world.

9. Opening petals of the crown chakra generates great illumination. The answer to an important life question can be attained now. You feel oneness with God and spiritual communion with the master teachers.

NU

The lesser known partner of Nut, nu is one of four pairs of creative forces that comes from the magic wand of Thoth, stirring up life in his cosmic cauldron. Those eight principalities form the Ogdoad. Nut is the watery sky mother, the ocean of stars (see page 171). Nu is the masculine principality of the flow, the swirling creative chaos before form. There are male and female elements of natural confluence, just as there are two rivers that flow through Kenya and Ethiopia to become the Nile. Nu is the infinite vibration that is the wave form of the space-time continuum.

One principle of masculine flow may be depicted as sperm swimming toward a destination. Another analogy may be the phenomenon that ripples through college football stadiums and is known as the Wave. Nu is a rapid, flowing out into an energetic line in order to create an impression. Conception, of course, is the big bang inside a womb. A small event culminates in a larger-scale phenomenon. Nu is the onslaught of waters flowing through the cataracts of Egypt, creating a crashing, great inundation that has a lasting impact on the building of civilization.

In the imagery on page 169, the energy of the great flood that is nu can be seen in the three hieroglyphic ripples of water that are his name. This image speaks of the great beneficence of the river that fertilizes the fields along the floodplains of Egypt. Three of anything means something endlessly multiplied. *N-n-n* or *nun* clearly indicates flooding, being overcome, even wiped away into nothingness. Our word *none* is derived from the multiplication of nu's energy. Those same fecund waters overflowed, swept away fields and houses, filled temples with mud, clogged the canals, and even caused the abysmal destruction that the biblical Noah escaped. Therefore, nu is an energy source that pulses in two directions both positive and negative. It is equally nothingness personified as well as the source of all things new.

1. A new season appears in your life. Energy flows to and from you. Enjoy every new opportunity.
2. Understand and use the law of polarity. What you perceive as opposition may be only a flow of energy in a different form. There are two sides of a coin, but only one coin.
3. A new life has been generated for you. Out with the old; in with the new. Catch the flow. Find opportunities to write, to paint, to meditate, and to develop your spiritual capacities.
4. Everything takes time. Prepare the ground, plant the seeds, then water and nurture them. Weed out the weaker plants. It's the same with your projects as it is with your garden.

5. Watch the ways that you experience flow in your life. How do you spend your hours? Observe the flow of words from your lips to the ears of others.

6. Family matters take on an urgency. A great flow of energy comes in that focuses on new situations. There are many new starts, lines blur, and emotions run high.

7. Be like the Nile inundation. Flow into a community, then flow out, leaving it better after you go. Flow invigorates and releases stagnation. Create a channel for coming in and going out.

8. In the Ogdoad, eight beings float within the cosmic waters. Examine the physics of light, darkness, time, and space to reveal a new understanding of universal law and mystery.

9. Say thank you to the universe for all of its influx and efflux. A season has ended. What did it bring? A new one begins. What is coming?

NUT

In ancient Egypt, the heavens are Mother Sky, or Nut, and the Earth is Father Geb. Imagine the night sky goddess arching over the Earth in the form of the Milky Way. She hovers over the land, touching earth only with the tips of her hands and feet. The stylized hieroglyph of the rectangle at the bottom of the photo abstractly refers to the sky goddess in a modified downward dog yogic pose. Nut is the Great Mother, the mystery of incarnation—how we come into being. Imagine the great star field of the big bang and the many stars and galaxies that are constellations of families. The ancient Egyptians saw each individual as a star soul born into earthly existence. Whether that soul lives now on the planet, has passed into Spirit, or is waiting to be born again, it is still an eternal being, a conscious spark of light that exists for all time in the star field or belly of the great goddess Nut.

In the Temple of Hathor at Dendera, the body of the sky goddess stretches across the ceilings, showing the constellations and ruling energies of each day, each week, and each millennium on this planet. All of this evolving consciousness is held in the body of the Goddess. Here lie the paths in and out of what we term reality. This dark, hidden body of the night sky is the deepest of mysteries. It is the embodiment of unconditional love itself. Nut, the cosmic mother of the universe, births all of her children; they are of every race, gender, and belief. She also births the karmic path of everything from plants to planets and from macrocosm to microcosm. She spins all of life out from herself, and she saw that it was good.

Neter, written simply *N-t,* was the original mother goddess, the flow of life swirling in liquid darkness filling the void. On clear nights in the desert you can see this and understand why the Egyptians saw the goddess Nut this way. N-t initiated the concept of the neteru; all of the gods or goddesses tumbled out of the belly of heaven. All these are the galaxies and stars that became a net of everything above and below. For example, the belt of Orion, the constellation Sah that the Egyptians equated with Osiris, was reflected in the three pyramids of Giza, and the circumpolar stars, constantly visible at night, were called the Imperishable Ones.

Remember that physics are the natural laws that we are able to see in action by their measurable effects in the physical world, such as the law of gravity. Metaphysics are what spiritual people refer to as the natural laws that determine how the spiritual and physical realms intersect.

In Nut's chapel in both Dendera and Edfu, the sky goddess bends above the Earth as the Milky Way, which, visible in the night sky, seems to touch the Earth with her fingertips and feet. The light from her body shines upon the holy sanctuary of the temple containing the goddess Hathor.

Physics and metaphysics are not so far apart; divine energy makes itself known in both.

Nut and Geb are the universal parents that created life on the planet. The Egyptians were one of the few cultures to suggest a female heavenly mother goddess. (The Iroquois also told of the birth of the earth plane energies by Sky Woman.) The early Nile Delta people envisioned a creatrix also called N-t, who later became the goddess Neith, an embodiment of the cosmic waters. She drew forth all life-forms from the net of her being, the watery depth of cosmic water. In *Imagining the*

World into Existence, I tell the fuller myth of Neith manifesting all life on the planet, but Neith and Nut are interlinked myths.

My book *Feasts of Light* offers the complete story of how Nut, the sky, and Geb, the Earth, create and birth five cosmic children—Osiris, Horus the Elder, Set, Isis, and Nephthys. It explains how Thoth, the moon god, played a chess game with Ra, the sun god, in order to win five epagomenal days into which these five children could be born. Thus the combination of solar and lunar calendars creates a way for us to account for earthly time. But Nut's mythic pregnancy with her children lasts for eighty years at the least; some say eons. Cosmic time and earthly time differ. Containing all that is, was, and will come to be, Nut is the fluidity and potentiality of life, both temporal and eternal.

1. The law of unity or the law of life explains that one creative force permeates all manifestation. Stardust atoms create being and return to the dust of the stars. Consciousness does not dissipate; it merely expands. Follow the law of unity to see how everything is connected. What you think is separate from you is separated merely by perception.

2. Heaven and Earth work together in a sacred marriage from which a new life emerges. Expect a new relationship with Spirit to manifest in earthly form.

3. The stars burn brightly, touching you with the flame of a holy, creative love. If you are inspired to create, do so. Combine the fire in your heart and belly to enliven your vision.

4. Mother's milk sustains her child. Nut, your cosmic mother, has more than enough nurturance to share. Remember that Earth mirrors Heaven. Work hard to draw down that formative energy and life sustenance. In such a loving way a baby suckles its mother, urging her milk to come.

5. Nothing remains at rest for long. Planets tilt, the sun flares, galaxies spin in spirals. It's all a dance, a cycling of time. Don't get carried away trying to make your life a permanent structure. It's already eternal; just enjoy the dance.

6. A spiritual union exists between the divine feminine and masculine. You

are called to explore the feminine face of God in all life-forms and in every person in your life—yes, even in the people who cause you to sigh with exasperation.

7. Inspiration is yours. Set aside work tonight to go out under the stars. With the awe of a child, lie down on the blanket to gaze into the night sky. Watch constellations wheel above you. Feel yourself both eternal and changeable. All is in divine order.

8. Do some useful work on behalf of the natural world and its people. Bake bread and feed the hungry, or whatever feels equivalent to your talents. Work and play. If you are so blessed that no difference arises between work and play, bravo! Thank Heaven and Earth for their gifts.

9. Pray by singing, chanting, or playing music. The sound of your voice is part of the symphony of the spheres. Step out today into the unknown, the vast unity and emptiness of the cosmos. A divine net will catch you and what you hold dear. Anything you don't need or is no longer of service easily turns to ash and passes through the net.

PER-Ā

From this word comes the word we know as *pharaoh*. It denoted a hero, a mighty warrior, that king who is depicted on the outer walls of the pylon of the temple. He is often seen riding in his chariot, his roaring lion beside him, his arm raised up, holding his mace to smite the enemy. The hero story of the per-ā is a demonstration of the Horus god overshadowing the pharaoh to conquer the god Set. *Per* is written as a hieroglyph of a house, and *ā* means "to emerge from a private place of rest (say, the palace) and to move into a public sphere with gusto." In other words, we conquer chaos by getting busy. The hieroglyph, as we can see, is written as a pair of legs striding through the doorway of a house. In some places, it used the hieroglyphic determinative of an arm upraised with a crook, bringing to mind Teddy Roosevelt's phrase "Speak softly and carry a big stick." It wasn't necessarily just about fighting, however.

To come forth boldly (rather than submissively) is the meaning of this hieroglyph. To go forth from the "great house" means to leave one's home or sanctuary and go out into the world to do something important. Sometimes it meant to pull oneself up by the bootstraps and carry on with one's business. At other times leaving the great house indicated the soul exiting the pyramid, or burial chamber. In yet other instances, it indicated entering into or exiting that great house in the sky that was the womb of the mother. Thus to leave the great house was to begin again, to be reborn.

When we start to stand with the Divine as co-creators of the world and the life we inhabit, there can be no timidity. To live a heroic life is not for the foolish or fainthearted. We must move forward boldly and confidently, knowing that Spirit is working with us and moving through us to overcome obstacles, to accomplish the things that will make our mark upon history in some way, as with Ramses the Great. Perhaps we are simply working to make the world a better, more efficient, more sustainable place to live.

The tricky thing about this hieroglyph is that it likewise implies going forth *into* the great house. That might mean the pharaoh going into his temple to pray. It might be imagined that he was accompanied into the temple with an entourage. For certainly there were many scenes of the Opet Festival at Luxor with its many beautifully decorated cattle, its fanbearers, dancers, and so on. However, only the pharaoh spoke to the god. Only the pharaoh entered the holy of holies to be with the god. Behind him, the priests in attendance shut the doors. In this same way, no one followed Moses to his tent of meeting; rather the people took it as a sign that it was time for them to go into their own private spaces and pray. In Luke 2:41–52 the twelve-year-old Jesus was discovered missing by his parents and later found teaching in the temple. Asked by his mother why he had left them, he answered either "I must be about my father's business" or "I must be in my father's house." Now, *per-ā* might be the perfect word for both meanings.

This could be a time of going into solitude and communing with a deity for prayers of utmost importance. This may also be an important moment for coming or going, for getting busy. In either case, see this as a sign that Spirit has important work for you, and know that it is time to get on with it. This work is part of your destiny, the reason you were sent here.

1. Chosen for a leadership role, you must leave the comfort of anonymity to come forth in greatness. You might hesitate, thinking "Why me?" or even "You must be mistaken." But there is no mistake. Why *not* you? All of us are called. Meditate on how you are best to do this great work.

2. A new partnership has formed—perhaps business, perhaps a matter of the heart. Someone calls to discuss plans together. You happily come forth from your house. You've been waiting for this opportunity to come along. Many hands make light work.

3. You, your god, and your spirit guides can accomplish great things. Get busy creating the life you wish to live. Prepare for a wonderful new project. If you just stay in your house doing the things you always do, you'll miss this creative time. If you are an artist, apply for grants. If you are a businessperson, take a walk and contemplate your stalled project from a new perspective.

4. Work, work, work. You are one busy little bee. You have much on your plate, yet you get it all done. You are able to multitask, which many people are not. Take care of the details. Before you step out the door know what you want to accomplish and how to accomplish it, then begin the work. Continue your walking meditations and pray with your feet.

5. Time to put on traveling shoes. Be visible doing the important work you are given to do. Take it to the next level or on the road. If it hasn't appeared yet, this dynamic work is coming soon, so get ready. In making yourself known this way, you are making Spirit's work known. A move elsewhere is possible.

6. Someone needs your assistance. Like a midwife called in the middle of the night, you know the request can't really wait. Go because the physical and spiritual work are aligned. As you go forth to attend another, the angels are attending *you*. If you wish to meet another in a creative partnership, the first move may be up to you.

7. Enter the great house through deep meditation. You may find yourself on a spiritual retreat to a monastery, or just spending a day visiting churches, cathedrals, temples, or mosques. A walk in the woods brings deep peace. When the chaos around you seems too demanding, retreat is what your soul craves. When you find yourself on the path of initiation, be spiritually brave.

8. The life you were meant to live waits for you to go out and find it. Are you willing to take charge of your destiny rather than wait for it to come to you? If you are not ready, you may not deserve it. This call to strive for what you want is a good thing—a kind of spiritual inheritance. You've worked hard, planted the seeds, and nurtured them. Do not fail to harvest what is now yours.

9. You have completed a large project, finished a major task, and/or concluded some karma. This hieroglyph could indicate retirement, leaving a relationship, or ending a role you have played. This is a fine thing. You do not leave in defeat. Congratulations for a work well done.

PTAH

Thought finds its form on Earth. As we've established, the Gospel of John 1:1 explains it this way: "In the beginning was the Word, and the Word was with God and the Word was God." The myth of Ptah and the Genesis story (1:2–3) recall the same event, saying, "The spirit of God hovered over the face of the waters. Then God said, 'Let there be light'; and there was Light." In the illustration provided, the final hieroglyph of Ptah's name is a determinative that shows a pair of lips spitting yods of light energy into space. Imagine the surface of water over which God intones the Word as a vortex of energy spinning light into the forms of matter, the stars and their planets. Rather than sucking energy inward as a black hole would do, it forcefully projects energy and matter outward.

According to the Shabaka stone, an ancient Egyptian relic, the god Ptah opened his mouth and light sprang from his lips. Ptah's voice vibrated across the waters in sound and light to create the world. When Ptah spoke the magical words of truth (*heka* and *ma'at*) over the void (nu, the water of nothingness), the light that sprang from his lips allowed the god Atum to see himself for the first time. In other words, Atum made the world, but first, Ptah made Atum visible. One might say that thought precedes action. His hieroglyph often includes a pair of pursed lips that seem to be spitting yods of light.

As architect of the world, Ptah became the patron deity of stone-masons, craftsmen, scribes, and priests. They were the metaphysicians who crafted, invoked, and operated the sacred energies within the temple. The generation of ideas, the enunciation of truth, and the energy to create order from chaos are the gifts of Ptah. Emblems of the Freemasons—the craftsman's square and compass—were the hieroglyphs of Ptah's name. The all-seeing eye that appears above the pyramid on the back of the U.S. dollar emphasizes the idea that if one can envision a better world and act upon it, that world already exists. The priests of Ptah taught the Greek philosopher Pythagoras name vibration and numerology. Names offered protection as well as informing one's destiny and the soul's progression.

Ptah stands upon ma'at, a solid foundation, the plinth of truth. He wears a gleaming sky-blue crown that represents his supreme power—the power of the universal mind to manifest thought into form. Tightly swaddled in mummy cloths, a symbol of his inability to move in a physical realm, his hands reach through the linen cloth to grasp his magical staff. On it are the emblems of the ankh, the djed, and the waz. These three symbols are the metaphysical tools he uses. Through thought alone, Ptah reaches into the unseen spirit realm and draws down through himself the substance needed to create. The energies of the chakras (the sacred centers of the body) are indicated on the scepter he holds. This staff of life aligns the heart and the solar plexus chakras, signifying united desire and will. The mind of God manifests through the use of ma'at, the feminine principle of unified desire and action. Ma'at is called the heart and tongue of Ptah.

1. Watch your words carefully; others are watching them. You create your reality with every word you speak. With your powerful voice, commitment to work for the common good, and your loving heart, you can become a spiritual leader among people.
2. Ptah created the world with two powerful instruments—his heart and his tongue. What does your heart desire to create? Affirm that it is so. How will this creation that springs from your heart nourish others?
3. The desire, the will, and the breath of life are the creative trinity. You must

take responsibility for bringing any life into form. Act upon what you know to be true.

4. Truth is the plinth upon which Ptah stands. Examine what is true for you. Let what is not true fall away. Speak truth always. There is no half-truth, only untruth. To speak when you know better is an untruth. Telling the truth requires discernment.

5. You busily create something new. Get your ideas down on paper and begin to work out the details. You gain momentum by speaking with the right people who align with your vision. Otherwise, safeguard the information until you are ready to bring it to light.

6. Someone in your community or family needs to hear your encouraging words. Our attention helps another focus their intention, to see themselves and their plans as having value.

7. Sometimes just as you are falling asleep you hear conversations being whispered in your ears. Pay attention. Write down what you hear. Spirit is communicating.

8. Before beginning a new project there is much to do. Asking for help is the best way to get the energy flowing for all and for yourself. Be clear about what you want done and how you would like it to manifest.

9. Say thank you and hallelujah. A project concludes well. One relationship is finished and a new one begins soon. Say thank you for all that you have learned through this work.

RE (RA)

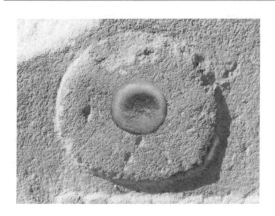

The main solar deity has two names: Ra/Re. Re, like the ray of a sun, which he is; and Ra, the sound of a lion roaring. The hieroglyphic name for a lion is in fact written with two *r*'s, the sound of a roar. Since the hieroglyphs often omit the sacred vowel sounds—the breathy elements of the language—we can imagine that the word we know as *roar* comes from the Egyptian word *re-re*. The ancient word, written with two lions or two *r*'s, meant "to cry out." Sometimes it is connected to the twin lion god and goddess, Shu and Tefnut, who were the first children of Ra according to the Heliopolitan myth. In other instances, the two lions sit back to back, one facing east and one facing west; or one crouching on its haunches in the desert sand and the other resting as the Leo constellation in the sky. These two lions of Re are known as Aker and are defined as limitlessness. Their names are yesterday and tomorrow.

In the myth of Hermopolis, however, Ra is one of the four pairs of creative substance of the universe that Thoth manifested while stirring his magic cauldron. How the universe came into being in this myth is similar to the universal big bang theory. As we have established, these eight creatures in four pairs of male and female essences were known as the Ogdoad, the sources of seed potentiality of beingness and non-beingness at the moment of Creation.

Their names are Ra/Ra-t, meaning infinite light; Kuk and Kuk-t, meaning infinite darkness; heh and heh-t, infinite time; and nu and nu-t, infinite space. (The *t* indicates the feminine state.) Of the eight beings, Ra and Nut become more well-known as divinities in their own right. Sometimes Amen and Amen-t are added to the pairs to replace Kuk and Kuk-t. They become the divine beings of non-beingness, the invisible god of the sky, and the invisible goddess that expresses itself as the vastness of the underworld.

If one studies gematria, one learns about the hidden gender of number—odd numbers being male and even numbers female. All beings operate through the laws of polarity and vibration. Ra (and Ra-t) are the infinite vibration of light becoming substance before light lowers its vibration to manifest into form. It is obvious that both seen and unseen forms exist in this bandwidth we call light.

In Egypt, Ra was considered the progenitor of light itself. Amen-Re represents the polarity of light existing in both its seen and unseen forms. We recall that in the Gospel of Thomas, Jesus reminds his disciple that he has come from the light. Light vibration is the building block of life in the known world. It is light desirous of the multiforms that created life. Think also upon the seven colors, the seven chakras, or the mystical seven flames before the throne of God. They may differ, but all are a part of the one light, the one Ra. The cells of your body require light to exist, as do plants. The atoms of our bodies emit sparks. The neurons communicate with each other across the synapses through light. Scientists have witnessed that at the moment of conception a flash of light appears.

The color spectrum is only a part of light's capacities. Each color has its effect upon our physical form. The unseen forms of light, especially those we know as ultraviolet, infrared, and x-ray, for example, appear at either end of the spectrum. We are probably more aware of the effects of the unseen light rays upon our body (x-ray and infrared, for example). The x-ray allows us to use light to see further into a form; infrared light becomes a heat-sensing ray that determines living or inert matter. Each of the colors of the rainbow that we can see have their own particular effect upon the body as well, although the influence may be subtler. For example, red colors energize, while yellows stimulate thinking, and so on.

Ra is ubiquitous in the Egyptian mythologies. In a desert climate, it's pretty obvious that the light can be both fructifying and deadly. The myths of Ra often refer to his various instances of being hot-tempered, egoic, and even jealously retreating when his pride has been wounded. The Ra in the myth sometimes comes across as a soap opera version of how difficult family dynamics get rolling. It's rather like *The Godfather* movie with Ra in the Marlon Brando role as the patriarch who is accustomed to getting his way, and moody behind closed doors.

Yes, solar light continues while we sleep. It is we who turn away from it! The family of Ra is fraught with competitive dynamics. The two sons of Geb and Nut (Earth and Heaven), Osiris and Set, vie for prominence in the earthly domain; their wives Isis and Nephthys become caught in the fray. All of this is the divine creative mystery of

Genesis in the Heliopolitan tradition. The entire family of Ra is called the Great Ennead. In the end of that story, after the battle between Osiris and Set, the young child Horus emerges as the hero who takes the place of his father, Osiris, on Earth and Ra in the sky.

The hieroglyphic symbol of Ra is a circle, and within the continuous and infinite circle of God resides a single point. This sole image refers to the big bang. First, there is the seed possibility of life, then: bang! Everything flows out of him and comes into existence all at once. A vibration, as if from a pebble dropped into a pool, endlessly ripples out, unified and perpetual, to the ends of the universe. All points of energy are connected by a central focal point. Intriguingly, NASA scientists have discovered that our entire solar system, which indeed contains a single star radiating energy outward, is ringed by a strong wall of hydrogen that has been pushed out to its outer edges by the solar wind. Beyond it lies interstellar debris and other matter that cannot penetrate that wall. The light of the sun creates a kind of golden ring bouncing off these collected hydrogen atoms.[39]

Ra may be seen also as God's eye. The central dot is the contracted pupil and the empty space within the circle is the cornea of the eye. Light is consciousness. While the ancient Egyptians understood light as the masculine Ra, there is also the feminine solar goddess. Ra-t, another name for the lion goddess Sekhmet, was the feminine mother sun, later demoted from goddess and called a daughter of Ra and his fiery eye.[40] Light is the life source. The agency of light acts upon every plant or animal, and changes it through photosynthesis. God said, "Let there be light." All Egyptian temples were designed to dramatically showcase the various aspects of light and the ways in which solar energy promulgates life through photosynthesis, seasonal and yearly rhythms, and the movement of the sun through the years and eons. Ra represents time itself—both human and divine. The circle surrounding the central dot demonstrates the principles of both eternity and temporality.

1. Illumination comes to you. A moment that was previously clouded suddenly becomes clear and you understand it. This represents the will of God. Your moment is now.

2. The feminine power of light grows within you. This is not solar egoic will-power, but the gentle fructifying power of the Goddess. Her gentle light stimulates, nurtures, and cultivates your life, whether you are aware of its presence or not. Use the power to enact the will of the divinity.

3. Light created universes. Inspiration comes. Infinite possible outcomes appear and gather like beads on a necklace. In its own time and according to each nature, all things come to pass. Joyful creation is not work. Radiate your creativity outward. Take disappointments lightly.

4. Light reveals by both illumination and shadow. Without shadow we could not see anything. All would be flooded in blazing glare and the shapes of things could not be perceived. To grow spiritually make use of the polarities of light and shadow, fullness and emptiness, activity and rest. How can your life be more harmonious with that integration?

5. Concentrate and focus your attention with a laser-like beam of energy. The mind works like a mirror of the mind of God set upon a focal point. Intention and attention define consciousness. Beam this light into the world around you. Create a spark in others.

6. Light gives itself with generosity. Healers manifest this compassion of light through mental, physical, and emotional work. Light workers often bear the burdens of others, yet instill humility and compassion into their communities. You don't have to be a Jesus or Mother Teresa to become a role model. Do the best you can for yourself, your family, and your community. Be the embodiment of light and love.

7. In rites, ceremonies, and meditations the magical power of light acts through ordered attention and focused intention. Candlelight services help to direct our energy. Observe how the light from a candle radiates through a room. You yourself are that candlewick and Spirit is the flame upon you to illuminate darkness.

8. All is God, life after life after life. The infinite play of light in your body emanates from the DNA of its cells. How do you embody light in your life? Consciousness is eternal—and yes, you *can* take that with you.

9. The unmanifested light beyond the veil is still entirely real and will reveal itself soon. A certain situation that baffled you becomes clear and you see things are they are. There is no reason to keep others in the dark.

REKHT

The hypostyle columns in the halls of Karnak bear this hieroglyph that signifies "the people in adoration." Rekht depicts a crested lapwing, a rather common delta bird. The bird appears to have its wings pinned, but raises up a pair of human arms. It has been suggested that this might be a gesture of submission, the way one raises one's hands in surrender, but with the brilliant star before it, I see the upraised arms as a gesture of adoration, or awe. To me this suggests surrender to a higher principle. It suggests that illumination (starlight) comes through daily dedication to a spiritual principle. It indicates priests and community members singing praises and chanting prayers for divine purposes.

Orators, lector-priests, cantors, and lay readers of ancient mystical literature in the temple were called the knowers of things. They kept lists of offerings, of praises, and even the names of the celebrants who offered temple gifts. The word *rekht* also implied tallying one's deeds, as in taking into account one's actions on a future "Day of Reckoning." From *rekht* we derive the word *reckon*. The phrase *rekht ab* meant "to know in your heart," implying clairsentience. This phrase may be what my grandmother meant when she just knew something, and said, "I reckon they love each other," or even, "I reckon she got what she was aiming for."

To the Egyptians, being a scribe was one of the most blessed professions because scribes had access to the wisdom of those "knowers of things"—the wisdom of priests, healers, magicians, dream interpreters, philosophers, scientists, poets, and artists. The word indicated one who was book-learned as well as intuitive. Being able to read nature, natural signs, and hieroglyphs was an honorable priestly profession, for one could ascertain the will of the gods.

1. Make a new beginning. Do not compare yourself to another. Embrace your uniqueness and the talents you have, all the while learning more by reading and meditating.

2. Cooperation gets things done. Co-create with God and cooperate with one's fellow man. Be at peace wherever you are. What you give, what you do, and what you say is returned in kind. Be kind and your karma will be kind.

3. Time to join with like minds to speak of spiritual tasks that matter. A book discussion group can get you on the right track. Creating an event that brings people together in joyous celebration becomes a tradition.

4. Never ever think your offering is not good enough, rich enough, wise enough, or important enough, or that your neighbor's offering exceeds yours in value. What comes from the heart through your capable endeavors is perfect to Spirit.

5. Look into accounting and reconciling accounts. Remember to tithe what you can to the temple or church. What you give returns in kind. If not giving money, consider giving your time. The law of reciprocity means you receive in like measure to what you give. If there is chaos in your life, consider what you are giving out.

6. Learn natural law and you will know great spiritual treasures. Use natural law to manifest for the world, and you will be returning a gift to God. This is a time of harmony.

7. This moment is your perfect prayer. What have you learned? What are you teaching? What is your highest truth? There is no room for regret—just learning love more deeply.

8. Wishing initiates action, but only action leads to success. If you succeed, praise the earthly and heavenly helpers who led your steps to the goal. Your soul's karma is a contract between you and Spirit. Your life is your best offering.

9. The world needs humanitarian aid. Pray for the world and learn the prayers and traditions of other cultures. Use your meditation to dream big for the planet. This is one of the highest forms of prayer. Really see it manifesting. Work magic with your heart.

REN

Ren means "the name" and represents the power of speech. One of the most powerful spiritual bodies on the mental plane, it uses the creative force of voice vibration. The hieroglyphic image of a mouth above rippling water says it all. Religious philosophy tells us that the genesis of the world began with the voice of God moving across the abyss. In the daily human realm as well, we have discovered that the words we speak create powerful vibrations and have an impact upon our environment. In his book *The Hidden Messages in Water* the renowned Dr. Masaru Emoto demonstrated this transformation by using magnetic resonance analysis to record either beautiful or disfigured molecular formations that were produced depending upon words spoken pleasantly or discordantly into the water.

Words offer powerful magic. Words speak to us in visible and invisible ways. With each repetition of a word, the sound vibrations attach to a name or object, and the words gain power through repetition. That is why Hindu chanting, which uses 108 mala beads, is so effective. Ancient priests chanted their prayers and incantations—literally "singing in" the energy of the Divine. This idea of enchantment involves using the breath and a tone and vocal pattern that dials in the vibratory energy.

In a literary sense, the sounds of the words bind the listener to a story. In a magical sense, the recitation of a "spell" binds the energy of the Divine and the heart of the speaker within a particular place or within an individual. Some of my earliest childhood memories were of my mother reading to me each night. I lay my head on her chest to hear not only her heart but her words. She literally spellbound me with her renditions of poetry when I was less than two. The only way I would eat those green beans was if she was reading me poetry. My mouth dropped open into the breathy *oh!* While I listened, she scooped food into my mouth. She fed me on poetry! Poetry was magical incantation—the proper words, the proper sequence, the proper intent.

When a religious person speaks of "heeding the call," he or she means that the voice of the Divine has called them and drawn them toward it. Dr. Helen Schucman penned *A Course in Miracles* by heeding that call when she heard a voice that identified itself as Jesus. It commanded that she take dictation, saying, "This is a course in miracles. It is a required course. Only the time you take it is voluntary."[41] In just such a way, the angel Gabriel appeared to the illiterate Muhammad and commanded him, "Recite." Thus began the Qur'an in an oral tradition.

Many traditions kept secret the true name of God as a protection against anyone usurping that name's divine power. Genesis 32 tells us that Jacob wrestles with a messenger of God, demanding that he bless him. Each fights the other, insisting on hearing his name. In the end, Jacob tells the angel his name (which means "Follower"), and the angel changes Jacob's name to Israel (meaning "Wrestler with God"). Conversely, when Jacob demands the messenger's name in turn, the messenger withdraws and disappears. For those who know numerology, the difference between the vibrations of Jacob as a 13/4 and Israel as a 28/10/1 is dramatic. The number four indicates struggles against limitations; the number one indicates a leader. Obviously changing one's name strongly changes the vibration of the individual.

Both Jews and Egyptians believed that naming and name vibration kept the universe in order. The chaotic forces ruled lower vibrations and the angelic forces were found in higher vibrations. Says religious studies professor Nicholaus Benjamin Pumphrey in his dissertation *Names and Power:* "The names of the angels, gods, and the stranger (in the Genesis story) were, however, kept a secret in order to maintain the structure of all existence because a lesser power could gain the name and disrupt the order of the universe."[42]

Egyptian gods, goddesses, and all children had multiple names. Some of them were secret names given to them by their mothers. Those names were hidden in their bodies, safe from anyone who might wish to attain power over the individual—even their own siblings. A myth of Isis and Ra found in the Turin Papyrus recounts the way in which Isis learned the god's secret name and so gained his solar power. Even in the throes of death and the near death of all life-forms should he die, Ra was reluctant to divulge his true name to his healer. Why? Because once Isis learned it, her magical power over life and death became as strong as his.

In the end, the two of them withdrew behind a cloud where he divulged his secret name and was healed. This story may refer to another Egyptian description of the first creative power of the universe. It claims: "My name is Heka." In other words, "Magic is my name." A magician might declare himself so by claiming *that* as his secret name, thus aligning with the co-creative energy of the universe.

Isis, of course, already knew the secret name of Ra. She had magically conjured the creature that bit him. "The Mistress of Words of Power" was bequeathed her magical ability by the god Thoth, who created the entire cosmos in his cauldron wherein all beings—divine and human—were magically and mathematically created. By having Ra divulge his name to her, Isis received divine affirmation of their similar abilities to invoke on multiple levels in Heaven and on Earth. Just as Jesus said "The Father and I are One" (consider the numerical power and unity of One) so did the ancient Egyptians assert in the Book of the Dead, "God is my name. I do not forget this name of mine."[43]

The vibrations of the words in the ancient texts were so important that the lector-priests, who may have sung the incantations to the Divine thousands of times in a temple, were required to carry the sacred scroll of hymns and to read from it exactly. They were not allowed to rely on memorization, as that might actually create a misstep and "disspell" the divine energy. The lector-priest was considered one of the most powerful magicians in the temple. Written spells of protection and healing were kept in divine storerooms to be copied onto papyrus. Some copies were dissolved in water to concoct a magical healing drink, or they were tucked into amulets worn on the body. The texts of the temple libraries were zealously guarded, and many an ancient Egyptian teacher refused to let his words be copied down.

The Nag Hammadi gnostic text *The Apocalypse of Peter* summed it up succinctly when Jesus advised Peter by saying, "Words are a mystery. Guard the words you hear! Keep them secret; do not tell anyone, for they are not for this time, but for the future."[44] These sacred words, the text warned, must remain secret. In profane hands, on profane lips, their true meanings vanish. The prohibition against taking the Lord's name in vain derives from those priests who used their spiritual knowledge for baser means. Perhaps the gift of tongues, or glossolalia, which is speaking unknown language while in trance, may preserve the vibrational intensity of the powerful words themselves. When spoken aloud the sound vibrations set the magic of the matter in motion, yet still hid the true meaning from profane ears.

One of the most profound uses of name power allows the dead to pass through the neterworld. It affirms the cycle of transformation and the understanding of our shared consciousness with the Creator. Speaking the names of the dead as we pass them in the cemetery offers a powerful prayer on behalf of the departed. After the tragedy of 9/11, the priestesses of the Temple of Isis in Los Angeles, an affiliate of the international Fellowship of Isis, gathered together through a call sent out by the late arch-high priestess Laura Janesdaughter. Using text from my book *Awakening Osiris,* we dedicated ourselves to pray for and invoke by name the soul of every individual who died in the incidents of that day. The Fellowship of Isis retains in its archives a copy of that ritual for those wishing to perform similar memorial rites.[45]

Perhaps a connection exists between the Egyptian hieroglyph ren and the oracular rune stones of the Vikings. The rune was a sacred image, like the hieroglyph, which telegraphed a whole constellation of meanings. There may indeed be something to the twelfth-century legend that an Egyptian princess named Scota was sent into hiding, thus becoming the namesake of her adoptive country. It is for this Egyptian princess that Scotland was named.[46] According to cultural anthropologist Ralph Blum, the word *rune* meant "a secret thing, a mystery."[47] Like the sacred hiero-glyphs, runes were used in Celtic rituals of healing, protection, enliven-ing, fertilizing, and carrying the dead into the next realm.

In certain written traditions, including the Hebrew language, the vowels of a name are considered the sacred soul of a name, the breath of the name. That is why ancient Egyptians did not write with vowels. Those breathy sighs were kept sacred, to be heard only between mother and child, or creator and creature.

Numerologists also identify the vowel numbers in combination as the soul urge, or authentic self. Each name you were called in your lifetime—your childhood names, pet names, married names, nick-names, endearments, roll calls, and so on—resonates to a different named energy. The numerology of your name becomes a kind of des-tiny. For example, I was not given a middle name by my parents. None appears on my birth certificate, yet when I was carried home from the hospital, my older brother, upon seeing me, exclaimed that he had a sister named Normandi _____. Like a fairy godbrother, in this case, he gave me a middle name to reveal my hidden potential that very few people know. The energy of that little-known name is hard to live up to, but it carries with it a vibration of great success after many trials. Most people would prefer the success without the trials, frankly. Taking on a new name changes your resonance, which changes your identity. Your street names, the name of your pets, your business name, even the pet name you call your car offers a different energy for your life.

Ren always reminds us to find our resonance, to speak our truth. The "Opening the Mouth" ceremony was an important rite of transformation that allowed the soul to affirm, pray, invoke, and thank— *especially* thank. In the Sanskrit, chanted mantras meant breathing with the *om* sacred vowels. In the Hebrew alphabet, those unwritten vowels became flames of light illuminating each word. In a meditative state, as you pray slowly, begin to see every word as a flame igniting a fire, or as incense curling from your lips. "Say my name that I may live," says the Coffin Text.[48]

1. Study numerology to unlock the power of your personality, your soul, and your path in this life. Find your personal power. You solidify your relationships when you invoke others by name. Greet those you have just met by name. Learning the names of group members shows a conscious and caring leadership that few possess.

2. Review your soul's progress through life. What was your name as a child? How often has your name changed, and when it changed did your life change? Did it pull you into resonance with another? What is your tribe's resonance? Your family's? How did you resonate with their soul ancestral story? Study your name and the name of a loved one to find how your souls intertwine.

3. Write something you can craft your resonance into—a prayer book, a family history, a short story, or poetry. Let each word become a meditation. Write from the heart to inspire others.

4. Language matters. Look up the meaning of any document or contract before you sign it. Find the word origin and meaning of the name of your street, your city, or even your name. If you are working on a large project, pay attention to the details of a plan of action. If you do not resonate with one of the tasks on your to-do list, rename the task until you resonate with it.

5. Take a look at the business of your life. Where did you agree to go? What did you agree to do? Check your schedule and contracts. If you are looking for a new situation, put yourself out there. Promote and Advertise yourself. Tell people what you do or want to be doing. Weigh the words you will use so that you may see how they sound in another person's ear.

6. Tell someone you love them. Say "I love you" often and act accordingly. Love yourself. Use affirming language to speak powerful sentences that connect your emotions to the heart of God.

7. Be filled with gratitude. Keep a gratitude journal. Write the names of people for whom you are grateful in your life. Other people are grateful for you. Did you know that? Feel their gratitude.

8. God is in the details. Notice the details. Soon you will hear words of praise for work well done. Singing a song like Woody Guthrie's "This Land Is Your Land" can become a powerful anthem for traveling through life, driving your car, or enacting your political inclusivity.

9. There is a time for silence. Is silence or speech appropriate now? Holding your tongue may keep you from wasting energy. Just doing the work can accomplish more than talking about it. Truth is always better than a half-truth, but measure your words and speak from the heart. Take a vow of conscious speech, purity of heart, and compassionate action.

SAHU

The high spiritualized form of the enlightened individual body appears in many cultures. Ancient Egyptians called it sahu. Mystical Tibetans call it the *Dharmakaya,* or truth body. Gnostic Christians call it the resurrection body. In Sufism, the Most Sacred Body is *wujud al-aqdas* and the Supra-Celestial Body is known as *asli haqiqi.* Taoists refer to it as the diamond body. Those immortals who have attained the enlightened form that may appear in earthly form or in heavenly form are called Sky Walkers (the *djedi*).[49] The word *sahu* also means "to travel," so another way to think of it is as the vessel that contains the soul that accompanies us on our endless voyage through the various states of birth, death, transformation, and rebirth.

The hieroglyphs that create the word *sahu* are composed of the sibilant *s,* represented by a folded cloth; a breathy, etheric *hu* sound; and a body form that is an outline showing itself to be a container for light. Sahu also indicated a garment of white linen worn by people of high wisdom or authority. In the spirit world, master teachers wear their energetic light codes, often appearing wrapped in a soft white aura tinged with blue when they draw close to us. This light technology helps to create a vehicle that can move at the speed of light—and via light—from anywhere in the universe. The "shining ones" of ancient times used these light bodies.

Some theosophical traditions posit that familiar constellations create patterns of light consciousness that imprint light codes on us. These include the clustered stars we know as the Pleiades, Orion, the Great Bear, and the Sirius complex. Master teachers can enter into human forms often using the DNA code known to them when they had physical incarnations. The sahu bodies of Jesus Christ, Mother Mary, Saint Germain, and others are notable examples of masters whose reappearance and sightings around the globe might be attributable to their using remnants of their DNA code to enable reappearances thousands of years after their physical bodies died.

Other sahu bodies project a humanlike form although they may have originated elsewhere. The masters use human vessels and intelligent lifeforms from elsewhere in the galaxy—as can any light being manifesting with intention from a distant, nonlocal earth plane. According to the theosophist Alice A. Bailey, the overseer of this sacred energy, known as Sanat Kumara or the Ancient of Days, has 144,000 light bearers working with him for planetary unfoldment.[50] A sahu is not a ghost. It is a traveler from the spirit world. When traveling in other dimensions, you can use your sahu as a vessel to move you not only through space but through time. Space and time are really the same thing. All beings come into form from timeless space and will return to timeless space. Actually one can travel backward or forward in time. We do it all the time—usually in dreams or visionary states, but sometimes in the physical as well. Déjà vu experiences and precognitive dreams are examples of that.

We have a sahu while we live, just as we have a soul, a spirit, a name, and a will. The reason we work on ascension processes while we are alive is to activate the use of the sahu and to equip it for the afterlife. The sahu contributes to our physical vitality while we are incarnate in a human body. It is one point of light on an interconnected web of light, like a pin on a map that grounds us in the local environment we inhabit in this incarnation. It provides the coordinates for a spirit to become reborn or even reconstituted into denser or subtler matter. It is the light that we send out in our vital, loving energy to others as we live, work, and cooperate with humankind in the task of bringing forth enlightenment on this planet. We use our sahu to protect and safeguard ourselves, our progeny, and those things about which we care deeply.

The ancient Egyptian tale of Khaemwast describes the high priest, magician, and son of Ramses II using teleportation to enact spiritual battle with a Nubian sorcerer trying to kill the pharaoh.[51] The Spiritualist prophet Andrew Jackson Davis describes how he flew through the air from Poughkeepsie to the Catskill Mountains forty miles away while in trance on March 6, 1844.[52] The Christian and Hebrew scriptures describe occasions in which Spirit teleported certain individuals. Elijah is saved from certain death through spirit teleportation in 1 Kings 18:10–12. In John 6:16–25, Jesus, walking on water, climbed into a boat with his apostles on the Sea of Capernaum and returned to shore with them, to the astonishment of the crowd. In Acts 8:38–40 the apostle Philip baptizes a man in Ethiopia and immediately teleports thirty miles away.

Above us, Sah was the starry light body of the ascended god Osiris appearing as Orion. Literally envisioned as a Sky Walker, the djed backbone of Osiris is seen as a pillar of light. The constellation moves through the night sky above the Giza Plateau, aligning perfectly with the three pyramids as the sash of Osiris, or the belt of Orion. It also dips below the horizon for seventy-two days before rising again in the east just prior to the helical rising of Sirius (Isis as Sothis). It appears that Sirius pushes the constellation back into the sky. When it stands erect above the pyramids again in midwinter, it is called the Risen One. Says the Utterance 466 of the Pyramid Text: "O King, you are this great star, the companion of Orion, who traverses the sky with Orion."[53]

The seventy-two days in which Orion is not seen in the night sky equal the days in which the spirit enters the underworld during the mummification process. Spiritualists believe that after transition a physical body should remain at rest untouched for seventy-two hours while the soul continues to upload its records to take with him. An individual consciousness needs at least seventy-two days to gain the knowledge necessary to maneuver through the spirit world. The immortal and incorruptible sahu functions as a messenger and guide to and from the hidden world to Earth.

1. Ascended masters approach, bringing light. Continue to be a light bearer for the planet, working to uplift those around you. Your community needs your leadership to unfold fully.

2. This energy is "out of this world." Prepare to meet one who enters your awareness, building consciousness of interstellar beings through meditation, dreams, or a physical contact. The encounter expands your understanding of your part in the unfolding of the universal mind.

3. Ancestral energy assumes a sahu form. One of the ancients or an ancestor

brings you information about your path. Creativity soars as your minds attune.

4. A particular spirit guide with whom you now work once lived an earth life in which he built up an abundance of spiritual wisdom and energy. He or she returns to work with you. Expect to see him or her appearing in a sahu form in meditation.

5. Build your light body now so that it can deepen its work on Earth. The consciousness you raise, the wisdom you gain, and the work you do here works for you in the future when you pass to the other side.

6. An angel, a healing presence, or a particular historical person in Spirit draws near to bring guidance, healing, gratitude, and comfort. Your accelerated vibration attunes you to their energy. Making the sahu connection part of your spiritual practice amplifies your progress.

7. In meditation you see Seven Ray masters who show you their faces, or who appear as flames before the throne of God. One at a time, study the energy signatures of these *cohan*: El Morya, Lord Lanto, Paul the Venetian, Serapis Bey, Hilarion, Lady Nada, and Saint Germain. One light may become brighter than the others. Determine who wants to work with you.

8. Master teachers appear in many spiritual traditions. Often a lost or ancient culture appeals to you because you experienced lifetimes there. A hidden wisdom tradition aids your unfoldment in this incarnation. You attune and enter this time of instruction. Take notes.

9. Nine great gods and goddesses draw near. Perform an Ennead Reading to see which divinities ride in the boat with you. Find images of these gods and goddesses. Create a meditation altar for them, installing a light in front of each image.

SEBA

Seba is the gateway to consciousness and higher realms of consciousness. If you work in deep meditation to access gods, goddesses, and
beings in higher realms, it helps to visualize a seba star gate, or portal
in consciousness that creates a passage from one dimension to another.
Whenever we travel to sacred sites we walk in and out of worlds. The
gods and goddesses who appeared on Earth in the physical forms of
their natures also had a stellar form, or akh. Ancient sailors used the
stars in the night sky as their coordinates in the vast Mediterranean
Sea. The texts and stars on the temple ceilings help us to negotiate the
waterways of the neterworld as we find our way to the Imperishable
Ones, those seba in the northern sky that whirl about the circumpolar
stars. The seba of the thirty-eight wandering deities, or constellations
that circle the equinox, appear as a calendar in the hypostyle hall of
the Hathor temple in Dendera. The qualities of beings associated with
these star portals are diverse.

All ancient temples with their complex doorways and halls were
aligned to the seasonal energy of the sun or to particular celestial lights,

such as the star Sirius. Ancient architects marked spring equinox by making sure that the Sphinx aligned directly with the rising sun. At winter solstice the arisen sun shines directly through the sequentially open portals at Karnak. The photograph of the hieroglyph reveals this open space with starlight shining through. When the sun precisely crested the horizon, the doors of the sacred shrine were opened so that the light struck the golden image of Amen Ra, indicating his return to full illuminated glory. Stars energies also streamed through temple doorways aligned to fixed star constellations like the Pleiades, the stars Deneb and Sirius, or those in Orion's Belt.

Certainly, an arit through which the soul passes in the underworld (duat) is a star portal; the underworld being duat and a star called dua. The seba can be used as a meditation or trance tool so that we may find entry into the neterworld, or the god world, or the inner world. Let's think of seba as "a room with a view." In the duat one had to know the names of the guardians of these gateways in order to open the doors to deeper levels of the subconscious and pass through.

The mouth is a portal, too. So it makes sense that Egyptians used the word *seba* to mean "to teach." Being able to say the right words, to ask the right questions, and to enunciate invocations to create alternate realities coincided with using seba as a doorway. The priestly rituals in the mortuaries and temples invoked the deities, allowed the priests to speak with them face to face, or assisted souls in transition. Papyrus scrolls and books were considered doorways as well. The many spells in the Egyptian Book of the Dead were the magical keys that opened gateways, books that needed to be read and internalized during life so that the knowledge therein could be easily spoken and its wisdom would assist one in the next life.

Seba shows the deep symbolic connections between image and speech, Heaven and Earth, and the portals between the living and the dead, and inner and outer spaces. Before the portals of interstellar connections, our psyches stand agog. In the 1994 movie *Stargate,* James Spader portrays Dr. Daniel Jackson, an Egyptologist who finds a stargate inside an Egyptian tomb and dials in an intergalactic connection. In *The Matrix*

Keanu Reeves's character enters portal after portal to find himself living and fighting bad guys in alternate realities. These ideas intrigue us because on some level we understand there is more to the universe than our earth reality. The unseen persistently knocks. Consciousness is a doorway to understanding how we not only move through space and time but create realities in space and time. The star portal may be the way in which we entered the hologram of our current life.

For this reason, indigenous shamanic cultures induced trance states via drumming, ingesting mushrooms, or drinking ayahuasca. Egyptian shamans had their own brews. Modern man has become fascinated with virtual reality games of avatars. A recent phenomenon in Japan involves individuals living their avatar lives while lying in "coffin hotels," their faces masked in AI (artificial intelligence) goggles. I understand the need to access interdimensional doorways, but that idea disturbs me, frankly. It can result in a type of altered state addiction that negates the spirituality of the world we currently occupy. And the neteru are here now inside the natural world. It isn't always necessary to access them artificially. Nevertheless, these avatar gamers are engaged in a life just as real to them as to those of us who dream we are awakened—or those "dead" who have simply slipped through a doorway into another room.

It takes time to adjust once we enter a new place. A variety of things carrying different vibrations, different auras and colors, and different energies confront our senses. It takes time to sort it all out. Being born is like that. The womb is a portal where the soul shifts dimensions from fluid to form. Death is another portal. For many it takes most of a lifetime to remember why they came. Do your soul work while you are here, and when you leave, don't forget to collect what experiences you came for and take it with you.

Star gates are not limited to space; they are movements through consciousness. If there is no past or future—only the eternal present in the flow of Spirit—then there is no "over there"; there is only here. Once we move our consciousness into the infinite, we transcend time and space. In deep meditation, your physical self grows heavy as your spirit lifts in order to pass through a portal to an altered consciousness. Come back and when you open your eyes . . . Wow! Is that where I am now? It's a shock when eternal consciousness returns to a temporal body.

Other beings, life-forms, or spirits use such portals to enter and exit our space. Spirits come into the séance room via their light bodies, moving through a particular astral door that is guarded by the medium's guides and protectors. In his book *The Inner Guide to Ancient Egypt*, written with Billie Walker John, author Alan Richardson suggests visualizing on a blank wall in your meditation room an image of the false door with its two eyes on its panels. Gazing into those hieroglyphic eyes "with your inward eye" creates an opening and assists one in seeing through solid matter into the next world.[54]

Any blank wall can become a portal if you place upon this blank screen drawn symbols attuned to your frequency. Writing your name, attributes, and any identifying imagery specific to you, for example, "*hem netjer* of Isis, daughter of _____ and _____," will create a seba gateway for you alone. If you wish to write an invocation specific to your portal and your energy, you may use the images of the hieroglyphs found in this book. The more you work with these hieroglyphs the more rapid and tactile their meanings become for you.

Your front door has a lock and key because you don't want just anybody coming through the door or the bedroom window. Learn how to close portals as well as open them. Seal them with an invocation, holy water, salt, smudge, or incense. Any tool works with intention. Use your spirit consciousness to affirm that this place is off limits to anyone but you alone. When you open a seba or circle, always be sure to close it down when you finish.

You can create a portal by drawing the seba hieroglyph on a wall with your finger as the entryway. Easily, the duat, a star within a circle symbol, can be imagined as the aperture of a camera lens, a way of focusing light energy coming in and out of space. Meditation on the seba hieroglyph alone can have the same effect, drawing us upward and out into the starry dimensions where other entities and ascended masters reside. Always travel in your light body with a particular purpose in mind. You are not going on vacation. You may want to meet and converse with a deity, collect a soul fragment for healing, or gain information about how to maneuver through upcoming personal or world events.

Once there, don't linger too long. Remember the way home. Close the door behind you when you leave either realm. Always move through these portals with a guide. You might use the jackal god Anubis, the Archangel Michael, or any other guardian of entrances and exits. When we travel on Earth, we must have travel documents, passports, visas, travel bags, and itineraries as well as companions and guides to new lands. When we travel in other dimensions the same is required. Do you have permission to go where you are going? Do you have a guide? What is the purpose of your visit? What are your itinerary stops, departure, and return times? Arrange your spirit transits so that you take with you both intention and protection.

1. The door to the future or past opens when you knock. This is an opportune time to begin anew. You find yourself working with altered states in your meditations. Rather than aimlessly surf the energy, stay focused on your intention. Go with gusto to find a key to unlock a mystery.
2. The mental plane joins the physical and spiritual planes, but you can't stay in one place to the exclusion of the other. Walk in two worlds simultaneously. Ancestors, spirit guides, nature beings, and star beings wish to speak with you. While much wisdom can be gained this way, always affirm your mutual purposes before you let them in or leave with them.
3. Many times portals open and words flow forth. Spirit taps your shoulder to asks you to use this channel for automatic or inspired writing, séance communication, or inspirational speaking. *Always* be sure you are in control of the portal. Choose a time and place of exit and return.
4. It's spring cleaning for the psyche. If you don't like where you are, change your thoughts, or rearrange the room where you spend the most time. Seal the entrances, exits, windows, and other portals, such as the television, mirrors, chimneys, and microwave ovens. If you do readings in your home, it's good to clear the area of unwanted energies or spirit people several times a year.
5. An open door brings new creative expression. See all humankind through

the eyes of soul. Open one door and many other doors open. Expect a new person to enter your life—perhaps even a child whom you will help to remember his or her soul purpose.

6. The family of humankind gathers to move the collective forward with harmoniously aligned states of consciousness. Not everyone understands that their thoughts generate a global consciousness. See an opportunity—or create one—to help others move their thinking up a notch. Ascended masters may wish to assist your group with planetary healing.

7. Ask and it shall be opened. A change approaches; your prayer is answered. The answer may arrive as a shift of consciousness, or as ascended masters, archangels, Pleiadeans, or others who step through the stargate to offer their help. Think through what can or needs to be accomplished.

8. Wise men follow stars. Studying the fixed stars or astrological alignments holds the key to opening a portal for you. The places you can go with astrological knowledge are endless.

9. Open the door to your spiritual classroom. When the teacher is ready, the students appear. Many want to learn from you. Accept this responsibility. Step through a doorway you were never sure you would pass through. It's time.

SEKHEM

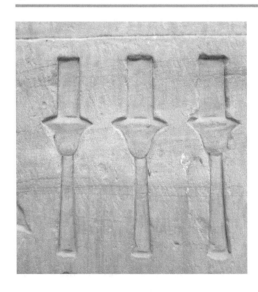

In the most well-known story about the goddess Sekhmet, the sun god Ra sends his eye, his daughter Sekhmet, down to Earth to teach the mortals a lesson. Because they have forgotten to honor him, he orders Sekhmet to devour them. Her name means "The Powerful One" and is written with the sekhem mace and feminized. This powerful sekhem mace operates for the pharaoh in much the same way as the goddess Sekhmet operates for Ra—as an emblem of his authority. When Sekhmet does as Ra commands and descends to Earth to teach the human hooligans a lesson, she leaves a trail of blood, which she finds exhilarating. So taken is she by the taste of blood that she nearly devours the world. She devours half of Egypt before Thoth can stop her. The mace, which symbolizes the divine power of Ra in pharaoh's hands, must also be wielded judiciously and carefully. Remember, however, the mace can have dangerous consequences if the pharaoh's authority is undermined.

Sekhem was one of the nine spiritual bodies. Every deity and every individual possessed a sekhem body, which was an active power. Linked to the desire nature, it represents will—specifically the willfulness and willingness to become active in order to attain a heart's desire. This hieroglyph of the pharaoh's mace head symbolized his sekhem; that is, his authority in the physical world, his ability to resist chaos, and the union of a divine will and his human will. Pharaoh and Horus were one and the same. Sekhem energy traveling between gods and mortals can be felt as a kind of force field. Similar to a kundalini energy, it can be recognized by the electrical shock one receives when in proximity to the sekhem energy of the Divine, or even another person. Thus sekhem is often equated with magic-making. Knowing the difference between willfulness and willingness is the key to understanding how to use this dynamic energy. Qabalist Jason Lotterhand describes it thus: "(T)here is only One Will. This One Will corresponds to the power of consciousness in the universe. Consciousness wills things and makes them happen. . . . As a microcosm, human beings have the same faculty, the ability to will and to create things that correspond to their will. This is why discipline is absolutely necessary for the individual."[55]

Many lion entities guarded, protected, and nurtured ancient Egypt. All of them manifested the solar energy of the Divine. The fire of the sun is dual-edged; it can burn and it can heal. While Ra is the masculine sun, Sekhmet is the feminine sun; yet she is equally powerful. Statues of the lion-headed goddess were erected at the borders of the country as a warning and deterrent to any invaders. The statues were magically charged to take care of anyone who would harm the country, in just the same way that a mother lion fiercely protects her cubs.

Often the sekhem instrument is drawn with two wide eyes, indicating that a divine spiritual willpower is being enacted. Some see Sekhmet as fierce compassion;[56] others see her as a goddess of war and pestilence. Of course, will is a tool, as the emblem clearly shows, and one's will may be used for good or for ill. The outcome depends on how it is wielded as one learns self-control and develops willpower. True willingness to be a vessel for spiritual work means to forget the mind candy and what the body craves for the moment. Focus your mental energy and will on a single purpose. Be willing to let Spirit use you as the instrument and then you will rise to the task at hand.

In thinking more about enhanced strength and the use of will, a quote attributed to Mahatma Gandhi came to mind. He identified the seven social sins as these: wealth without work, pleasure without conscience, knowledge without character, commerce without morality, science without humanity, worship without sacrifice, and politics without principles.[57] Sekhem is doing more than using an electrical current of energy to conduct work in healing or magic. He is employing discernment as well. More than a list of social sins, these concepts help us to think about how best to craft our own personal metaphysical ethics.

The phrase *will do* means that if you can control your thought and will, deity will help you do anything. Spirit controls the medium and the medium mentally controls his or her own mind. Study the Chariot card in the tarot to understand sekhem and the power of mind and will.

---

1. Yes, sometimes it really feels like being on a mission from God. You are appointed to an important role in your community. Use your power

In Abydos, Pharaoh Seti I demonstrates that he understands how to use the living sekhem by uniting the divine will—depicted by the god Horus on his standard—and his earthly human will—depicted by representations of himself upholding both the sekhem and the standard on which the god appears. The two images of Seti I kneel upon the plinth of ma'at that represents cosmic order and truth.

wisely, always aligning your will through prayerful consideration.

2. Andrew Jackson Davis, the founder of modern-day spiritualism, advised, "Under all circumstances, keep an even mind."[58] On the physical plane, balance your energies between action and rest. A wise leader knows not to push. Gain control of your inner and outer nature. Work in accordance with natural law.

3. Deep spiritual healing moves through the physical body but originates in the mind. Imhotep considered himself a child of Sekhmet and Ptah. He was honored for his life's achievements as a genius of architecture, science, healing, and magic. Let your creative output be of the highest intention and enacted with passion.

4. Some things are worth striving for. You control the output of energy you need. Certain mental and spiritual techniques can rev up the engine so that you can break through any blocked energies, or your own barricade of restlessness and procrastination.

5. Ideas without action plans vanish like wisps of smoke. During ritual offerings, the *hem netjer* priest waved a sekhem paddle above the offering to stoke the fire beneath the incense. Symbolically, he fans the fires by applying his will and energy to enact divine plans.

6. Heal yourself by releasing any stagnant energies, ideas, and commitments. Wield your will like a machete to clear out the old, tangled jungle of your life and cut a new path. Resurrect yourself from your worn-out heap of desires and things that compete for your attention.

7. Let your life passions pull you toward Spirit. Allow Spirit to move through you and about you while you listen and wait on the will of God. Get to know the Seven Ray energies and the ascended masters associated with them. Protect your cubs.

8. Rest to avoid burnout and combat destructive tendencies. Practice fierce compassion. Heaven and Earth are the two eyes through which the gods see. These eyes of the jackal Anubis see in the dark as well as the light. Discernment must precede action.

9. Every now and then ripping, tearing up, and shredding will get rid of physical, emotional, and mental clutter in a quick manner. Bless and release what no longer serves you.

SE-SHEN (LOTUS)

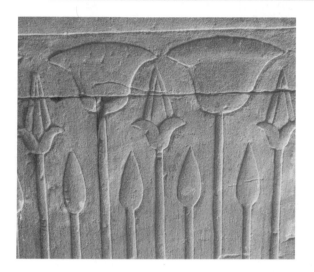

From the depths of the celestial waters of nu at the dawn of Creation, the blue lotus arose. The lotus and papyrus together evoked the joy, the fertility, the perfection, and the pleasure of life along the Nile. In the hypostyle halls of Karnak, tall columns of closed and open flowers symbolized the beauty of walking through the gods' world at the dawn of Creation. In the temples of Memphis, Nefertum, child of Sekhmet and Ptah, wore a blue lotus as a crown. His name meant "the beautiful completion."

Courtesans are often depicted sniffing the pleasing aroma of the lotus or wearing the flowers in their hair. The blue lotus, or *Nymphaea caerulea,* also contains the psychoactive alkaloid apomorphine. Recent studies suggest using blue lotus for treating such diverse things as social anxiety, erectile dysfunction, alcoholism, and Alzheimer's disease. In Greek mythology, the narcotic lotuses eaten by the crew of Odysseus created a dreamy, soporific effect.

It took many thousands of blossoms to create the subtle fragrance of the lotus. Distilled and stored in precious flasks, blue lotus oil became a prized commodity in magical life. The sacred flower was said to elevate the consciousness and attune it to the highest spiritual mind, aiding one in attaining a vision of one's role in the infinite scheme of things through deep meditation. It was used as an aphrodisiac, creating a sense of gentleness, relaxation, and peace.

Author Murry Hope linked the Egyptian blue lotus to the Hindu myths of the flower that grew from the navel of Vishnu. It represented the mandala-like quality of the universal energy unfolding in all four elements and encompassing all kingdoms. Within its many petals resides the all-pervading wisdom that connects all things in mind, body, spirit, and the ethers.[59] In meditation practices the lotus links to the seventh, or crown, chakra that opens the mind for contact with higher mind. Deep and intentional meditative practices can continue to unfold the lotus blossoms for greater understanding. In *A Treatise on Cosmic Fire* Alice A. Bailey elucidates the shakti or kundalini that H. P. Blavatsky refers to as the *fohatic* power. The merger of the fires of the body and the fires of the mind, she says, result in the unfold-ment of the egoic lotus and the twelve petals of wisdom, love, and sacrifice.[60]

Long regarded as a symbol of the sun, the flowers close at night when the sun god Ra retreats and rise to open in the morning light. Growing with its roots deep in the muck of the riverbed, the lotus is a flower of transformation, of turning a negative into a positive, or of rising up from the muck of one's life. Sadly, since the damming of the Nile, blue lotuses no longer grow in Egypt. An ancient proph-ecy said that Egypt would enter a death when the lotus no longer grew; however, when the blue lotus returned to the Nile, so would the ancient knowledge and power return to the land of its origin. At the current time, blue lotuses grow primarily behind the Nile dams in southern Egypt. Several horticulturalists in Egypt have created pools where blue lotus are grown, cultivated, and pressed into precious lotus oil.

1. Life is good. Enjoy the moment. New things begin to arise, bud, and grow. You will see them flower and manifest as you desire. All is in divine order.

2. Enjoy this peaceful time with loved ones. Make music or have a sweet romantic retreat. Hold hands with those you love. Sniff the head of a new-born. Celebrate togetherness.

3. Creativity blossoms! Amid celebrations and gatherings, life appears in full flower. Your joyful exuberance draws the right people to you. Conversations create new ideas and opportunities for all participants to flourish.

4. You work hard and have been on overdrive. Treat yourself to a pedicure, a massage, or a mini-vacation. If you find yourself near a hot spring pool, immerse yourself in it. Slough off fatigue and worry as you rise up rejuvenated and open to life like a lotus flower.

5. Change approaches. Transformation is essential to your situation. A better and more reliable structure is in the offing. When other things disappear, this change sticks around.

6. Beauty, harmony, and love abound. A wonderful partnership, a fresh start, or an addition to the family is near. You have sacrificed for others and their needs, so enjoy this sense of renewal. Investigate aromatherapy or visit a spa to discover some beautiful new healing treatments.

7. Deep insight, intuition, and revelations seem to open themselves in your dreams. Your creative ideas surprise you. Visions of new possibilities pop into your quiet meditations. Write them down! This is the perfect time to take spiritual advice and ground it in practical application. That is the source of magic.

8. Your hard work paid off. When obstacles arose, you overcame them and stayed true to your vision. Enjoy your success and share the wealth. Know that the lotus consciousness you cultivate blooms both in Heaven and on Earth.

9. You long for world peace and envision a way to create it. You will do your part to make that happen. Perhaps you are a philanthropist, a humanitarian, or an ecologist at heart. Out of this need to end ignorance and suffering, a new vision of unity occurs.

SE-SHESHET

Musician priestesses of Isis, Hathor, and Bast rattled their sistra in festivals to the Goddess. The sound of a sistrum shaking was a joyful noise of jubilation, healing, and shaking things up. Similar to the clapping and tambourine music that accompanies a gospel service, the rhythmic sounds of the sistrum and bone clappers raised the vibration in the temple. Shaking a sistrum, called iri sekhem, literally meant "to do the power."[61] The sound awakened the slumbering deities and drove out negative energy. Thus sistra make dandy instruments for clearing houses, along with holy water and other practices.

Made either in the shape of an ankh or the sekhem, the sistrum enclosed, in a loop, three or four metal bars with either seeds or disks across the bars. When shaken, it created a rattling effect like the sound of wind blowing in the reeds, an onomatopoeia of the sound that the sistra and blowing reeds actually make—s-sh-sht.

More than a simple musical instrument, the sistrum also contained magical properties. The handle often depicted on both sides the full face of the goddess Hathor, including her little cow ears that emphasized the properties of hearing. Because Hathor was the beloved of many of the male deities in Egypt, a sistrum with seed rattles and Hathor's face was used in fertility rites. Hathor's child, Ihy, whose name means jubilation, became the sistrum player extraordinaire. At other times the sistrum was surmounted by the cat head of Bast. Bast statues often depict her surrounded by kittens and holding the sistrum. The baby rattle was an ancient Egyptian phenomenon as well.

Isis rattles the sistrum that depicts the goddess Hathor.
Hathor's cow ears emphasize the action of clairaudience,
or sacred hearing, of conversations with the Divine.

As a magical instrument, the sistrum's jangling vibrations averted the energies of chaos and disaster. These calamities might include the approach of snakes—which the sistrum scared away—or attacks by wild animals. Or it might be a disaster such as a windstorm or sandstorm and all manner of negative manifestations of the god Set. Who can be angry when the goddess Hathor is shaking her sistrum and her hips in a joyous dance? The rhythms of the cosmos are implied by the sistrum. The four bars of the sistrum, said Greek historian Plutarch, represented the four elements of fire, air, earth, and water.[62] This instrument makes it clear that things need to be shaken up, rattled about, and set into motion to prevent stagnation and death. In other words, change and vibration are part of the same natural law.

1. A change in leadership can counter stagnation. You may need to step forward to be the one who shakes things up. You are progressive, courageous, and a little rebellious. Curb the rebel within but stand up for what is right. Today, begin something new.

2. End separatist ideas. Find joy in family and partnership. Sensual, musical, and intuitive, your feminine nature exudes confidence. You are pliable but not breakable. You know how to keep your own counsel. *Shh-shh* is the sound of the sistrum.

3. A creative idea evokes a shift in the way you currently operate. Be playful and discover a unique truth. Be joyous. Paint, dance, or make music. It is possible that the coming birth of a child will bring great joy.

4. All work and no play make Jack a dull boy and Jill a dull girl. So make some fun—not just have it—*make* it. Invite a few close friends over. Caretaking children can actually be relaxing if you engage with their creative impulses. Put away your paperwork and allow joy to find you.

5. It's time for a vacation or an adventure. Travel to a place you've always wanted to visit. Right now, you are at your social best. Join a new group of friends in dancing or camping. Try your hand at creative writing, or dream up other new ways of getting your inner joy out.

6. A new relationship may be in the offing, or an old relationship may experience a shift. Not an end-of-the-world scenario, it offers a change for the

better. Dance improves your physical health. Sensory feasts, sensuality, and love improve your emotional health. The family unit expands.

7. Do something different—change your look, retire old ideas, or rearrange your office. Refresh your altar. Now would be a good time. As you make changes, new spiritual energies enter.

8. You've already planted the seeds of creative transformation. Slow but steady growth in a home or business begins. Plans are in motion and you will soon see results. You grow materially and spiritually by leaps and bounds through gratitude and reciprocity.

9. Eliminate clutter, cut the deadwood. Revitalization begins with getting rid of what no longer serves you. You can make a change in the world or have a restorative impact on your environment by helping others to see alternatives. Be the change you wish to see.

SESHET

Ah, the lady herself appears. Seshet, the Female Scribe, Mistress of the Libraries, and companion of Thoth, kept the Akashic Record. She marked the years, the days, and the soul story of each individual on the leaves of a laurel tree. This Tree of Life lived eternally throughout each incarnation. As the divine recorder of events she appeared as early as the Second Dynasty (2890 BCE) when she and Pharaoh Khasekhemawy established a temple that unified Upper and Lower Egypt.

Sometimes called the Lady of Lists, Seshet maintained the per ankh, or temple library, of every deity; kept record of its festivals; safeguarded all the liturgy, hymns, songs, rituals, and magical healing recipes; accounted for every offering; and recorded all of the divine myths as well. When a new temple was laid, she consulted the stars, the oracles, and the previous plans. She and the pharaoh initiated the first measurement of its foundation. Securing the stakes, they lay the groundwork for the entire temple, aligning each sanctuary to the star whose light embodied the divine being to whom the temple was dedicated. The Egyptians were known to align their temples to particular rising stars that were dedicated to the divinity worshipped there. Because even fixed stars wander through the sky over the course of centuries, however, the Egyptians would build a new temple next to the old one. The new temple would intentionally be a few degrees out of alignment with the old one in order to keep the holy of holies sanctuary—where the divine image resided—aligned with its determined star.[63]

High priestess of the Egyptian mysteries, the knower of secrets, omens, and oracles, Seshet preserved the hidden wisdom. In fact, any mystery was called a seshet and its hieroglyph was the rolled-up papyrus scroll tied with red string (as seen in Heka on page 103). These sacred texts were stored inside a niche carved into the wall of the temple; the niche was also called a seshet. The goddess wore the leopard skin of the high priestess. This indicated that she, too, knew the mysteries of initiation that the pharaoh and high priest had learned, having passed through the gates of death and returned.

Side by side with her dear companion Thoth and considered his consort, Seshet carries Thoth's record book. Sometimes she holds the notched palm frond, making her measurements or tallying accounts. She plays a major role in nearly every temple, but for some reason she is often overlooked. Like Ma'at, she is mistaken for a mere principle rather than a powerful deity. Seshet remains hidden to all but the wisest. Alongside Thoth, this goddess of magical practice, astrology, and numerology invented the hieroglyphs. An ancient woman wearing the leopard-skin robe was a high priestess initiated in Seshet's mysteries.

In Kom Ombo, Seshet and Horus are seen working together to establish the boundaries of the temple. She wears the leopard-skin robe indicating that she is a keeper of the mysteries and Akashic Records. The leopard spots resemble stars.

On her head she wears a diadem that appears to be Hathor's cow-horn crown turned upside-down. It expresses the energy of the Taurus constellation that also contains the Pleiades. The seven stars appear as a flower with seven petals inside the horns of Seshet's crown. The Pleiades stars were known as the Seven Hathors who appear as dancing goddesses tapping frame drums and singing in the Temple of Isis at Philae. More importantly, they stand as the seven columns outside the Mammisi on that same island, guarding the shrine that contains the story of Isis birthing Horus. Like fairy godmothers bequeathing the child its fortune, the Seven Hathors attended the birth of every child.

In the land of dreams and death, these seven goddesses also guard the doors into the seven halls of the underworld, or the realm of the unconscious. It was important to honor them as gateways and to speak their names. The Coffin Texts tell us that Seshet opens the door of heaven for us.[64] It is easy to see, then, that her library contains a collection of mystical and prophetic writings about the beginning and the end of life, both human and cosmic.

1. The magic is just beginning. It's time to begin to write a new chapter in your book of life. What are you aiming for? You are blessed to be able to create it. Work with Seshet to see it manifested and recorded on the leaves of the Tree of Life.

2. Together you and a companion of equal strength embark on a powerful work. You are never alone in your endeavors—your guides and your collaborator's guides are with you to advise you and make sure that the work or the life that you make together is of the highest and best quality.

3. Create something beautiful today, tomorrow, this month. Remember yourself as a star seed planted on this Earth to grow and do some wonderful work for the benefit of yourself, others, and the planet. Love and be joyful.

4. Now you can lay the foundation for a work you have long desired. Organize your inventory, set plans in motion, and envision the process fully—what and how much you need, how, where to attain it, and who will help you. Ask for divine support. You are building an eternal structure.

5. Passing through a symbolic doorway, you enter into a new stage of life. You may be uncertain as to what comes next, but know that you may call

upon the Divine with every step. Although you feel you are going it alone, you are receiving help from beyond.

6. After a time of trial with your health or a relationship, you come out on top. It was part of your karmic agreement to have passed through this period. Now that the crisis is quickly concluding, take time to heal and consider your soul contracts.

7. You were bequeathed seven great wishes in your lifetime by the Seven Hathors who attended your birth. To attain each gift may have involved a difficult passage, but you have succeeded with divine help. Think back on what these agreements may have been. Perhaps you have completed them all and received their wisdom. Perhaps you are only beginning to understand them. Meditate on the highest and best plan for yourself and the planet.

8. As the karmic equalizer, eight symbolizes a force that creates as easily as it destroys. Karma is another word for work. You do reap what you've sown, so always plant seeds of love, harmony, and compassion. The spiritual and material worlds mirror each other. See what comes up for you in the next three weeks and you will know what you need to do next.

9. As you conclude a chapter in your Akashic Record, think of all you've accomplished. Analyze it, reap its benefits, and decide where to go from here. Consider a future harvest and sort the "god" seed from the bad. Distribute rewards to the community or family. Your legacy is love.

SET

The warrior Set used force and will unwisely. The youngest male child of Nut and Geb, Set felt that he played second fiddle to his firstborn brother, Osiris. Impatient for his own birth, Set used a bolt of lightning to pierce a hole in his sky mother and emerge from her side. When he touched the ground, it scorched and turned into desert. Set ruled the red sandy desert, whereas Osiris ruled the fertile black alluvial soil. Set murdered Osiris twice, trying to become the ruler of all of Egypt. He battled Horus for the right to rule after Osiris was dead.

Set has been demonized and seen as equivalent to Satan. The myth portrays his story as a battle between good and evil—a reasonable interpretation. There is the possibility that, like the Genesis story of Cain and Abel, the myth of Set and Osiris pits the genetic family of hunter-gatherers, of which Set was one, against the family of agriculturalists, of which Osiris was one.

Historically the desert, which belonged to Set, was once an ocean bed that later turned into a lush savannah filled with game and green fields. Then, due to climate change, it withered and became desert. Without grasslands to keep the soil in place, the winds whipped the sand into dunes and the seasonal khamsin windstorms blew violently into the farmland and cities, smothering fields and houses alike. A god of sand and windstorms, Set needed to be mastered to prevent the fertile black land from filling with the saline desert sand or clogging the waters of the Nile that needed to flow to the fields.

In the underworld, Set most often appears as a serpent with knives in his back, to indicate that he was being put under control. That begs the question: Were all serpents evil and an aspect of Set? No. Isis and her sisters often appeared in serpent form and were highly protective of that which they held dear. A-Set, or Isis, sometimes shares the same throne hieroglyph with Set; in both instances the seat establishes a foundation. With Aset, the throne hieroglyph indicates being placed upon a throne, whereas with Set the seat indicates sitting a person down and keeping him in his place. In both cases, the seat is a symbol of authority. In addition, the word *set* meant "to sow seeds," or, as tobacco farmers say in Kentucky, "to set tobacco." It had to do with making the tender seedling into something permanent and growing.

A second hieroglyph identifies Set as a strange-looking animal that has baffled Egyptologists. None agree upon the animal that it represents, although most agree that the animal originated in the desert. Sometimes Egyptian symbols used hideous combined creatures to represent whatever power had few redeeming features. The anagram of the goddess of truth, Ma'at, had a hideous form called Ammit, the Eater of Hearts, in the underworld. The Papyrus of Ani shows a composite lion, hippopotamus, and crocodile form—without human attribute. Similarly, the Set animal appears to combine three desert creatures: the aardvark, hyena, and jackal. Perhaps this image depicts the mysterious salawa, a canine creature with forked tail and square ears. The salawa was described as a mix of jackal, wolf, and dog—a creature as big as a donkey that loved the taste of blood and reportedly attacked children and killed livestock. While many still believe it to be only a mythical creature, the locals of Sohag in Upper Egypt found and killed one of its kind in 1996. Other sightings of the salawa came from Armānt near Qena.[65]

Sometimes called Seth by the Greeks, Set's human form appears with the desert animal's head. Possibly our Set, who hunts desert hare, boar, and wild beasts, still possesses certain human qualities that are not simply chaotic and destructive, but that might be considered protective. Edfu marks the site of the predynastic temple complex of Set; it now lies beneath the Temple of Horus there. The current structure symbolizes Horus eventually conquering Set and thus unifying the nations of Upper and Lower Egypt. When his city is under siege, the First Dynasty pharaoh King Scorpion aligned his energies with the warrior energies of Set by depicting him on his mace head. Early on, even into the Fifth Dynasty, the god Set was depicted as a friend of the dead, uniting with Horus to hold the ladder on which the soul ascends to heaven. He protected the life-giving desert oases and was a powerful ally to Ra, preventing him from being hypnotized by the serpent Apophis during his night sea journey.

Astrologically Set's energies run parallel to those of the Roman god Saturn, whose planetary energies represent limitations, boundaries, and the ground itself. The hieroglyph of set may also be written with the sign of a knot, symbolizing that which binds and holds us tight. Some hieroglyphs for set depict arrows piercing an animal's skin. The same hieroglyph indicated the burning desert sands or anything that burns.

In a tarot deck the Devil card and Saturn exhibit similar properties. Set appears in the ancient myth as the brother filled with greed and selfish will, who deceives Osiris, betrays, and murders him, then severs his body into fourteen pieces. No one wants to see his or her life falling apart or to feel limited, bound, or restricted. Sometimes the Devil card denotes a loss such as the passing of a loved one, the end of a relationship, or a deep inner conflict to which one is blind. Limitation, restriction, and decay all are attributes of the planet Saturn.

It is not always bad to be limited or held back. In a way, the universe may be doing us a favor. Exerting control over oneself can be a positive trait, unless you use it in self-harming ways, like anorexia. Limitations can be caused by out-of-control appetites. Set, you see, is about control. Who has the control—you or someone else? And is it the right or wrong time to use that power? According to the myth, Set's major downfall was ego—that is, overreaching for what was not rightfully his to attain. When Set appears he is more likely to raise his head in an unhealthy way if ego infiltrates a situation. Esoterically speaking, personal limitations in our thinking, our compassion, or our will tend to bind and restrict us. Ego results in a loss of face, a loss of relationship, or a loss of spiritual balance. When Set appears, take a hard look at the circumstances in the situation around you.

1. Being a leader means gaining respect through reasonable action, not by forcing outcomes. Step back and look over the plan or situation. If you were not in the picture, how would the events transpire? Rein yourself in until you can see clearly what the best outcome may be. A good leader leads and models how to be a mentor.

2. Darkness works in partnership with the light. At the equinox day and night reign with equal power. Set and Horus may battle, but each holds up his side of the ladder to heaven. In whatever situation you face, equal balance

offers a solution to reach heights further than you can see now. Work with a former adversary and cooperate to find mutual gain.

3. The poet John Keats spoke of the creative power of negative capability. By it he meant holding in mind two opposing facts without leaning more toward resolution on one side or another. Such mental balance draws a taut string between the polarities. You may be called to mediate a dispute. Survey the situation first; consider the desired outcome and the energy of each. Use any limitations to find a middle ground that can create a solution.

4. Slow down. Don't be in a hurry to attain a desire; build a secure foundation first. You don't want it to fall apart or have to go back for do-overs. When life's events seem to fall through, don't be angry or worried. Ask: What am I learning from this teaching moment?

5. Now, *really* slow down. Stop. Look before you leap. I once saw a woman stomp angrily down the middle of the street in an ice storm because her car was encased in ice and she didn't have an ice scraper in her car. Her foot-stomping anger so unbalanced her that she fell and accidentally slid down the entire hill on her rump. Do the necessary work to remove the obstacles in your way.

6. Before rushing into a partnership or relationship, pause. Use this time for self-examination. You know the type of individual you want to draw to yourself. Are you the type of person that individual would want? If not, consider working on yourself as Spirit directs. Spirit is the true partner in any relationship.

7. Whatever setbacks you face, know that Set is teaching patience and compassion. If we act in ways that hurt others by stirring up jealousy, Set will cut us down. Do a number on Set by giving to someone who least expects it. Trust Spirit. Share the wealth.

8. With so much riding on the line, pay attention to details. Don't forget to pause in the midst of crisis, or to give gratitude after success. You can never fall out of God's hand. If you have many things to do, do one thing completely at a time. Multitasking may cause you to lose focus and energy.

9. A time of limitation ends. The missing piece or right answer appears. Take a deep breath. Empty it all the way out. With the next breath, begin again. Past dilemmas all lie behind you.

SHEN

The shen appears as a circle of protection similar to those ritual circles a metaphysician draws before beginning any ceremony. The hieroglyph may include a drawn arm holding a magic wand. One works inside the circle so that standing in the light, one invokes the god force. The symbol of God itself is the circle of being, the life force energy without beginning or end, but ever present. A magnifying glass is a circle that creates a focal point to amplify the solar energy beamed down upon a subject.

The collar of talismanic beads worn by the pharaoh created a circle of protection around him. Not simply decorative, Tutankhamen's shen collar depicted the winged vulture Nekhbet, an image of the Great Mother gripping two shens in her talons. This symbolized her eternal protection and the golden light of eternity.

The pharaoh's head placed inside that protective collar acts much like the central dot inside a circle that denotes the image of the sun god Ra. The implication is that pharaoh is the perfected solar light itself. He is the sun around which the planets, or beads upon the collar, are positioned.

Shen also represents a trajectory that includes the concepts of the alpha and the omega—the beginning and the end, the one and the many.

The shen encompasses the All within itself. It points to a cyclic return to its origin, or to a new beginning. This eternal movement within the shen is likened to a moon making a circuit around the Earth; or the Earth traveling around the sun. It indicates the circuit of stellar energies that rise and fall in the constellations that represent the neteru in the sky. In all of these circumambulations, the principle of eternity appears.

An elongated circle can be stretched into the protective shen called a cartouche. Since the beginning of the First Dynasty, the king's list in Abydos has been filled with cartouches of the pharaohs, thereby elevating the names of these kings forever. Travelers to Egypt often return with gold or silver cartouches that contain their names and the names of family members to offer a charm of protection, in the same way that Tutankhamen's golden necklace protected him.

1. A powerful leader receives divine protection in order to lead his people. People gather themselves around a leader they can trust. The leader protects the ideals and freedoms of the individual and each individual protects the authority of the leader. Such protection hinges first upon a correct alignment with the Divine.
2. You receive a gift from God. A drop of wisdom descends into the pool of the mind. It ripples out across the waters of the psyche, creating concentric circles of energy that reach a far shore. Receive that wisdom in meditation. Disseminate that wisdom in response.
3. Ra radiates power, like the solar energies that pulse outwardly from the sun in all directions. Three powerful circles contain the inner-connecting spheres of body, mind, and spirit. Where there is a trinity of energy much can be attained. Three people can accomplish a great task together.
4. Imagine wearing a beaded necklace composed of four strands. The power of the circle comes equally from all four directions, is drawn over you, and is placed upon your shoulders. Nekhbet's wings lay across your back as a sign of protection.
5. Travel plans arise very quickly. Before you leave, and before returning home, put a circle of protection around yourself, your luggage, and your group. The shen is flexible; its protection can travel with you and stretch to hold more people within its circle.

6. Surround your family with divine protection. If worries abound, carry a ring of hematite, or wear a silver and turquoise bracelet over which you have invoked protection. The wedding ring is a sanctified circle of god energy between you and your partner that cements a vow to honor, protect, and cherish. If you give a necklace, bracelet, or ring to a family member, it is a similar vow of love.

7. Choose an object, god, or goddess that evokes eternal, divine energy and attach it to a bracelet, necklace, ring, or something that represents Spirit. Bless it with holy water and wear it always. Every time you touch it, remember that you are dedicated to and protected by the Divine.

8. The shen circle is an eternal presence. While love never ends, at times it might appear to be creating a circular pattern of waxing and waning. Love is our greatest power and protection against all that is not loving.

9. At this time in your life you may wonder, *Will the work that I do and have done last?* As one thing draws to a close, a new beginning finds you. Perhaps your work has reached a culmination for now. Rest, but not too long; then begin again.

SIA

While the phonetic images drawn on the facing page indicate that the wisdom of Sia is that of a beardy philosophical god, I rather like the somewhat unusual and rare hieroglyphic image of a backbone and spinal cord that appears at the bottom of the photo taken inside the Pyramid of Unas. This hieroglyph signifies instantaneous knowledge and reminds me of the shivers one gets down one's spine when standing in the presence of or hearing words of truth. Sia, whose name means "the knowing one," offers high wisdom, spirit communication, and contact with the masters. This is the image of the mind on fire, consciousness at its highest manifestation. As divine beings, Sia, Heka, and Hu are three essential divinities needed for magical practice or any creative work.

Rather than conjecture, what Sia perceives is clear truth as it exists within the god-force energy of Ptah. Sia and Hu work together. In the cosmology of Memphis, these gods precede cosmic creation. Sia is the wisdom and intelligence within the heart of Ptah, and Hu is his tongue. As one entity, the two gods Sia and Hu may be thought of as Ma'at—the heart and tongue of Ptah. In this case, however, Sia stands at the head of the trio, preceding Hu and Heka. We must perceive truth rightly before our voice can be authoritative or our utterance effective.

In the Book of Gates, Sia and Hu ride in the solar boat of Ra during the night. As it is with Ra, so it is with the individual soul after death. Neither the weakened sun nor the deceased are able to speak for themselves. It is Sia who perceives clearly, who knows the truth. In the Coffin Texts Sia becomes instrumental in the opening of the mouth ritual. This makes it possible for the dead to speak his conscience during the weighing of the heart before Ma'at.[66] Sia knows what the outcome is before any other god does. As one's conscience, he becomes one's fate. In some cases, when the dead cannot speak, Sia speaks for them.

In particular, on a daily basis, Sia recognizes and uses energy patterns, knowing when and where Spirit is present in a particular situation. Another way to think of Sia in a human sense is as clairvoyance, clairsentience, or clairaudience. Sia relates to a gut feeling or the equivalent of the prickly skin we feel when we recognize that our perception is right. When one connects deeply with Sia, the power of the mind creates a brilliance that seems out of this world. The knowledge appears to come from beyond us. In Arabic the name Zia means "brilliance or glowing light."

Growing in relationship with Sia and allowing that stellar—even intergalactic—wisdom to move through us prepares one to take on the role of sage. In Pyramid Text Utterance 250, Unas took the form of Sia and carried the Book of Ra, or the knowledge of the light.[67] Often Sia is equated with the study and writing of wisdom texts—whether those texts are comprised of inspired literature, inspirational speaking, automatic writing, or trance channeled words.

1. A wise one, magus, or master appears and inspires you. Important information is conveyed through reading, perceiving, and thinking, and then gaining insights. Or the insights may simply drop in as cosmic recognition. Record these insights; they will benefit many.

2. The spiritual work and training you have done consistently with your guides has given you new insights, preparing you for an initiation. Even though you may not recognize that master teacher with whom you work, you know that a higher energy has prepared you for the next step in your spiritual development.

3. You may affirm, pray, or invoke, but what do you get? Proper attention to divine intention is required to manifest anything. Do you *know* that it is right and in divine order? Do you get goosebumps when you are in the presence of spiritual truth? Without that knowledge, you're wasting your breath.

4. Find a box in which to keep some sacred objects: a scarab, a piece of malachite, a seed crystal, a seed of corn. The objects may be whatever signifies talismanic power for you. Use this box to hold your affirmations, dream statements, and desires. Lay your intention in the box, close the lid, put it on your altar, and know that it is done.

5. Something you wish to change isn't changing. Change your perception of it. Meditate on your situation and be willing to make a radical departure in your approach toward it. If that doesn't change things after twenty-eight days, move on.

6. Deeply listen to Spirit, focus your mind, and will yourself to be present. In this way attend all your conversations with your partner, your child, and your friends, especially those with whom you disagree. Goodness results from seeing goodness in others. Listen for Sia in all situations.

7. Using this divine power of perception, something new enters your life. You learn a new skill, a metaphysical tool, or gain a spiritual understanding. Meditate with Sia for three months. Lift your mind and your intention. Be quiet. Read, write, and be inspired. Observe the differences.

8. Certain circular breathing patterns move your meditations into a higher stratosphere. You may wish to read Stephanie Clement's book on various meditations. (While its title, *Meditation for Beginners: Techniques for Awareness, Mindfulness and Relaxation,* implies that it's for beginners, it is not.) Work on getting your mind higher and your ego out of the way as you meditate to gain a more light-filled body. Keep circulating the breath energy through your body and grounding it deeper into the Earth. The higher and deeper you go, the more you circulate the life force wisdom.

9. The truest wisdom can be expressed this way: Love your life. Be in the world. Recognize that the All comes from Spirit. Sia was formed from the mind and body of God. In the Qabalistic tradition, yods of light, or god seeds, emanate from Yahweh and are planted in all things.

SOPDET

The ancient Egyptians called the goddess Isis Sept or Sopdet when she manifested as the star Sirius; the Greeks identified her as Sothis. Sirius appears as the brightest star in the night sky of the northern hemisphere from the midwinter to early spring. While its light shines blue-white primarily, it rapidly flickers in rainbow colors. These unusually multi-colored flickering lights have on occasion been reported as a UFO! The light appears in sharp rays; therefore, some Egyptologists suggest that the tall hieroglyph that depicts it is a thorn. It may be an elongated pyramid similar to those of Nubia. The brilliance of this star is noticeably missed when Sirius rises too close to the sun; then its light is overtaken by the sunrise. The all-important heliacal rising is the day that the sun and Sirius move far enough apart for the first time in months so that Sirius can reappear as the predawn herald of the New Year.[68]

Among all ancient Egyptian festivals, the Coming Forth of Sopdet, which marked the New Year, was the first continuous and oldest celebration. Sopdet heralded the coming flood, four months of inundation, and the subsequent renewal of the land. Our first ancient records note its appearance near the summer solstice around June 25. At the present time in Cairo, Sirius rises again on August 3, although because of two modern dams the Nile flood no longer inundates Egypt.

The rise of our Dog Star Sirius in the Canis Major constellation set the calendar of Egypt. In the beginning Egyptians kept three calendars. A lunar calendar governed by the moon god Thoth designated twelve temple months in the year, with thirty days in each month and ten days in a week. In a mere ten years that would make the calendar fifty-two days out of sync. The solar calendar of Ra attempted to fix that by adding five epagomenal days to equal 365 days of the year. The most accurate calendar, however, proved to be the cycle of Sothis. While we use 365.25 days a year, accounting for a leap year, the solar years still slip somewhat, never arriving to the point where they began until 1,461 civil years have passed.

Because of that, the Egyptians kept a calendar that denoted Sirius as its starting point, as well as relying on solar equinoxes and solstices. It has been suggested that the Egyptians might be one of the first cultures to abide by a "two sun" solar system. It isn't that outrageous a thought, considering that our weaker sun might be orbiting as part of a sun in a much stronger galaxy. Sirius is our nearest solar sister, a mere 8.6 light years away; yet it is 71 percent larger than our solar system's sun. That may because Sirius is comprised of not just one sun, but three suns that orbit around each other. A more explicit description of the dual sun solar system, and how Sirius and our sun interrelate, may be found by visiting the website of the Human Origin Project—an online media platform and global community exploring the origins of humanity.[69]

All that may explain why Isis as Sopdet attains such importance— even at the dawn of Egyptian history. Through their oral tradition, the Dogon people of Mali preserved stories that articulated that at the dawn of time their Nommo ancestors came to Earth from Sirius. These beings were born as twins into amphibian-like bodies, a bit reminiscent of the paired serpents and frogs that evolved in Thoth's cosmic soup. The Dogons first noticed the consistent rising of Sirius, and knew it to be a double star—Sirius A and B—the Dog Stars attributed to Anubis and Isis. The Dogons also, without the aid of telescopes or scientific knowledge, deduced that there was likely a third sun, Sirius C. Sopdet suggests not only sudden cosmic awakenings but potential contact from and with extraterrestrial energies. Robert K. G. Temple's book *The Sirius Mystery* further examines this controversial idea.

Perhaps the myths of intrigue between Isis and Ra actually reinforce the idea of the dual suns. Which was more important—Ra rising daily in a repetitive but somewhat imprecise calendrical pattern, or Isis rising as Sopdet/Sirius, consistently marking time? In Egypt the New Year (*wen repet*) was marked by the arrival of massive floods that lasted nearly four months during the season of inundation. The summer rise of Sirius and the imminent flood coincided with the swelling of the Nile's two major tributaries: the Blue Nile, carrying rain from Ethiopian monsoons, and the White Nile, carrying melted snowcaps from Mount Kilimanjaro in Kenya.

Once the two gushing rivers merged and surged forth from Khartoum, all work stopped. When the Nile receded, having washed away old, unstable structures, it deposited a rich black alluvial soil to renew the land and ready it for plowing and planting. The rise of Sirius marked a time of rest before the coming renewal of work and its promised abundance. Around 3500 BCE, the star Sirius marked the New Year when it rose in June in the early degrees of Cancer, just after the summer solstice. By 650 BCE, during the reign of Pharaoh Psamtik I, the star rose in the later degrees of Cancer, around July 17. Today Sirius rises in the sign of Leo on August 3, just two minutes before sunrise.

After having fallen beneath the horizon for seventy-two days in midspring, the reappearance of Sirius coincided with the rise of the constellation of Orion, or the god Osiris. Isis as Sopdet appeared to lift Osiris out of the Nile waters where myths tell us he had drowned. The star goddess rescued him and resurrected him. Just as the star Sirius was seen to push this constellation upward at dawn, so did Isis lift Osiris until he appeared to stand upright in the midwinter sky. Osiris has thus attained ascension and resurrection. Theosophist Alice Bailey avowed that the master teachers of the spiritual hierarchy that works with our planet Earth came from their homeland in Sirius. She called Sirius the star of initiation that worked upon the "Christ principle in the solar system, in the planet, in man, and in the lower forms of life expression."[70]

1. Sopdet heralds a new beginning; prepare for an important task ahead. Anticipation helps to ready us to open new ground.

2. An important contact draws near—perhaps a spirit messenger, an ascended master, or a star being. This communication begins a beneficial partnership. Alice Bailey and her teacher D. K. had such a partnership.

3. Three stars comprise the Sirius star system; a similar triad of energy increases the brightness of your spiritual work. While one individual may outshine another, the synergy of all creates a brilliance to the work. What matters more: Being the central star or getting the work done?

4. After the new energies come, the plan for using these energies must be followed. In like manner, through the divine guidance offered in meditation to Peter Caddy, Eileen Caddy, and Dorothy Maclean, the Findhorn

community, the renowned intentional community in Scotland, was created by them and flourished.

5. Your personal projects get a boost. Make use of this time. It flows quickly at first. Be ready to catch some inspiration, then continue to harness the resources that it offers.

6. The Great Mother cares for her children. Her energy flows through you to your family. Nurture some new projects and tend the garden. There is no more important work than the support that we give our communities and our families. Isis is with you.

7. Tap into the inspiration, divine guidance, and master energy available to you now. Go into your sanctuary to commune with the Divine. Light a candle and peer into its flame. Undisturbed time to meditate is needed. Your guides will reveal three important things for you to attend to.

8. The light reaches into the furthest corners of a dark room when amplified by the lantern's glass globe. Clear away anything that keeps your light from shining brightly. Success comes when you wipe away worry and clutter. Just keep shining your light.

9. Isis, the Divine Mother, wraps her arms around you. She stands with you as you tend to those in need. Know your great love burns brightly throughout the universe. The Goddess sees and knows all that you do.

TA

In hieroglyphic form the ancient Egyptians depicted the Earth they knew by drawing a path with green growth on either side of it, surrounded by mounds of sand. Of course, Egypt is a desert whose land only flourishes near the banks of the Nile. Ta is the ground of being. It is matter in the natural world. When Osiris, the firstborn son of the sky goddess Nut, stepped down to Earth, a garden sprang up beneath his feet. Like Adam, he was the first son born into space and time. In the tarot cards, Westerners see the Empress card as embodying this fertile Mother Earth. For ancient Egyptians, however, Earth was the god Geb. Later, Osiris became the earth god. Rather than seeing Mother Earth, the Egyptians saw green growth as analogous to seeing the Green Man. Osiris and the ithyphallic god Min both appeared as the sprouting grain.

What holds us in place on our planet? What keeps Earth spinning around the sun? Gravity. We don't usually think of it this way, but we are held here by a mysterious, unseen pull. Ta shows us the mystery of presence, place, and time—the here and now that is space and time coalesced. There were many lands in Egypt: the Land of the Dead, that is, the western lands (*ta manu*), the Land of the Gods (*ta neter*), the Land of Eternity (*ta neheh*), the Pure Land (*ta ab*), the Red Land and the Black Land (*taui*), the Land of Mystery (*ta sheta*), and so on.

Many paths in the spiritual or geographic landscapes crisscross. We establish markers even in psychic spaces to know where we've been and which roads lead where. Ta reminds us to do as Ram Dass said, "Be here now." *X* marks the spot, but it also marks the point between past and future events, as well as forking paths.

Ta also represents fire and the heat of transformation, which is understandable because the core of our planet is a constant crucible. When we think of Egypt's climate, we know it primarily as a hot and dry land, except for those places where the Nile flows and greens the alluvial soil. Those products of the Earth that sustain life were ta. Ta is bread, and bread is wheat baked and transformed through fire for the nourishment of the body. Ta is both physical bread and the bread of heaven. It is what is consumed in order to sustain us.

Learning earth magic means to learn practical metaphysics and medicine. We must be careful in our use of the Earth's resources and energies; these have the power to heal us or kill us. Understand that the Earth is a sentient being. It even has a heartbeat. Precisely, Earth's heart is 7.83 Hz, which the Hindu rishis said was the resonance of the Sanskrit *om*. Called the Schumann resonance, this heartbeat can be perceived from space as high as sixty feet above the globe.[71] Earth has a heart, a consciousness, and a cosmic plan or will of its own. It lives as we live, and we do a disservice to ourselves when we undertake anything that harms it. Natural law teaches that consequences follow actions. It teaches that wisdom abounds in every living thing. Caretaking our planet is the most important work that we can undertake to serve Spirit.

1. Love is the first natural law. Weigh every action by asking "Is this loving?" Wake every morning saying, "Who can I love today?" A powerful love pulses between parent and child, and between Earth and those who care for it. Do no harm. Help the Earth support your desires.

2. The law of karma promises that kindness will be returned, and that harm returns harm. When Isis taught her son Horus about reciprocity, she suggested, "From pigs you get pigs; from wheat you get wheat. Never the other way around." Every action reaps action in kind.

3. All we could ever need, Spirit supplies according to its divine laws. As any farmer would do, tend your garden with care. Pull weeds, nurture what you hope to bring to fullness, harvest, and share your bounty. Keep joyously working in your garden and success will come.

4. Psalm 92:12 tells us to flourish like the cedars of Lebanon; Osiris flourished like a cedar in Lebanon. Growing into your fullness, how do you nurture others? How do you use the life you have been given? What sparks or stimulates your life? Are you treating your body so that it can support you? What spiritual waters purify you and quench your thirst?

5. How we organize our working and living spaces determines what Spirit will bring. Express your sense of place. Help others see that Earth's environment reflects how we treat each other, ourselves, and Spirit. Climate change is a part of a symbiotic relationship. Consider your carbon footprint. It is possible to move into a more eco-sustainable environment in the future.

6. The law of oneness is this: namaste. The goddess in me sees the goddess in you. Practice your connectedness. Hug a friend; hug a tree; hug a beautiful pet. Feel it deeply. Listen to each heartbeat. Share the wealth with others, and share the responsibility for attending to life's details.

7. You find your true spiritual path when you commune with nature as you walk in the woods or work in your garden. Set business affairs aside for now and turn inward. Read and meditate so that you can connect your spiritual goals with your reality.

8. Build a solid foundation for your personal or business plans. The pieces will fall into place. Review and rework ways to fertilize your seed idea so that it can grow more abundantly. You will soon see rewards.

9. You have come to a crossroad and now must choose a new path. Right? Left? Straight ahead? You may choose to end one direction and take up another. This is no dead end, but a point of departure, connecting previously opposing paths. Breathe and be filled with gratitude and mystery.

THET

The hieroglyphic emblem called the knot of Isis is well-known. Linguistically, however, no other ancient Egyptian words relate to any of its spellings as *thet,* or *tyet, tuyet, tit,* or *tjet.* We don't know the origin of the word. Some Egyptologists believe the thet to be a stylized ankh, but I'm not sure that was its purpose. The ankh already has a long-standing history, meaning, and iconography. The thet amulet came into prominence during the New Kingdom and continued in importance through the Greco-Roman period.

A mysterious emblem, thet relates solely to the mysteries of being female. Often the emblem was worn about the waist of a queen or priestess, attached to a belt. Author DeTraci Regula, a priestess of Isis and director of the Isis Oasis Retreat Center, explains how the thet was a sacred knot that was used to keep garments tied. In her book *The Mysteries of Isis,* she demonstrates how the ancient and modern priestess uses the thet knot as part of her ritual robing.[72] An amulet worn by women, it evokes the kind of strength that Isis needed, given that she was a single mother, a widow, and a larger-than-life community figure working for social justice. All of these roles are exemplified by modern women of the Red Tent Movement, whom I associate with the thet.

The knot of Isis was often accompanied by the djed of Osiris. Its shape may be derived from both the sistrum rattle (emblem of joy) and the ankh (symbol of life) with its transverse arms curved downward. With its life-giving, pleasurable properties, scholars have suggested that it is a variation of the hieroglyph of the womb, or that it was a cloth to catch the menstrual flow (not so pleasurable!). Translated loosely, *thet* meant "life, fecundity, and well-being." When used in conjunction with the djed, the thet suggests the binary nature of life itself—masculine and feminine. Djed and thet combined in iconography, as it is on amulets and furniture in Tutankhamun's treasures, may suggest the sacred marriage representing the staff of Osiris and the womb of Isis. Crafted in wood and painted in gold, these probably were magical amulets to assure fecundity and resurrection.

Knots, considered magical in ancient Egypt and elsewhere, were used for binding and releasing energies. The goddess Neith (N-t), considered one of the oldest deities in Egypt, wore upon her head a shuttle used for weaving and tying knots. She represented every type of cloth and binding in the ancient world—from fishing nets to linen knits. The binding knot of life force energy was hers. Neith wore a patterned, loosely woven green dress into which she reached to pull out all the creatures of the Earth. Every living thing was her own creation. Netting, knitting, and knotting were, in particular, Neith's creative talents. Bedouin women of Egypt are likewise highly skilled with needle and thread; their embroidery and stitching are legendary. Words spoken over a cord or thread while tying knots has a binding effect. Likewise, words pronounced upon untying a cord release the power once bound. Indeed, Isis priestess, hermetic adept, and author Isidora Forrest asserts we moderns still use these binding rituals in handfasting and marriage ceremonies wherein we "tie the knot."[73]

The Pyramid Text of Tetà speaks of Isis and Nephthys tying cords and performing a magical spell over Osiris.[74] This referred to tying his mummy wrappings as the sisters were credited with creating funerary rituals for their brother in all the cities in which his body parts were found after Set murdered him. This spell alluded to the insemination of Isis and the resultant birth of Horus. A carnelian or red jasper thet was often used as a funerary amulet of protection. Wrapped within the mummy cloth and worn around the neck, it provided a kind of fortitude or a girding up of energy. The magic was intended to counter any attempt to desiccate the body in a similar way to Osiris having been torn asunder by Set. The thet amulet reads: "You have your blood, O Isis; you have your power, O Isis; you have your magic, O Isis. This amulet is a protection for the Great One which will drive away whoever would commit a crime against him."[75]

1. One who has come of age is tying things up to begin pulling together a new project. The thet announces the capacity for leadership by a strong woman.

2. Partnership occurs between equals. This tie binds two energies to do the work that follows. The marriage rite binds a couple's creativity into

eternity. This Isis energy works in a physical partnership or unifies Heaven and Earth.

3. The knot that binds the hips of the Goddess may indicate children to come. Capture a creative flow by nurturing your creativity and manifesting love. Work a simple spell with your female friends by knitting together and discussing plans or future dreams.

4. Become grounded in one's femininity. What is it that women sit upon? The boundless creative source of their own energy! There is your throne, mighty Isis. Be in your own flow to build the foundation of the life you desire.

5. Change, flux, and movement appear. Untie any knots that bind you to what does not serve your life or the Goddess. Craft a new life for yourself and bind it. You may be moving into a new flow of energy or pattern of thinking.

6. Make a commitment to healing, to family, and to self because you are a vessel of divine love. Embody strength. If you want love in your life, then be love. Live love. Love everything.

7. In this commitment to divine union and to one's own sovereignty, take care that you do not give away that sovereignty when you love. As Khalil Gibran has said, "Let there be spaces in your togetherness. And let the winds of the heavens dance between you."[76]

8. Commitment to one's community and to the Divine within and without is a magical binding of Earth and Heaven. You have the ability to achieve your desires. Use feminine wisdom, strength, and power, not an aggressive way of striving. You are under the protection of Isis.

9. Acquiring the wise blood means you are listening to the wisdom within. This includes elders moving through menopause or andropause. Wisdom comes in dreams. The kundalini energy rises, curls, and folds back on itself. To further open your crown chakra, wear a thet amulet anointed with jasmine or spikenard.

WAB

A wab or uab priest or priestess held a temple position of high esteem. Wab means to be a pure one, ritually washed and fasted, and engaging in one's spiritual functions with ritual attention. The white robes of the priest or priestess were made of fine linen. In general, this hieroglyph refers to being clean, holy, and ceremonially pure. The long tradition of purity required daily bathing rituals. Thus the hieroglyph illustrates waters flowing from a jar and being poured over one who enters the temple.

Although beer was a staple in the Egyptian diet, only small amounts of wine were drunk. The priest or priestess followed a simple vegetarian diet. According to the prohibitions of a deity's particular temple, certain foods and drink were forbidden. Certain meats, such as pork, pigeon, sea fish, ewes, and sacred cows, were not eaten. Vegetables that produced strong odors, such as beans or garlic, were not eaten. Again, the prohibitions depended upon the particular temple. Sexual abstinence was required during the period of time that one served the temple.[77]

The god Thoth cleanses the aura of the pharaoh to magically purify him.
As high priest of the temple, the pharaoh may now attend
the god because he is "a pure one, washed and fasted."

Only the high priest or funerary priest who understood certain
shamanic rites might wear the leopard-skin robe over his white robe,
indicating that he had passed through certain initiations. Many priests
or priestesses served the temple as lay ministers for several weeks out of

the year on a regular rotation. Even as administrators, wab priests and priestesses did not enter into their duties lightly. A lengthy training in meditation, metaphysical studies, and the responsibilities of their particular jobs were required. Sometimes these tasks followed particular family members. For example, the daughter of a priestess whose needlework most appealed to the god and goddess might follow in her mother's footsteps to become a seamstress, working with the fine linen of the neteru or royal family. A miner followed his father into the mines; a scribe studied to be a scribe under his father. Those who could afford to send their children to scribe school did so because being a scribe led directly to temple service, which was considered an easier life than that of stonemason, miner, soldier, or sailor.

The wab priest in training had administrative duties just to keep the temple running, such as checking schedules and inventories. A few priests or priestesses attached to the temple were devoted to specific

The son of the pharaoh wears the leopard skin of the high priest and offers incense to his father, Osiris, wrapped in his mummy cloth. We know that he is the son of the mummy by his braid, which indicates that he is a child (becoming a man who will take his father's place).

deities, which gave them specific duties. For example, the priest of Sekhmet was often a healer or physician, while the sem priest presided over the funerary rites. The hem netjer was the high priest or priestess allowed to enter the holy of holies and attend the altar and statue in the absence of the pharaoh, who when present was always the highest servant of the god or goddess. The hem netjer was seen as the permanent holy guardian of the temple. And the hem-netjer-tepi, or so-called first servant of the god, was the firstborn son of the pharaoh who accompanied his father in ceremony as a means of learning the rites that he would engage after his father's death. At the time of his father's death, that son acted as the sem priest for the king's funeral.

There were also cheriheb, or lector-priests. The lector-priests read the rites of the day (at sunrise, morning, noon, sunset, evening), paying homage to the divinity of the temple, of the season, of the month, of the day, and of the hours. Often these were sung or chanted hymns of adoration. These lectionaries were kept on scrolls in the library of the temple. As many times as the priest or priestess read these texts, they were never intended to be memorized, but always read exactly as was written from the script in front of them to prevent some minor change from occurring through a slip of memory or tongue.[78]

1. Called to a higher purpose, now it is time to deepen and develop your spiritual practice. You are asked to step up to the task of leading others in the development of their spiritual practices, according to your gifts.

2. You are doubly blessed. In your community there is a priest/priestess or minister whose gifts are many and whose service is one of compassion. You are asked to shadow that person in order to learn their tradition, practices, and prayers. Perhaps you are called to become a midwife, a hospice worker, or a spiritual counselor.

3. Use holy water to bless a new home or car, christen a child, cleanse a building, or dedicate yourself to a more sacred path. Before beginning his work, the ancient scribe poured an offering of sacred water from his ink jar and said a prayer of dedication to Imhotep and Thoth. If you write or paint, find a ritual way to incorporate these activities into a daily practice.

4. Someone may ask for your help in building a firmer foundation for their spiritual practice. The undertaking of this work may begin as simply helping to organize others, or acting as an overseer of some spiritual tasks. Remember to keep your eyes open and learn to see what is really being placed before you. You are engaged in an apprenticeship with Spirit.

5. Confusion and a whirlwind of recent events have clouded your thinking about a particular situation. Rectify any errors of thought or action. Release illusions and judgments about others. A change of heart and a brand-new start are measures of purification that are needed now.

6. Put your best foot forward. You are called to enter into a deeper relationship with Spirit by entering into a deeper relationship with others. Accept this higher calling. Know the difference between helping and interfering. Never lose sight of the fact that as you help others, your most important relationship is between yourself and Spirit.

7. Before beginning a new spiritual task, undergo a purification. Spiritualist Andrew Jackson Davis reported that his spirit guide Galen, the ancient Greek philosopher and physician, was the teacher who advised him to keep an even mind in any circumstance. Clean up your routine, attend to your nutrition, and take a balanced approach to work, rest, family, and self-care. Clear your body of toxins; clear your mind of toxic thoughts. Discernment is key.

8. Accept one's spiritual responsibilities and duties. God is in the details. All we do—from sweeping the floor to painting a work of art—must flow from focused attention. Many religious traditions encourage one to see the spiritual in the ordinary. You may wish to follow an ethical pattern of spiritual practice, such as the Buddhist Eightfold Path. Ask yourself, "How is the spirit world presenting itself to me daily? What practice does it require of me?"

9. Whether you have consciously thought about taking the next step toward beginning a specific religious practice—or even ordination—it is certainly a possibility. Your commitment to a deep spiritual discipline calls you. You have much to offer your community, yourself, and deity. Relinquish your hesitation.

WADJET

Whenever wadjet appears, abundant life arises in surprising ways to open you up to new life, new discoveries, and new possibilities. The cobra represents primal fire goddess energy. Nearly every culture of the world offers a divine feminine in the form of the snake. The Mayan moon goddess Ixchel watches over women in childbirth. In northern India and Bengal, the Hindu goddess Manasa provides abundance and fertility. Ananta was the serpent who fell from heaven to encircle the world; the Hindus saw her boundaries as limitless. In Crete the serpent priestess appears adorned with snakes in each hand, slithering up her arms, around her shoulders, and girding her waist; her wide-eyed gaze portrayed the snake-charmer priestess as a prophetess.

The oldest serpent goddess in Egypt is Neith, the Great Green. All of the goddesses in the ancient Egyptian pantheon, however, can be indicated by providing a hieroglyph of the serpent at the end of her name. This rearing cobra, with its hood extended, denotes an enormous amount of power that can be used wisely or not so wisely. Remember how Isis placed a serpent in the path of Ra in order to learn his secret name (or perhaps to teach him not to be so arrogant). Thus did the Jews give the woman Eve the unappreciated task of listening to the serpent in order to awaken Adam from his blissful ignorance. "Be ye wise as serpents," advises Mathew 10:16, meaning that it is good to be careful and alert, and keep your ear to the ground.

In ancient Egypt, Renenunet, goddess of the harvest, assured protection and future abundance. Meretseger, the winged serpent called the Lady of Silence (a female Quetzalcoatl), kept watch over the necropolis of the Valley of the Kings. In ancient Alexandria, a Hellenized version of Isis as serpent appeared as the harvest goddess Isis-Thermuthis. The Two Ladies, Wadjet and her sister Uto, the fire goddesses of Upper and Lower Egypt, became the twin serpents upon the healing staff of Asclepius, the Greek physician who mastered the healing arts of the ancient Egyptians. Because the snake sheds its skin and rejuvenates itself, this creature epitomized the female power of regeneration and birth. Philo of Alexandria believed snakes lived eternally because they constantly shed their skins. As they shed skins, they shed their old age, thus making lowly serpents the most spiritual of all creatures.

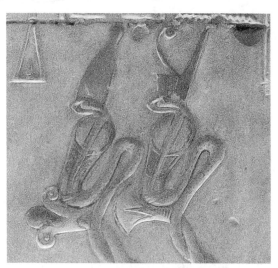

These two serpents, known as the Two Ladies, wear the crowns of Upper and Lower Egypt respectively. They are depicted as entwined about the caduceus of Thoth in Abydos.

By nature the serpent mesmerizes with its sensual rocking motion and hypnotic gaze, as it rears and arises. Its energy can be both dangerous and protective. In the papyrus swamps the cobra guarded mythic Horus, the child of Isis. As an embodiment of the pharaoh, Wadjet guards and protects the pharaoh, the living embodiment of Horus.[79] She appears as the uraeus: erect, alert, and with hood extended at the pharaoh's *ajna* center where the wadjet serpent both protects him and enlivens his psychic powers. Its ever alert and aware presence indicates a readiness to invoke visionary powers of seeing, or conversely of spitting fire into the eyes of enemies. (See the cobra on the forehead of Pharaoh Seti I as he offers ma'at to the gods in the figure on page 153.)

Likewise, she protects her children in the afterworld. Says the Book of the Dead: "[She anoints] thy head with . . . flames. She riseth up on the left side of thy head, and she shineth from the right side of thy temples without speech; they rise up on thy head during each and every hour of the day, even as they do for their father Ra, and through them the terror which thou inspirest in the holy spirits is increased."[80]

Wadjet signifies the zap of the life force moving through you. These energies are available in meditation, but also on a daily basis. The powers can be so strong that you are advised to ground yourself by lying in the grass whenever you start to feel overwhelmed by them. The wadjet cobra is associated with the color green, or the life force energy moving from the root chakra upward. The connection between the life force energy and the physical appearance of the spinal cord certainly demonstrates serpent power. As manifestations of kundalini energy, the chakra energies that the serpent awakens are relative to each plane of human consciousness: sensation, emotion, reflective intelligence, intuition, spirituality, will, and intimations of the Divine.[81] Sometimes wadjet can be identified as a rising green flame. Snakes rear up to receive the spiritual energy from Heaven and they lie down to receive the energy from Earth.

Often winged, Wadjet possesses the qualities that we understand to be dragon energy. She's not dangerous except to those who are afraid of or unaccustomed to the electrical current that she brings. The energy can be creative, innovative, or destructive. Certainly, when a real snake appears on the path and catches us unaware, it sends an electrical shiver through our system. To be caught unaware in some instances can be deadly. Snake dreams are among the most common, but because snakes are often well-hidden and overlooked, to dream of a snake is to awaken us to a very important situation or message from the world of Spirit. Sometimes it informs us of what we have overlooked or need to avoid; sometimes it announces an awakening to mystical insight.

The snake offers a different kind of seeing—a kind of thermal sensitivity. You may feel a charge drawing you to or repelling you from others in the room. Perhaps you feel a change in temperature that others do not feel—a zap, a kind of sensitivity to light, to flashes, and to pressure. All of these are clairsentient ways of knowing. Serpents have that kind of knowing because they live close to Earth, feeling their way along with bellies on the ground. With some practice in meditation you will be able to sit on a winged serpent—your own dragon—and astrally visit key people and places in the spirit world.

Associated with visionary capacities, Wadjet is called the Lady of Flame or the Veiled Priestess of the Oracle Temple. Those who practice ceromancy by reading the serpentine drips of candle wax, the flickering flames of lit candles, or the wisps of smoke smudged onto a card are practicing the visionary arts of ancient oracles dedicated to the *naga* and serpent goddess. Green candles work especially well with Wadjet's energy, but white candles do just fine. Some astrologers attribute to Wadjet the eccentric, eclectic, and electrical energy of the planet Uranus. Expect the unexpected energetically. On a physical level, as you work with this energy, keep all doctor appointments. It's a safety hook. Be easy with yourself as the energy pulses can whack you out of balance.

1. When Wadjet appears here she signifies the uraeus on the pharaoh's brow. Unique forms of leadership are represented. Accept the call. She protects you. Sudden flashes of intuition may be experienced. Your spiritual sight increases.

2. Wadjet emphasizes spiritual unity with a partner, a possible deep love

connection, certainly one that is protective, spiritual, and intense. There may be a physical zap of energy between you and another individual. If this is not a love connection, then it may appear as a deep friendship that is an ancient soul remembering.

3. Creativity appears prominently with flashes of ideas that seem to burst into your consciousness from out of nowhere. You may even experience an insight or a form of intuition that borders on trance—the kind that gets so strong that you feel a strong zap up your spine, so much so that you practically jump. Creative visioning and shamanic travel are on the horizon.

4. The foundation of your world is rocked. You experience energy surges, possibly even neuropathy or adrenal rushes. The quake of energy awakens a protective response. Keep your eyes open, and do not lash out without first perceiving the situation correctly.

5. Travel in the astral is possible. You might have out-of-body experiences, lucid dreams, or deep shamanic visions. Telepathy abounds, but it may come so fast that other people feel left behind in confusion. Unusual energy shifts, ideas, and unusual solutions to problems arise. Slow down so that you are able to communicate your new understanding.

6. Your magnetism draws others, sometimes more so than you would like. You are deeply solitary, creative, intuitive, and visionary. You or a family member may experience being a little too much out of the body. An elder may have a neurological dysfunction, or a child might be suffering emotional overload. Wadjet can help you and them to find a balance.

7. Unique spiritual gifts unfold quickly. This suggests an opening into clairaudience, clairvoyance, or other clairsentient gifts. In addition to intuition, other avenues may be astral travel, precognition, and remote viewing. For those trained in mental mediumship, Wadjet may announce coming demonstrations of physical phenomena.

8. A zap of insight clears an obstacle. Impressive powers of focus, concentration, and mental planning are yours. If you work with this energy, the sudden amplification of consciousness can help you attain an understanding of your part in the divine plan. Here we see enlightened determination to do important work on a planetary level.

9. Something abruptly ends that needed to end long ago. A change for the better occurs. A decisive use of will brings this end about. Courage amplifies a sudden movement forward. Rather than focusing on the dramatic upheaval, focus on adapting to transformative change.

WAZ

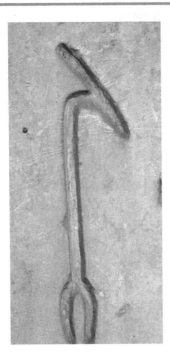 

The waz scepter does not show the head of a serpent, which is a different shamanic tool. A waz scepter represents the magic power of dominion over the Earth. It has the head of the Set animal, which is sometimes a scary energy. In this case, however, we see an implement made of iron, forged in fire. Perhaps this is why the suit of wands in the tarot deck is equated with fire energy.

Much like the bones of Set, or the bones of Earth, the iron that the priests of Ptah used to smelt into Egyptian magical wands had a meteoric origin. When a meteor fell from the sky in a streak of fire, it was said to be Set piercing the side of his mother, Nut, the sky, to descend to Earth. Yes, there can be a violence to such energy. The metal in a waz scepter carries an ultrahigh vibration as matter from the outer depths of space tends to; but it can be mastered and controlled to gain dominion on Earth.

We can make weapons of war with Set's iron or we can create magic by using its vibrations. We do this by using the magnetized energy that is part of a magic wand's power to either attract what we want or repel what serves no purpose. In other words, a waz scepter functions along with the law of vibration. The energy of waz equals the energy of change. One can use a waz scepter to set into motion a transformation of a negative into a positive. It can work the other way, but why fool with that karma?

Iron waz scepters may also chain an entity and hold its energy in one place in order to master it or keep it still. In other words, the old priests and kings grasped the staff tightly at the neck of the desert jackal or Set beast. In such a way they mastered Set by gripping him around the neck in a choke hold. Some Egyptologists say that the pronged end of the waz scepter was used to snare and pin serpents to the ground, another way of controlling Set.

Certainly, the dual ends of the scepter indicate several other possible meanings. For example, if the energy is moving from the ground up, it is the merger of Heaven and Earth energy. We have two feet on Earth and one head in the Heaven-scape. The law of polarity is also seen in this staff—and possibly it may indicate a dowsing rod or the possibility of forking paths. Think for a moment upon the meaning of the word *irony*. When a situation is deliberately contrary, it creates irony or forking paths. Ironic events are those that seem Sethian or contrarian in nature; that is, the opposite of what is expected, not merely an amusing coincidence. Although not necessarily connected linguistically, the connections between the *iron* of the waz scepter and the *irony* of the contrarian Seth can be seen hieroglyphically as similar in tone.

As with many hieroglyphs, double meanings abound. The hieroglyph for waz means both "mental and physical well-being." Waz also means "to crumble to ruin or decay." A young man at the height of his power uses his scepter as a sign of authority and power. An old man leans upon it, using it as his cane.

1. Power, leadership, control, and the mastery of negative forces come to the fore. This is a time of learning to lead. Coaxing, as with a shepherd's crook, rather than shocking, as with a cattle prod, better accomplishes the task of managing others.

2. Coins have two faces; everything has two sides. In thinking about a stalled project, investigate which side your projected energy falls on. Use your energy to unite, not divide.

3. Contentment comes following a push forward to get a stalled project moving. What you want and are willingly work for comes to you successfully. Put the pedal to the metal.

4. A firm foundation prevents the collapse of a project. Build a strong foundation for a temple or a spiritual home. You work hard to establish an idea or an institution that can be built upon. Develop mastery over your limitations.

5. A change in directions and energy comes. Set your mind upon that which you seek to manifest. Then set your course with a steady application of energy. Master the chaos that swirls around your project by seeing both the god and the devil in the details.

6. The most important use of our power is to align our energies with ma'at. The true spirit of the heart lies in the ability to master our own self-destructive nature—those qualities of procrastination, anger, fear, and ego. Self-mastery is the most precious power we will ever control on Earth. Look within and find your purest motive in all you do.

7. Open yourself to Spirit. Listen. Use both ears. Use your discernment. Feel Spirit moving through you and through the words and actions of your community representatives. Do that which Spirit commands—do no evil. If something truly needs to be mastered, delayed, or held back, do so—but use powerful, prayerful discernment in determining this.

8. Work your altar. Do your job. Make magic of the highest order. Like the tarot Magician, lift your magic wand high; let the lightning energy of Spirit move through you. Complete the divine plan and follow the path that Spirit has laid out for you. Work with love, knowing that each detail, no matter how minor, matters to the overall scheme of things.

9. Your work is complete. An enormous task has been finished. Because you have kept your faith and tended to the work at hand, a well-deserved rest is within sight. Congratulations on living a spirit-filled life. A significant problem has been diverted or a long-desired outcome has been attained.

ZEP TEPI

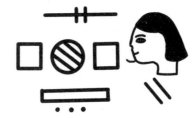

The Egyptian New Year began when the Nile River overflowed and fertilized the land. Once a year, during the dog days of summer, the furiously flowing Nile seemed to shoot forth through the cataracts of the Nile near Aswan. In the photographed image above, flowing water from a jar suggests that the liquid is moving quickly, almost as if carried on a pair of legs. The triplicate ripples of water suggest the multiplied, overflowing quality of the rising river as it inundates the land below it, represented by the hieroglyphs of the valley. This overflowing water jug became the icon of the Aquarian age and its forthcoming renewal. The line drawing above offers yet another way of seeing this word. While the first four glyphs are phonetic, one can clearly see the land below and the seed that will be fertilized by the water of the inundation. The hieroglyphic head is used to designate something that is "ahead" of another thing, something that comes before. In this case, the year begins with a flood; the season of inundation comes ahead of the season of sowing.

Zep Tepi harkens back to an Egyptian genesis story of the creation of the world. At that time nothing existed except the waters of Heaven and the waters of Earth. Then Atum cried out and light leapt from his lips. His voice vibrating on the waters set the creative act in motion. The waters of Heaven and Earth parted. His winged soul, filled with creative desire, flew out of him. Birdlike, it soared until it saw a mound of earth arising from the waters. The akh bird, or phoenix, landed upon this place and made a nest. Upon this benben stone, or primeval hill, the pyramids were built to remind us of the first time when the Land of Khem—Egypt—emerged from the waters.

Thereafter this Golden Age called Zep Tepi became known as the First Time. One legend says that gods and goddesses arrived in their fleets, landing in Egypt. Were they Atlanteans fleeing a sinking continent? Or star people voyaging across celestial rivers of light in their craft? Or magi escaping an inundation that fractured their homeland? Some theorize a prehistoric time when the land bridge spanning Europe and Africa sank. The plains of Giza and the Sahara Desert were flooded around 36,400 BCE, trapping the sea creatures. This area later became the famous western Sahara Desert Valley of the Whales.

According to several researchers—among them former investigative journalist and Egyptologist Armando Mei—Zep Tepi is an actual historical period traced back specifically to 36,420 BCE.[82] It was then that the god Osiris was said to have first stepped down upon the soil of Egypt, bringing ancestral knowledge with him. Many ancient texts refer to Zep Tepi, but its first reference derives from the earliest known writings in the Pyramid Text.

Every year when the Nile predictably flooded after the rising of Sirius, this prehistoric cataclysmic event (the flood) and its attendant mythology was recalled. As the waters subsided, leaving their alluvial soil, all seemed to be renewed. The waters quenched the parched land's thirst. Old and worn structures were swept away. The mud brick houses lost to the flood were rebuilt every year after the river receded. This annual event resulted when the melting snows of Kilimanjaro (the White Nile) met the surging monsoon rains from Ethiopia (the Blue Nile). Both rivers surged downstream, merging and crashing together at Khartoum, the origin of the river Nile proper.

Thankfully for the ancient Egyptian farmer, this Zep Tepi in ancient Egypt repeated itself every summer at almost the same time. Once the river washed everything away, then reclamation began, along with seeding, growth, and abundance. After the harvest came the drought, before inundation began again. The cycle denotes both beginning and completion. The astrological image of the zodiacal sign Aquarius refers to the two sources of the Nile that the god Hapi pours from the amphorae he holds (see page 256). The earliest known hieroglyphs for the word indicating *abyss* or *inundation* was the word *nun,* inscribed with the hieroglyphs of two flowing streams of water. Our concept of none or nothingness comes from this image of the abyss in which there is no difference between Heaven and Earth; all is vast oceanic emptiness.

When one thinks of the Aquarian Age, we feel simultaneously a kind of terror at the dissolution of our way of life as we know it now and an exultation over the coming revolution of higher spiritual awakening. An age, a cycle, a phenomenon that repeats itself, destroying in order to liberate and reshape us—this is the meaning of Zep Tepi.[83]

1. The gifts of the Nile flow into your life in whatever way rejuvenation comes. What begins now sustains you. The work may ebb and flow, but what remains will be life-sustaining.

2. A phenomenal rejuvenation comes from two divergent resources meeting. The past and future intersect. You have never felt more in balance in your life than where you are now.

3. Prepare your boats. The flood approaches—not in an apocalyptic way, but in a "what floats your boat" way. You enter a creative wave, so prepare to

The Nile god of abundance, Hapi, summoned the two living streams of water to create the Nile floods. His full breasts and belly symbolize the fecundity of the land after the inundation.

ride it through the crest. If certain things flow out of your life, rest assured they are making way for the new.

4. Now the flood approaches. Gather the resources that will sustain you. Stock up on what secures your future—whether these things lie in the material world or in the realm of ideas.

5. Things are astir and changing quickly. Keeping a record of these fast-paced events helps you stay on top of things. If this Zep Tepi refers to work you do with others, delegate, but don't forget to celebrate the wins and the new vitality that these changes bring.

6. If you've been worried about health, healing comes. Do your part to find balance in your life. Eliminate those things that overwhelm you: too many projects, too much self-doubt, or standing too close to the forest so you can't see the trees. The right amount of sleep, of sleeping in, of self-care, of exercise, and joy does wonders.

7. Objectivity and a change in perspective will get you back on track. Your world vision promotes global peace, universality, and a compassionate understanding that all souls flow from the same source. We may divide into many rivers, but ultimately, we all return to the same place. Unify a group by accepting the uniqueness of each individual in it.

8. Release what no longer serves you. Sort through your junk drawers, closets, boxes under the bed, and files at the back of the filing cabinet. If you haven't needed it for six months, let it go. Success comes from having only what serves you readily available. Don't waste energy trying to find what you need or save what you do not need.

9. Start again. After a difficult end, a renewal brings light, and a rejuvenated spiritual energy flows back into your life. Have no fear. Transformation and renewal are natural cycles. After an ending, there comes a predictable and welcome beginning again.

THE LAYOUTS

TOOLS FOR DIVINATION

In order to enhance your understanding of the hieroglyphs, study the various layouts of the readings before you begin to use them. The layout of a particular reading offers a pattern of interpretation. Sometimes the hieroglyphs themselves suggest a particular pattern. Two examples are the Dendera Zodiac Layout and the Djed Pillar Layout, which resemble the traditional horoscope and Tree of Life patterns for reading cards. Other patterns are derived from Egyptian geometric shapes or images found on temple walls. I have adapted and used them all in an especially Egyptian manner, drawing on the energies of the Egyptian hieroglyphic designs of the temples or images they emulate. A brief history of the rationale for each layout and a sample reading are included.

THE DENDERA ZODIAC LAYOUT

The traditional horoscope layout designating the twelve houses of the zodiac can be found in the zodiacal ceiling of the Temple of Hathor at Dendera. That zodiac has recognizable images of the Aries ram god, Amen; the Taurus Apis bull representing Osiris; the Gemini twins, Shu and Tefnut; the Cancer sign of Khepera; Leo, the lion, the celestial sphinx; Virgo, perhaps as Isis carrying Horus; Libra as the scales in the neterworld where the heart is weighed; the Scorpion goddess Selket; the pharaonic archer in his chariot as Sagittarius; the goat khnum as Capricorn; Hapi, the Nile River god, as Aquarius; and the two Sobek crocodiles swimming in opposite directions taking the place of the traditional fish of Pisces.

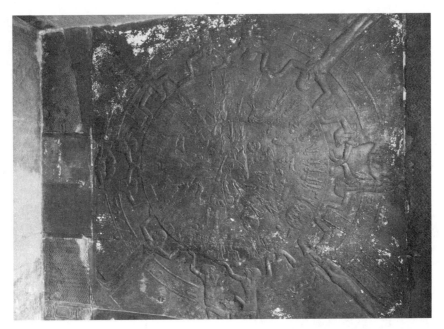

This zodiacal ceiling at Dendera offers a complete map of the ancient sky; all subsequent zodiacs are based on it. The original ceiling is housed in the Louvre. This exact duplicate was inserted into the temple ceiling and was blackened to match the original ceiling that had accrued centuries of smoke damage.

The Meaning of the Houses

The house meanings for the Dendera zodiac reading and a traditional zodiac are as follows:

1. **Aries**—How you begin things, present yourself, how others see you, general outlook
2. **Taurus**—Money, finances, personal values, possessions
3. **Gemini**—Siblings, neighbors, environment, short trips, communications, thinking, messages, letters, writing, speaking
4. **Cancer**—Home, foundation, domestic life, mother, nurturer, real estate
5. **Leo**—Creativity, lovers, hobbies, fun, physical children, children of the mind
6. **Virgo**—Everyday activities, pets, daily work, health, service, workout routines, food

7. **Libra**—Marriage, significant partnership, business partner, counselor, contracts, legal issues

8. **Scorpio**—Partnership, money, sexuality, metaphysics transformation, addictions, inheritance

9. **Sagittarius**—Long-distance travel, foreigners, publishing, education, religion, personal truth

10. **Capricorn**—Career, success, public recognition, reputation, father, authority figures

11. **Aquarius**—Friendships, associations, networks, groups, hopes and personal goals, humanity

12. **Pisces**—Intuition, illusion, dreams, hidden things, unconscious mind, karma, spirit, prisons

13. **East/Ascendant**—Your mask, what others see, how you wish to be seen

14. **West/Descendant**—Projections onto others, the mirror of partnerships, opposites

15. **North/IC**—Who we are in our private self and how we connect with our ancestors

16. **South/Midheaven**—Our life path and work in the public eye

17. **Center/The Imperishable Stars**—The stars around which all else moves tell us what the whole matter really is about

Your Dendera zodiac reading could be considered an astrological transit of your natal birth chart. The twelve houses represent common areas of focus and the hieroglyph that falls in that house reveals the energies that you may be experiencing at this time. This layout works well when you have multiple areas of concern. Referring to the layout figure above, draw fourteen cards, one at a time, from the deck of sixty hieroglyphic cards that you have created or purchased. (Again, should you wish to purchase a deck, please see the ordering information at the back of this book.) Place the cards 1 through 12 in a circle, following the pattern in the illustration. Then place an additional card in each of the four directions (cards 13 through 16), denoting the angles of the astrological chart.

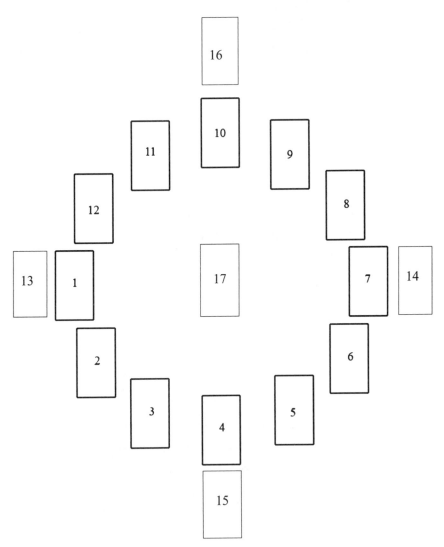

Dendera Zodiac Layout

These angles can be seen on the Dendera zodiac as the four Horus figures who uphold the circle of sky. A kneeling Horus appears in each direction—east on the ascendant, west on the descendant; north at the *imum coeli* (IC) or "bottom of the sky," and south at the midheaven (MC), or "top of the sky." For me it makes sense to lay out the hieroglyphs in polarities of east and west followed by north and south (these four "outly-ing" cards) because when I read an astrological chart, I look at the cardinal points in pairs of oppositions. The ascendant is all about the individual whereas the descendant focuses on that person within a relationship. The IC describes how an individual feels within themselves, their inner world, whereas the MC shows how the outer world tends to perceive that individual. These two points may also be thought of as home (one's personal space) and career (one's public space).

I also place one extra hieroglyph in the center of the reading (card 17), which I take to be representative of the Imperishable Stars, the North Pole around which all the other stars move. This card holds the central space in the Dendera zodiacal ceiling where the crocodile god Sobek and pregnant hippopotamus goddess Tauret reside. It expresses one's North Star, the reason one came into this lifetime, the lessons one is to learn and to which all the other cards refer. I think of this card as representing the duality of what might be considered the north and south nodes of an astrological chart.

Following are some sample readings, so you can get a better idea of how this all works.

The Question

The querent wanted a snapshot of where he was currently on his spiritual path, how to develop mediumship, specifically physical mediumship, and what the influences were that he needed to consider. Having been a student of Spiritualists who reportedly developed themselves sufficiently in order to produce psychic phenomena (such as skotography, apports, and spirit art), he was specifically interested in being able to manipulate physical matter by spiritual means.

I laid out the cards for him, drawing Ptah first, Ir-is second, and so on and so forth. The following is an interpretation of how the energy of the hieroglyph, combined with the meaning of the house in which it falls, offers up a full articulation of the answer to his query.

The Reading

House 1—Ptah. Others see you and know you as a serious student of the natural laws of mind and vibration. Thoughts are things.

Mental mediumship and physical mediumship both work on the power of thought vibration. Although he is an incredibly powerful creator god, Ptah is physically bound—even as the mediums of the last century were bound to their chairs while working in trance. He creates nothing except with the power of thought. His lapis blue skullcap sprinkled with gold stars indicates that the law of mind is the beginning of all life; this is how the Divine created the world in the beginning. For example, when we focus directly on a beam of light, it appears in a wave form; but when we look away, the light particles scatter into a random state. It is consciousness itself that trains the mind to perceive and create meaning. Physical mediumship is consciousness in motion.

House 2—Ir-is. In this house, usually attributed to how we spend our money, Ir-is shows you spending your time and energy delving into your psychic work. During your meditations work to attain that high vibration energy you seek in order to manifest phenomena. It is less about moving or creating the physical object on which you should focus and more about creating the state of mind in which matter can come into form. The astral realm, the realm of ecto-plasm, is the plane that separates the mental plane from the physical plane. In the mind we see things as symbolic. On the physical plane we see things as material. In the astral realm, we see physical objects begin to both dematerialize and rematerialize. The same thing that happens in trance is what happens when you dream. We send ourselves out into the astral while our conscious minds are asleep. Allow your conscious mind to sleep as you work. Again, frequent deep meditations are your most valued resource.

House 3—Khepera. It takes superhuman energy to create physical phenomena. A dung beetle has a superhuman strength just to keep pushing something that is ten times its size into form. If you are launching a big project, combine energies with those in your community to get the ball rolling. This house corresponds to the people closest to you (like-minded brothers and sisters) and to the patterns of communication in which you are engaged. Sitting in a circle will keep the ball rolling so to speak. The internet is not necessarily the way to generate the energy you want, although it is an energy wave form. However, it is not reliable. The dung beetle says have your "crap detector" on. There may be too much background interference.

House 4—Heru. This desire of yours to manifest spiritual work into physical form lies rooted in the alchemical theories of the Renaissance, which of course derived from Egypt. Heru indicates that you are on a hero's journey; yet you must begin with a solid foundation. Create a space in your home where you can do the work. Ritually prepare the room for your work and dedicate it to nothing but your express purpose. That's why mediums built physical cabinets as dedicated containers for energy. Find out what the physical mediums of old used in their séance rooms, and set up your environment similarly. Do you know how to use your trumpet, crystals, gemstones, holy water, and candles? Are you as well-connected to your spirit guides as Horus was connected to his father Osiris? He spent years in the astral state being trained by Osiris to do his work. Is your physical body, your home to Spirit, in condition that's good enough to create the manifestations you desire?

House 5—Arit. Interestingly, in the house of what we normally consider "creative fun" you have one of the more difficult cards. However, this is the perfect card for one who now engages in the serious work of creation that also falls in this house. Understand, first of all, this work is neither a game nor entertainment. We enter it with intention. Why are you trying to manifest physical phenomena? Is it idle curiosity, or to contact the spirit world and demonstrate that consciousness creates reality? Attaining such proof is a harsh test. It's hard on the body. It requires huge reserves of energy. Like walking through fire, it has its risks. You must be fully protected, grounded, and connected with your spirit guides. When you open that door, you have to be ready to deal with the energies coming through. More than that, you will be criticized by those on the outside who accuse you of fraud, of lying, or stretching the truth.

Walking through fire means accepting the risk of being burned. You have to have a pretty good reason to walk through fire.

House 6—Nut. The goddess bends over the Earth and embraces it. The stars in the belly of the sky mother are all the souls that ever were or will be. This position reminds you that your meditations and Spiritualist practices must become a daily, or nightly, work to expand the mind and consciousness so that it fills with possibilities. Your work requires a huge expansion of energy and a devotion to it that is like the full-time, all-consuming devotion of a mother to her child. This daily devotion changes our routines and habits. To grow this child of your desire into a fully realized being, daily mental expansion and commitment are required. At the end of this work, which occurs over time and with great outpourings of energy, you will be totally changed.

House 7—Per-à. You open the door. You close the door. Thus begins a relationship or partnership with another. It is important that you create a partnership with one whose work ethic is close to your own. Do not change partners with whom you are working. It's a bit like finding the right marriage partner. You want to work with someone who shares your creative vision and is not just throwing their energy around willy-nilly as a dalliance. You open the door to another person's energy, and when you find that it works with yours, close the door and work with only that individual. That said, also pay attention to who in your environment is coming and going around the field of energy in which you are working. It's pretty hard to sit still and meditate with intention while there are others in the house playing with the dog or doing dishes. The same is true with the spirit guide with whom you work. Is the energy of that guide compatible with yours? Is it long-standing? Do not try this guide first, then that one, as if you were trying on hats. This relationship must work on a deep, sustained level.

House 8—Osiris. We enter the house of mystery. Recall the story of Osiris and Atum, seated in the underworld, the hidden world, the realm of the subconscious. They are co-creators working in tandem to create a visible world that has its roots in the invisible. Here in total darkness nothing seems to be happening, yet everything is happening. A dark room aids in seeing the gathering ectoplasmic energy. Study the metaphysical principles that are eternal principles through which the world comes into being. If physical phenomena occurred in the past, they can occur again. Energy cannot be destroyed. It simply reshapes into something else. That means that sometimes things will disappear and rematerialize. Atum points to the energy of dematerialization and rematerialization. Osiris is the changing form that comes in and out of being.

House 9—Shen. Metaphysical protection is required both inside a circle and around the room in which you are working. This highlights what was said in House 3 about the need to be vigilant. All spiritual work must be done in a true circle, for it is like a focal lens of energy. Your spirit people are also sitting in a group with you. Be sure you are including their group in yours. Whatever you do, don't talk about your spiritual practice to those outside your group. If you are working from a distance, be sure that your computer settings enable your intention to have your group be a closed one.

House 10—Hotep. If you are looking for accolades, stop. If you are wanting to bring people together for a common goal, proceed. Think deeply about why you are trying to materialize physical objects. The point of the work is transubstantiation. Think about Communion Mass in which bread and wine are transubstantiated into the body and blood of Christ. Are they actually? The reality is that what is being created in the Communion rite is the community itself. Attention should be on changing ourselves, the shift in our consciousness, attaining the peace that passes understanding. At Abusir a huge alabaster stone carved in the hieroglyphic shape of hotep offers peace in all four directions. Its crystal structure holds the memory of every offering made at that altar. When activated through ritual, it becomes a gigantic magical peace machine for planetary healing. If you can create physical phenomena, then also use the energy you have generated to shift world consciousness, to feed the hungry, uplift the poor in Spirit, and to bring together in harmony those disharmonious aspects of the local and the world community.

House 11—Manu. You are crossing the great divides in race, religion, and culture all over the planet. This has to do with ferrying information—and sometimes objects—over distances of time and space, and over longer distances between the spirit plane and the physical plane. Manu speaks to ferrying the boat in the neterworld, carrying souls across. Consider the materialization of spirit guides and protectors from another realm as forms that can be ferried across the great waters for the purposes of healing, rather than simply moving objects through the dimensions. As with any spirit work, test the spirit to see whether it is appropriate to ferry that energy into the physical or spirit world.

House 12—Benben. The physical container houses the spirit, which is eternal being. Inside the Great Pyramid lies a granite sarcophagus, which becomes a spirit container in which waves of surging energies converge to transmute form. The granite sarcophagus in the King's Chamber is an initiation chamber. Our bodies are also physical containers for spirit. What your work is really about is undergoing an initiation for a spiritual purpose. Every initiation is cloaked in secrecy. Rites of passage precede initiation. There is a reason the twelfth house is called the house of secrets, the unconscious, and mystery. Deep transformation is taking place, which defies articulation. What happened inside the pyramid was not intended to be discussed publicly. Yet the pyramid itself was a structure that attests to the profound and enormous impact that the studies and work in metaphysics has on the physical world. Prepare to be changed at a fundamental level. Benben says this is deep transformative work, but warns you to be very careful about what you do and how you do it, so that you do not get incinerated in the process.

East—Waz. Part of your desire to attain this form of mediumship is because you believe it will confer some level of mastery that others can perceive. That is one reason to do it. If what you are doing aims to develop your mediumship to gain a deeper understanding of your capacities as a spiritual person, then by all means do it. But remember how Aaron threw down his rod and it became a serpent, then pharaoh's sorcerers turned their rods into serpents? This was a spiritual competition. Is that why you are doing it? Of course, Aaron's serpent swallowed the other serpents. Do you have true spiritual power, and does it matter if anyone really believes you?

West—Heh. If you pursue this project you desire, you must be in it for the long haul. If the point is to shift consciousness, then there is no changing your mind about changing your mind! We create reality both past and future, but all we have is the now. You must commit to the present. The spiritual development you seek is always part of the present moment in which you are living.

North—Akh. In your private connections with the ancestors and the masters, you work with the energy of the phoenix, the co-creative mind, the highest intelligence possible. This is the essence of alchemical transformation. Throughout history similar groups have worked in this way—the Brotherhood of Light, the Theosophists, the Golden Dawn, the Society of Inner Light, and others. Study daily to attain the highest understanding of the work that you can. Read Clifford Bias, Annie Besant, Manly Hall, as well as Gurdjieff, Ouspensky, and ancient sacred texts. Expand your understanding. Keep burning toward the light.

South—Atum. To the outer world it may look like nothing is going on. That's fine. Keep it that way. The true work of Spirit is the powerful work of the light hidden in plain sight. Atum represents the metaphysician's four powers: to know, to will, to dare, and to keep silent. It has been shown that dispersion of matter in the universe resembles a giant quill feather. The invisible breath of God is what moves each rib of the feather and keeps it in motion. The ordinary eye doesn't see that. Always stay open to possibilities you've yet to imagine. It is not up to you to determine the final form that your mediumship takes. It is up to the Divine. Atum created out of his desire for communion with another like him. Be that spiritual partner Atum seeks. Sometimes that looks like emptiness, because it takes an empty glass to hold what will fill it. Live beyond explicit expectation.

Center—Re. Fundamentally, your question is about understanding light as consciousness itself. Through our various forms of consciousness (that is, supraconsciousness, subconsciousness, and ordinary attentive consciousness), we can remain both open and empty. All potential manifestations of light occur in this way. Form is a concentration of energy into shape. Thought manifestation is a result of the concentration of mental energy in order to materialize. Truly we are thoughts in the mind of God. We are the forms of divine thought. We are made of light, co-creating and playing with the energy of light in the world. Your daily life is already a manifestation of thought and form.

THE DJED PILLAR OR TREE OF LIFE SPREAD

The Djed Pillar (also called the Tree of Life) refers to the tamarisk tree, wooden column, or coffin in which the god Osiris was encased. Divine beings of many traditions live within or upon the Tree of Life. The Yggdrasil, an immense mythical tree on which the Norse god Odin hung himself, was said to connect the Nine Worlds. The physical life of Jesus ended on a wooden cross. In the ancient Egyptian myth Osiris was trapped in a coffin that was enclosed inside a tamarisk tree. This tree was cut down and became the supporting column for a residence built by King Malcander and Queen Astarte after the coffin had floated out of Egypt and landed on the shores of Byblos.

The Djed Pillar symbol helps us to see the process of spirit manifestation. Energy moves up and down the pillar through the four worlds or layers of embodiment: The upper plane of Spirit contains three spheres that form a triangle pointing up toward the crown of the tree. The second mental plane is represented by three spheres that form a downward triangle. The astral plane, or emotional realm of existence, is likewise

Pharaoh Seti I celebrates the festival of Raising the Djed,
which is depicted here in Abydos. The djed festival, also known as
the heb sed, celebrated the rites of renewal of the pharaoh's vitality
and dates as far back as the early Old Kingdom. Here, the djed
clearly shows the four layers of existence that are likewise depicted
on the Qabalistic Tree of Life.

represented by three spheres whose triangle points downward. Finally,
the physical world in which humans live and in which the Tree of Life
is rooted is a single sphere that, like the trunk of a tree, holds the whole
Tree of Life in place.

Energy moving up and down the Tree of Life is analogous to angels ascending and descending the ladder as they did in Jacob's dream. Our manifest world is made by the divine spark flowing down from the highest spiritual dimension, crossing the veil into the mental realm, moving through the emotional or astral realm, and entering into physical form. In Qabalah the energy known as the lightning flash demonstrates the pattern that we use to create our lives, moving from the spirit realm into manifestation in the physical realm. Conversely when we pass from this earthly plane into Spirit, our consciousness moves up through the emotional/astral realm (where it also goes in our dreams). It continues on through the mental realm of thought and will before it then moves into the spiritual world. Our desires, thoughts, and actions exit with us.

Further study of the mystical teachings of the Hebrew text known as the Kabbalah (or the non-Jewish mystical Qabalah) can deepen your understanding of how to interpret this hieroglyphic layout. The further you go with that study, the more you will get out of this layout. The Jews, despite their historic differences with the Egyptians, lived in Egypt for many centuries. Moses was received into the mystery initiations and trained with priests in their temples. There are many things that the Jewish people learned from the Egyptians, and some of that information now resides in their Kabbalah. This is a blessing, for in many cases the ancient Egyptian wisdom became lost after the burning of the libraries in the Christian and Muslim eras.

Each circle on the Tree of Life represents a jewel or sephira operative on one of the four planes of existence. The Qabalists see all of the sephiroth together as aspects of the Divine Creator and the spiritual plane as a divine, archetypal world called Atziluth or the World of Emanations. The mental plane called Briah is a creative world, or the World of Schema. Yetzirah, what we deem the astral or emotional plane, is seen as the World of Formation and of the angels. These upper planes culminate in the physical world, the World of Matter and Action, which the Qabalists call Assiah. I have explored the Egyptian connections to each sephira in the Tree of Life, comparing them to the

Egyptian spiritual bodies. (For more information on this, see part 2, "The Bodies of Light," in my book *Dreams of Isis*.)

The Meaning of the Sephiroth

1. **Highest Ideal, Inspiration.** Spirit lives here; the ego cannot accomplish anything at this sephira as this is God's territory. What lies at the source of the situation appears here. The meaning of an event, a life, a path is revealed. Purpose as it flows from the divine hand will answer any question. How do we resolve a dilemma? This is the best possible outcome.

2. **Wisdom and Creative Outpouring.** An outpouring of creative energy from the world of spirit enters the picture. The active, invigorating principle of Spirit and its desire for life appears. Wisdom, it is said, is the ability to see something from God's point of view. Desire enters—desire strong enough to create a world, but as yet without object. The Qabalah would define this as a yod, or god seed.

3. **Understanding and Form.** The inner knowing and understanding of life can reveal the true basic structure of a thing. Here is where we first encounter limitation and boundaries that we will experience in the world of form. Also we are shown how we create a vessel for creative outflow. No essence can be contained without some form. How we come to terms with these limitations (lovingly) becomes who we are.

4. **Thoughts and Virtues.** Proverbs 23:7 summarizes the co-creative power of thought: "As a man thinketh, so is he in his heart." Here we find the ways in which we can arrange our thinking rightly to gain recognition and control over our lives. Here our resources appear, as do human helpers and spiritual assistance. These opportunities and gifts flow when we are in flow.

5. **Will and Determination.** What prevents us from attaining our desires? Where do we meet our challenges and conflicts, and how must we readjust to these obstacles and frustrations? How do we handle anger, aggression, and belligerent opposition? The answer to

all of these shows us how we are as leaders. Handling these habitual frustrations through the proper use of will strengthens us.

6. **Self (Tipareth).** How others see you falls here. The central issue, your health, and your purpose are all reflected here in this mirror of the Tree of Life. It is the central point of the pillar, the heart of the matter. This position reflects the pivot, or point of balance, between our spiritual selves (higher mind and god seed) and our lower natures (desires, emotions, and the physical world). The degree to which we are willing to sacrifice to accomplish our goals falls here.

7. **Artistic Higher Self (Netzach).** Whom you love and what you gravitate toward instinctually finds expression here, as well as where you find your inspiration and the people with whom you are in relationship. One's pleasure-seeking and sensual nature appears in this sephira, as well as one's harmonic responses to beauty.

8. **Creator, Designer, and Scientist (Hod).** Sometimes this is called splendor. It is the realm of communications and creation. The magician and sorcerer alike inhabit this world. Knowledge of truth or falsehood is expressed here through symbol and music. Our moods, visions, fantasies, and clairvoyance all reside in this sephira. Here is where we fall into a trap of succumbing to our perceptions and impressions, rather than seeing and communicating with clarity and love. We make our plans by using accurate perception and correct ambition.

9. **Psychic Self (Yesod).** Here is the mirror that reflects the above and below. How accurate that image is depends upon how clean the mirror is. Our emotions and desires often cloud our vision, creating what Alice Bailey termed *glamour*. But the imagination lies here as well, and dreams and illusions. Sometimes one's past lives show up here as influences.

10. **Physical Self (Malkuth).** At this point, whatever plan you have worked on comes into form. Who you are becomes a reality based on all the thoughts, feelings, and consciousness that preceded it. Here is the physical body, one's daily life and habits that have created the situation, or are the outcome.

The Djed Pillar Readings offer ways to see the resonance that a situation has on all four planes. It speaks to how the situation began or how it is evolving, as well as what is shifting. In some ways reading a Djed Pillar is similar to what one sees in the aura of Kirlian photography. The energies manifesting on the emotional and physical planes lie closer to the individual, while what is taking shape in the spiritual and mental planes is further out in time. To determine how a project will manifest—that project being either your life at the current time or something you are working on bringing into manifestation such as a book—begin to lay out the hieroglyphs from the top sephiroth in the spiritual plane or plane of conception. You will simply shuffle and pull ten cards, one at a time.

There are two ways to lay out the cards for this type of reading. As in the figure on the facing page, you can start at the top with number 1 and work downward from there, as just mentioned. In this case, you are consulting the Tree of Life in order to foresee what might transpire in the future around a particular issue or issues.

Or you can read this spread from the bottom up, starting with the number 10 at the bottom and working upward to number 1 at the top. When reading from the bottom up, one can glean an understanding of what is happening now and how its origin began in the spirit world and manifested in thought and deed. This is a good way to try to understand how the current situation we are experiencing in our lives derived from our feelings and seed thoughts, which is a great way to explore karmic action.

In brief, to see the past and/or what is happening now, read from the bottom up; to see the future, read from the top down.

Pulling additional glyph cards may clarify issues of timing that are often part of a question. The querent might wish to know *when* something will happen. The djed has a long base like a tree trunk. In this, the roots of the tree connect it to the foundation in the past, while the furthest branches at the crown of the tree higher up represent the more distant future.

Draw three cards together to represent the emotional triad of the

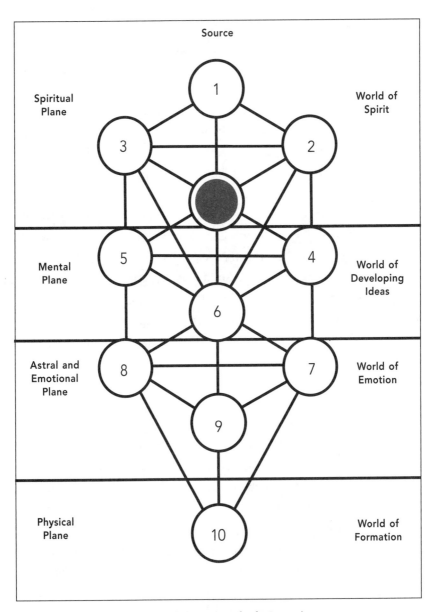

Djed Pillar or Tree of Life Spread

astral plane. These represent how one's *feelings* are contributing to the growth of the tree, while the next triad in the mental plane shows the more immediate future based upon our *thoughts*. This might show how one's thinking can shift the situation as well. Again, the upper triad in the spiritual plane is the more distant future and the likely result based on the current moment. Recognize that may change if emotions and thoughts change. Because of this, it makes more sense, when doing a Djed Pillar Reading, to read from the bottom up if you want to see these alternatives.

There is a point in the Tree of Life where the intersection between the mental and spiritual worlds appears. It is called the *Da'at*. Qabalist Mary Greer says of Da'at, the crown of the Tree of Life, "It is the inner, hidden knowledge of the potential of your highest self."[1] It can be used in Djed Pillar Readings after the other ten cards have been interpreted and fully explored. Greer warns, however, that this knowledge cannot be used for personal gain or ego gratification. This is about how your soul wants you to use the information for its own development.

One might ask the question: So how do I integrate all of the aspects of this reading at this time? Fan out the remaining cards after the reading, then select one card randomly. The meanings associated with that card will reflect the synthesis of all of the aspects of the reading.

The Question

The querent had recently completed an associate degree in graphic design. Hoping for a new opportunity, she left a job that was physically demanding and not in alignment with her desires. She moved out of state and temporarily into a family member's home, but after six months still had not found the right new job and living situation. She was again working a temporary job not in her field and receiving minimum wage. Rather than finding the change she had hoped for, she had less money and less independence than before. There seemed to be little opportunity where she now lived and she was becoming increasingly depressed. She wondered what the future held at the present time and what she should do to manifest a job and a life more in alignment with her desires. The querent was not well-versed in the ideas of thought manifestation, so, in this case, I chose to read the cards for her from the bottom of the Djed Pillar up. I hoped that would help her to discern how she got where she was, which might illuminate what she could do to reverse the situation she was now in.

The Reading

10. **Physical Self—Dser.** The current situation appears stagnant. A vast empty landscape lies before you, behind you, and all around. You seem to be following illusions and chimera. This indeed is a time of test and trial. You have a difficult time determining what is real and what is not. What you think you are seeing is not accurate. Let go of your fantasies. The emptiness of the desert becomes an opportunity for you to enter a vision quest. One thing is certain: You cannot stay in this desert. You have to do something. You must move out of this stagnation in order to survive. In your deep meditations you may encounter a true helping hand if you let go of having things happen your way—and only your way. Let God step in.

9. **Psychic Self, Imagination, Glamour—Kheper.** Transformation and creativity are a part of your psychic self. The dung beetle lays its eggs in a pile of manure, but soon enough the dung ball cracks open and a golden-winged beetle flies out. You do have the capacity to take a situation that is not to your liking and turn it into something useful. First you have to know where the crap is and how to use it. Something true and golden lies inherent in the illusion you now carry. Kheper may help you sort out illusions and escapist fantasies and see what you need to do to create the change you want. Identify the negative state of your current situation by asking yourself: What is not working? What is the lesson I gain from being mired in the muck? How can I turn a negative into a positive? Really get into your journal and come up with some truthful, soul-searching answers. This transformation will take time, but if you do your part, the situation will indeed transform.

8. **Designer or Creator Self—Nu.** Nu represents the creative chaos before form. You can tell things are changing, and yet you feel yourself going in circles, not yet sure of what is taking shape, almost as if you were caught in an eddy. You try to feel your way out of the chaos, but you don't know which way to turn because everything keeps shifting. Rest assured, a new life is coming. You must let it flow toward you and accept it, rather than put things off until later.

The fear you feel around not knowing who, where, or what to do actually is creating the chaos. Don't fret. Begin to craft your ultimate goal. Allow what you thought you wanted to shift as well.

7. **Artistic Higher Self—Sopdet.** Working with Isis as the star goddess Sopdet can help you access a higher creative vision than you have right now. It seems as if this vision has been searching for you, even shining a spotlight on you, but you have had a hard time seeing it. The answer to your quest can be found right under your nose, but you aren't aware of it yet. You are brilliantly creative; it's just hard to see that truth about ourselves sometimes. Where is your joy? Work with that energy. Ask yourself, "How do I create a life that will bring me more into other people's awareness, and how should I handle myself when the light shines on me?" Begin now to lay out your plans, creating a vision that is attainable. By the time July rolls around and Sirius is rising in the sky again, you will have attained your goal.

6. **Self and Heart's Desires—Atum.** Basically you are stuck in hiding mode. Come out of your shell and recognize the power that you do have. Infinite potential is here, waiting for you to decide. You could create any life you want. You have talent and vision, but self-doubt keeps you in a rut. Atum is the beginning and the end—the exploding big bang as well as the universe collapsing inside a black hole. Your life is what you make of it. You can work with or waste your potential. Are you sending your energy outward, or are you folding back in on yourself? Like Ptah, Atum speaks the world and the light into being. Hear yourself saying what you want.

5. **Willpower and Determination—Ib.** Steve Jobs believed that "The only way to do great work is to love what you do. If you haven't found it yet, keep looking." Commit your will to attaining your goal and nothing can stop you—except what you think. If your thoughts say, *Oh, I'm not good enough,* or *I don't want to work that hard,* or *I don't want anyone to tell me what to do,* that is willfulness holding you back. Determination means putting your heart and soul into what you want, going for it, and staying the course because, ultimately, you love what you do. Money is not the motivation; money

is the outcome. A love of the work and living the life you deserve must come first.

4. **Thoughts and Virtues—Heka.** Make up your mind. That's it. The mental vibration is what makes our lives happen. Thoughts are things. Know this as a fact and keep this idea in mind. Every day do something toward manifesting your goal. If it helps to put a little magic affirmation in your wallet alongside of your money, then do that. Write down your goals and every full moon examine them again. Are you getting closer to your vision? How can you bring more magic into your life? Know what you want, be willing to make it happen no matter the odds, then go about your business knowing that the universe and Spirit have got your back.

3. **Creative Form—Akhet.** A naturally creative person, you live closest to your spiritual self when you give yourself permission to make beautiful things. You have a vivid imagination. Make sure you are using that imagination wisely. Allow yourself to shine at the proper times. Akhet indicates that creation is cyclical. Sometimes the sun is rising; sometimes it's setting. The wisest use of your downtime is to spend it gestating an idea, letting it grow a little more daily. You won't see immediate results, but like the return of the sun after midwinter, you will soon begin to feel the growth within, moving closer to your goal, your personal summer solstice. Have patience and use the time you have available wisely. Your aim won't be immediately apparent to others, but don't stop working your own kind of magic to make it happen. Feed and nurture your vision every day. Don't despair because you can't see the outcome just yet. It is coming. The most important thing you can do is create a container for the form to fill.

2. **Creative Power—Seshet.** The goddess of scribes, artists, and librarians lends her power to you now. This is a good omen for a graphic designer, visual artist, or writer. Seshet is your guiding star. She operates in similar ways to the artistic Greek muses and to the Seven Hathors, the fairy godmothers of ancient Egypt. Seshet tells you that you are destined to do the work you long to do. Keep reaching for it. Do not let the material concerns of the world trouble

you. Find a form in which you can put all of your creative energy.

1. **Highest Ideal and Inspiration—Ast.** The goddess Isis, who overcame loss, stagnation, and isolation, became the most beloved goddess of all Egypt. She represents any woman who has ever had a challenge to overcome, who has felt that she had to go it alone at times, and at other times had to rely on the aid of her sisters and the advice of the neteru. She managed to get what she wanted by never giving up. Isis is your guide. She will help you succeed in any challenging situation. Find a role model, a woman who is older than you, perhaps, who works in the field you wish to work in. Ask her advice on attaining your vision. Isis sends you assurances that you can find your independence, nurture your creativity, and attain your dream.

THE SPHINX READING

What walks on four legs at dawn, two legs at noon, and three legs at eventide?

THE RIDDLE OF THE SPHINX

The answer to the riddle of the sphinx that's given most often is "man." As we have mentioned earlier, man begins life as an infant crawling, then spends the majority of his life walking upright, but grows old and walks with a cane in the end. A more in-depth answer would say that the riddle actually is about understanding the concepts of time and fate.

In *Oedipus Rex* by Sophocles the adult Oedipus leaves home in order to spare those he believes are his family from their predestined fates. On the road he encounters a charioteer and argues with him about who has the right-of-way. The argument ends when Oedipus slays the man.

Next, on his way to Thebes, Oedipus comes upon the sphinx who controls the city. The road to Thebes, ancient Luxor, is lined with an avenue of sphinxes, many of which are ram-headed rather than lion-headed like the famous one in Giza. There are different sphinxes in Egypt. The lion-headed female, which this myth refers to, may be the goddess Mut or Sekhmet. In the story, the sphinx stops all travelers.

They must correctly answer its riddle. Those with incorrect answers are gobbled up by the sphinx. Now this part of the story refers to Ammit, a creature of one's destiny in the underworld who is part lion, crocodile, and hippopotamus. She gobbles the heart if it weighs too heavily on the scales of truth. Killing someone in a road rage argument, obviously, would be some bad and weighty karma.

The sphinx recites its riddle (on facing page). Oedipus answers correctly "man." His answer frees the city from the domination of the sphinx, who throws herself off a cliff. Yet the story is not over. Once in Thebes, the heroic Oedipus marries the queen and is given the dead king's throne. Of course, we know how that story ends: the man Oedipus killed on the road was his father and the queen he marries is his mother.

The ancient Egyptian myth based on that same riddle speaks to the triple aspect of the sun god Kheper-Ra-Atum. As Khepera, the dung beetle crawls over the horizon on four legs, pushing the sun above the horizon ahead of it. It walks upright in full strength as Ra at midday. As the weakening setting sun, Atum, whose name means "completion," walks with a cane in the evening. Such is the fate of all humankind—past (Khepera), present (Ra), and future (Atum). Ra, of course, has the most lasting influence. All that we can control is what we do in the present, which determines our future. If we wish to know why the present is so difficult, we must look upon what we have done in the past.

Another tale, this one about the Sphinx at Giza, describes a frustrated young prince named Tuthmosis, hunting in the sandy western hills outside Heliopolis one hot day. Wondering what he must do to claim his rightful place as pharaoh, and when this would happen, the prince falls asleep in the shadow under the rocky chin of the Sphinx. He dreamt that the giant statue told him that he (the Sphinx) would make the young prince a pharaoh if he cleared the centuries of accumulated sand from around its neck. Naturally, this prince did this. When his elder brother was ousted as crown prince, Tuthmosis IV became pharaoh, succeeding his father Amenhotep II. The dream stele he erected between the paws of the Sphinx in Giza recounts the story of his prophetic slumber.

Between the paws of the Sphinx, Tuthmosis IV erected an epigraphic stele documenting a dream that foreshadowed his kingship in 1401 BCE. Edgar Cayce prophesized that one day the Hall of Records established in the time of Imhotep (circa 2700 BCE) would be found beneath the Sphinx.

Another interesting fact about the Sphinx is that it faces due east. At the spring equinox, the rising sun shines directly between its paws. All this makes a Sphinx Reading the perfect three-card layout for a past, present, and future determination. The reading is not intended to answer questions that pertain to the long-term. However, for short-term questions which, like a day, have a clear beginning, middle, and end, it's ideal.

Ask a process question, such as "How will my job interview go?" Then shuffle the cards well. Fan them out and randomly pick from the deck three cards to represent the beginning (past), middle (present), and end (future). *Always* pay close attention to a card that flies out of the deck "by accident" while shuffling because often it is very significant in that its meaning may really speak to the situation at hand. Also, if this happens, it may indicate you are finished shuffling and you can use that card for the first card.

Another way to read with three cards is to designate the cards as desire, dilemma (or situation now), and outcome. This will tell you

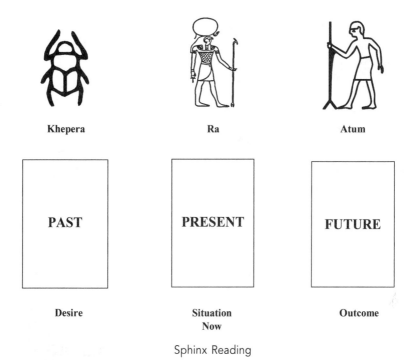

| Khepera | Ra | Atum |

| PAST | PRESENT | FUTURE |

| Desire | Situation Now | Outcome |

Sphinx Reading

about the thing that you want to accomplish, what stands in the way, and what you should do for a beneficial outcome.

The Question

In this case the querent was an older woman who had long ago given up on the dream of ever attaining her doctorate. She devoted her time to raising her daughter and working a job. The unfinished education, which she had always wanted, still gnawed at her. Now her daughter had grown and things had changed. An opportunity for her to complete her education had arisen. She wondered if she was too old, if it was even necessary or just a frivolous dream. She began the program but had paused after some struggles to ask if she would complete her dissertation within the next year as she hoped.

The Reading

The Past—Anpu. The way has been opened for you. The dissertation that once seemed so out of reach has now come into view. You have already set out on this new path and are feeling your way through it, moving cautiously but deliberately. Your inner guidance urges you to proceed.

The Present—Het. At present you feel you might have bitten off more than you can chew. Het reminds you that this kind of work is a trial by fire. There are many hoops through which to jump, many obstacles, and many tests now. You worry that there is not enough time to complete the work on schedule. You wonder if people are expecting you to fail, even setting up roadblocks. This is part of the trial by fire. Even if there are delays, the final product is a refinement, a smelting of gold. It may take a little longer, but just keep going.

The Future—Ib. While some delays do arise, based on how you negotiate the fire altar, ultimately you attain your goal. It will be to your heart's satisfaction. You gain that which you seek.

THE CONVERSATIONAL READING

Sometimes having a simple conversation with the cards is most effective. This can be a variation on the Sphinx Reading. Just ask, "What should I do about a particular situation?" then draw three cards. You can designate them as past, present, and future as we previously did. Or you might create a kind of sentence structure from them consisting of a noun, verb, and object. So and so (noun) does (verb), and this happens (object). It is entirely possible to keep drawing three cards as noun, verb, object, as if you were building sentences until you have uncovered a paragraph of information. Yet a third way of having a conversation is with a partner, where one of you draws three and the other person draws three in reply. This endlessly fun process also sparks very deep conversations.

The Question

I used this method recently when I had a meeting with some board members about how to move forward with developing a program where I teach. My mentor had recently passed away and I wondered, "What should I become aware of with regard to this upcoming meeting?" The matter in question as I did this reading had to do with the intellectual legacy of my mentor.

The Reading

While shuffling the cards, the khat card flew out. Because one of the images that sometimes appears on that particular khat card is a mummy lying on a lion bier, it indicated to me that the message I was about to receive was from someone who had died. I interpreted that flying card to mean that the person had not been dead long. Khat is the corpse itself around which the spirit is still moving. When the soul begins to move farther into the spirit world, it becomes represented by a khaibit. Later, it may appear as a ba soul, which is more well-adjusted to the spirit world.

Having the khat card fly out from the deck (in addition to having the khaibit drawn, as we will see below) certainly clued me in to this obviously being an answer from my mentor, Rev. A. Win Srogi. He had died only three months previously. Spirit also drew my eye to the fish on the khat card, suggesting that if I thought something was "fishy," I needed to keep my eye on the situation.

The three conversation cards were: ib, khaibit, benben. The interpretation is as follows: Your heart (ib) is pure and you weigh things in the balance. Keep yourself on an even keel. An individual who is alive and well in spirit form will assist you (khaibit). This individual may even be your mentor who is still close to this earth plane and has unfinished business. In the end, the structure that is in question (benben) has been crafted over time to withstand the test of time. It may appear to go up in flames, but in truth it will return slightly changed but still vitally important in its influence. The legacy will not be easily destroyed.

THE DAILY
NUMEROLOGY READING

This is a one-card reading that can be used for any day based upon your current numerology for the day and year. Try this technique for a week.

Each number will be unique and you may find a kind of resonance in the patterning.

✦ First find your life path number by adding the month and day of your birth.

   Example: September 24 becomes 9 + 2 + 4 = 33 and reduce it to a single digit, as follows: 3 + 3 = 6.

✦ Now add the current year (not your birth year) to the life path to find your personal year.

   Example: 2 + 0 + 1 + 8 = 11 and reduce to a single digit: 1 + 1 = 2; and 6 + 2 = 8.

✦ To figure out the number of your current calendar day, add the month and day to your personal year.

   Example: April 14 becomes 4 + 1 + 4 = 9 and 9 + 8 = 17 or 1 + 7 = 8.

✦ Now pull one card to determine your message for the day and read the numbered oracle.

The Reading

On April 14 in my personal year 8, I drew the card Anpu. When I looked at the meaning for 8 Anpu, it seemed to be saying to me that I was to find a precious resource buried in my hidey-hole. Because I am in an 8 personal year, I am in a manifestation phase, and Anpu suggested that I might need to dig a little deeper into a situation.

It turned out that a few weeks before I drew that card, I had run into an old friend who suggested that I might have unclaimed funds in the treasurer's office in a state where I no longer lived. I forgot about her advice, but one day—after a little bit of digging—I was able to confirm that this was true. I sent off my request for unclaimed money and received the check in a couple of weeks.

Thank you, Elaine and Anubis!

THE ENNEAD (JOURNEY) READING

In Heliopolis, the cult city of the sun god Ra, nine primary gods and goddesses rode in the solar boat at the beginning of time. Called the Great Ennead, they were deemed the nine most important deities in all of Egypt. Each of these has been called, by the Egyptians themselves, simply aspects of the one god Amen. One might think of them as the parts of Amen that split off from the One. A Hymn to Amen in chapter 90 of the Leiden Papyrus says: "The Ennead combined is your body. Every god joined in your body is your image. You emerged first. You inaugurated from the start, Amen, whose name is hidden from the gods."[2]

The Great Ennead of Heliopolis were the sun god Ra (Amen); his children Shu, the air, and Tef-Nut, the moisture; their children Geb, the Earth, and Nut, the celestial heavens above; and their children who first inhabited Egypt: Asar (Osiris), Ast (Isis), Set (Seth), and Neb-Het (Nephthys). Horus the Elder is not counted in this grouping except as he appears as the earthly manifestation of the solar god Ra himself.

The Ennead rose to importance in the Old Kingdom and remained so for thousands of years, well into the Greco-Roman era. The Ennead is a permanent structure, a foundation, and a complete picture of the self. This particular reading can be used to determine your life destiny as the light being (Ra) riding in the solar boat. Think of your body as the vehicle of your movement throughout your life. The Ennead Reading does not tell you what events will happen or when, but points to the reasons you were born, your karma in this life, and the likely experiences you have based on certain qualities of being.

Because the energy of these neteru ride in the solar boat, sailing across the sky from east to west, and then throughout the underworld, sailing through the stars, this layout additionally seems well-suited to anyone contemplating the taking of a particular voyage. Again, it does not speak in sequences of events, but rather of the qualities of how an event might be experienced. The journey you wish to explore may be a physical one or it may be metaphoric. I often use this layout to give me some idea of what lies ahead whenever I take a trip to Egypt.

The accompanying layout depicts the nine energies that ride in the boat of Ra. Ra defines the purpose; Shu, the inspiration; Tef-Nut, the willpower needed; Geb, the work itself; and Nut, the birthing of the journey. Asar (Osiris) defines the cultivating; Ast (Isis), the giving; Set (Seth), the limitations; and Neb-Het (Nephthys), the hidden aspect.

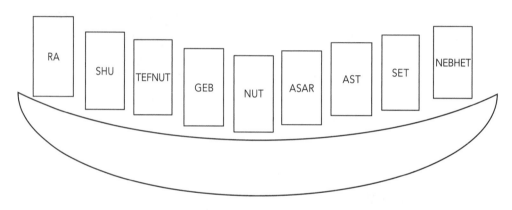

Ennead Journey Reading

The Question

A teacher had for some time contemplated the establishment of an Egyptian mystery school, which would educate and ordain priests and priestesses. The work was inspired along the lines of other orders similar to the Temple of Isis in California and the Fellowship of Isis in Ireland. She wondered how it might be to become the "captain of one's own boat." To create such a group, who might join this crew of seminary teachers? Specifically what qualities were needed on its operating board?

When I drew the cards for this reading, the first one I drew was Se-Sheshet. The second one was Wadjet, and so on and so forth.

The Reading

RA (AMRN)—Se-Sheshet. Called to return to the lost wisdom of the Library of Alexandria in a metaphysical rather than academic way, it may be necessary to shake things up, to teach the mysteries differently than they have been taught in the past. All the while, one must curb the rebel within, but certainly it is time for the work to begin. The rattling wake-up call has begun.

SHU—Wadjet. In the seat of inspiration wadjet's visionary, kundalini energy opens the third eye and a new vision emerges. The work has begun and will continue to evolve through a meditation. Working in partnership with another can bring ideas into form.

TEFNUT—Seshet. Seshet says pay attention to recordkeeping, contracts, bylaws, and any legal paperwork that needs to come together and be filed. Whoever is the secretary will perform the yeoman's job. Getting the details of the paperwork right matters, so that what is desired can be easily accomplished without having to redo. That requires a bit of research, studying, and modeling one's work on the records of similar groups. Be joyful about the work because when Seshet appears, the work is divinely ordained by the Lady herself.

GEB—Akhet. Geb lays a golden egg. This is big work—raising personal and planetary consciousness. This high magic of priests and priestesses needs a practical, down-to-earth form. Fundamental lessons should be offered in pastoral care, counseling, daily services, and temple rites, sacred calendar, astrology, liturgical music and dance, and so on. The enlightenment of all is the work of the dawning new age. Healing Earth itself is a part of this magical endeavor.

NUT—Ast. Isis appears in the position of Nut. She is the reason for and the process through which this work manifests. The Goddess herself asked for it to be done. Invoke her at every meeting. Ask "How does what is being taught empower women, and communities, and children? For those are Isis's domains as Great Mother. The power of feminine wisdom is on the rise and women are moving into seats of power. Isis no longer appears as the throne simply to confer power to a son or husband. Isis works for the common good, overseeing the cultivation of consciousness and planting the star seeds of illumination as Nut. The Goddess indeed is coming to the fore of our consciousness.

ASR (OSIRIS)—Ren. Learning the Book of the Dead and all the books of the afterlife becomes important as we assist souls in transition, which will be one of the most important aspects of this priesthood. If one trains priests and priestesses, and ordains them as initiates of the mysteries, they may offer the ancient rites of the dead to assist souls in transition. Clergy become death doulas as well as midwives tending the birth of children, celebrants of the daily rites and prayers of healing, counselors, and mediums. It behooves them to begin creating their own psalter. They must be able to speak well, work well with others, sermonize, eulogize, and pray extemporaneously.

AST (ISIS)—Hotep. The most important aspects of one's ministry as priestesses and priests of Isis is the promotion of unity, social justice, community, and peace. The person who has undertaken this vow will have acquired a wealth of life experience and performed the personal and communal work necessary to become an emissary of peace, love, and compassion. This work will not be a solitary practice, but within the context of a larger community. Indeed, group work becomes all important. We want those who study to go out and do some humanitarian work as well, with individuals who are disadvantaged. It is easy to share love with our friends and family. It is vital to share it with the poor, the dying, the imprisoned, and the marginalized. It is especially important to bring the message of love and compassionate care of the world to those who are privileged and those who see themselves as entitled and tend to scapegoat others. The way to change them is to love and educate them. There is no fear of harm when love and peace are our religion.

SET (SETH)—Hu. Hu in the place of Set reminds us that whatever we say is brought into manifestation because it comes from the breath of God. Therefore, any negativity must be culled. What we say is what we do. Our word is our bond. Political jockeying must be dealt with, differences understood and laid to rest. Egos must be restrained. Let there be no dissension among members; idle talk will weaken the organization. Meditation before a board meeting has a calming effect as it brings us into resonance with each other and with our spiritual source.

NEB-HET (NEPHTHYS)—Ba. It all comes down to the development of the soul. We must be doing the soul's work on Earth, working through lifetimes of missing the mark. The spirit that began the Fellowship of Isis with Lady Olivia Robertson and her brother Lawrence Durdin-Robertson must be restored to the work we do. There are no outsiders. We are all capable of joy and meeting the Imperishable Ones and our loved ones in Spirit so that we can bring messages of hope, light, and personal responsibility.

THE OGDOAD READING

The Ogdoad Reading refers to the eight paired cosmic principles both male and female that appeared as serpents and frogs in the magic cauldron where Thoth first conjured up his creation of the world. According to the cosmology of Hermopolis, this binary division forms all life in the universe. One can think of the cosmic soup in that cauldron as the big bang. Our universe came into being through the hermetic principles of cosmic polarities—the juxtapositions of time and space, darkness and light. We know the time as Heh/Hehet; space as Nun/Nunet; darkness as Amen/Ament; and light as Ra/Raet.

How life begins in the cosmos is the macrocosm of the microcosmic beginning of human life at conception. In the secret cauldron of the mother, a cell divides to create an embryo that grows into a being. Life begins after a sperm and egg meld into a kind of tadpole-looking creature, whether that creature becomes a frog, a bird, a cat, or a human. There is a little chant that goes with this particular Ogdoad creation of the universe. The cosmic progenitor proclaims: "First, I was one, then I was two, then I was four, then I was eight, then I was one again."[3] Sounds like cells dividing to me. Because Thoth is a god of scribes, healers, and accountants, the stories that combine myth, mathematics, and physics make sense as a lesson in understanding what creates a physical form.

This Ogdoad Reading works best when used at the beginning of a project that needs a certain span of time to unfold. Like the creation of anything, you will be looking at both the positive and negative (or masculine and feminine) aspects of where the project will occur (space), when the project will occur (time), what benefit will be derived from it should it succeed (light), and what either partners with it or crosses it (darkness).

You will be pulling four cards in total (time, space, darkness, light). Try to think of the entire reading not as positive and negative events, but as poles that represent an array of opportunities that will affect the project. I might lay the cards out in pairs of oppositions. As I read the hieroglyphs, I want to be sure I am looking at both the positive and negative aspects of the situation.

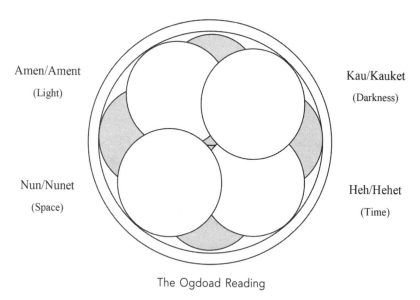

Amen/Ament
(Light)

Kau/Kauket
(Darkness)

Nun/Nunet
(Space)

Heh/Hehet
(Time)

The Ogdoad Reading

The Question

I live in a very old spiritual community. We have a lot of old buildings in need of repair. How can I raise money for a historic building renovation?

The Reading

Time—Wadjet and Kheper. This project has a deep and far-reaching spiritual vision. Wadjet, the winged serpent and third eye in the position of time, suggests that this fundraising and restoration are definitely possible, even though it seems improbable. It shall unfold in its proper time; it shall unfold because Spirit wants it to. In your rush to try to get things off the ground, it is important not to overlook the details. It is important to see things from a number of perspectives and points of view.

Keep in mind that this is a process of evolution, not a product. The process will take time to evolve. You may have to overcome the multiple opinions of others who think it's a lost cause. The dung beetle keeps pushing, and if it keeps pushing, letting itself be guided by right timing and optimism, the current situation will transform. It takes as long as it takes to go through the great process of alchemy. It takes time for a dung beetle to emerge golden and winged from its pupa. In its own time transformation of a negative into a positive happens; then something golden and winged emerges in our lives. When it does, people may be surprised.

Space—Re and Ast. I need to be specific about which building needs the funding, although I may not yet know where to find the money (that other material concern). Ra (Re) occupies the masculine position and Ast, or Isis, the feminine position. A man of enlightened vision may come forward to assist, and a woman may also nurture the project. These two individuals establish a charitable foundation, and are willing to help to create the community that can move the endeavor along. Two resourceful people may be relied upon. This man and woman are strong archetypes who have influence and authority.

Remember, however, in the myth Isis usurps the power of Ra by learning his secret magical name. Ra, it seems, withdraws, a little petulant. Egos in conflict will not help the project move along; in fact, it may stall it. Yet it will take a very powerful voice to energize others, shine a light on its potential, and get the ball rolling.

It may be necessary to speak as one voice about the project in order to raise the funds. The powerful voice will raise the energy and the money.

Darkness—Sopdet and Nu. Some things are still a mystery, and events related to this issue will unfold in their own time. Consider that Sopdet is the star Sirius that heralds the inundation, or nu. Both hieroglyphs point to the flood and inundation. Sufficient funding will come. This seems to say, again, that all is in divine timing. Both images refer to the stars in the night sky that herald the coming flood in July or August. Is there a way to consider astrology as a possible influence on the coming renovation? Will that help us to decide the right timing for these changes to occur? Perhaps Sopdet refers to July or August—the time when Sirius rises—as a possible critical turning point. In addition, the nu hieroglyph holds an image of a vessel full of water overflowing. Sometimes that hieroglyph means abundance, but an abundance of what? Could there be a problem with the roof and water leaking in? Are the plumbing pipes sturdy? What is the cost of installing a sprinkler system in such an old building? Perhaps there is mold in some of the rooms where the roof leaked, which would create a huge problem that needs to be taken into account before any restoration can begin. These are all potential problems that can't be answered yet because the building in question is locked and abandoned at this time.

Light—Shen and Heru. By shining a light on the importance of the longevity of the building, much can be accomplished to showcase the community. The community has been here for over one hundred years and the shen indicates a need to protect its heritage. The name of an entity or individual written into a cartouche, or elongated shen, affords protection to the name. In ancient times the shen assured a long life to the pharaoh whose name it contained. Perhaps this indicates that preservation can come from a benefactor whose name would be attached to the donation.

The shen also protects the name of the 130-year-old entity known as Camp Chesterfield, where this building is situated. Even the sign at the wrought iron entrance gate identified the community as "A Center of Spiritual Light."

Finally, we see Heru, a hero of a sort, a visionary, a person who becomes part of the legacy of this place. Again, it could also be that a man comes forward who wants to be recognized for his contributions to the camp by having his name attached to the building that he is willing to invest in. Or it could be that money is offered as a memorial in the name of another individual. Either way, it looks as if the hero will appear from out of nowhere.

Fingers crossed!

NOTES

INTRODUCTION TO THE HIEROGLYPHS

1. Ellis, *Imagining the World*, 64.
2. Pound, *Literary Essays*, 25.
3. May, *Courage to Create*, 124.
4. Ouspensky, *In Search of the Miraculous*, 280–81.
5. Hauck, *Emerald Tablet*, 45.
6. Ellis and Scully, *Union of Isis and Thoth*, 22.
7. Lesko, *Great Goddesses of Egypt*, 196.
8. McGrath, "Seshet: Mistress of the Books," *We Are Star Stuff* (blog), last updated October 28, 2017.

THE UNIQUE MAGIC OF THE HIEROGLYPHS

1. Andrews, *Animal-Speak Pocket Guide*, 10.
2. Assad, "Sleep in Ancient Egypt," 13.
3. Faulkner, *Ancient Egyptian Pyramid Texts*, 166.
4. Lamy, *Egyptian Mysteries*, 78–79.

THE HIEROGLYPHS

1. Herodotus, *Histories II*, 73.
2. Herodotus, *Histories II*, 74–76.
3. Herodotus, *Histories II*, 74–76.
4. Clark, *Sacred Tradition*, 391.
5. Lichtheim, *Ancient Egyptian Literature*, vol. 3, 132.
6. Gardiner, "The Graffito from the Tomb of Pere," 10–11.

7. Aragorn, "Eclipse over Amarna," Earth Mystery News website, last updated August 22, 2017.

8. Naydler, *Shamanic Wisdom*, 164.

9. Wilkinson, *Ancient Egyptians*, 266.

10. Ellis, *Feasts of Light*, 45–51.

11. Ellis, *Feasts of Light*, 45–51.

12. Meyer, *Gospel of Thomas*, 50.

13. Ellis, *Awakening Osiris*, 84.

14. Lucretius, *On the Nature of Things*, 90.

15. Budge, *Egyptian Book of the Dead*, 471.

16. Frankfort, *Ancient Egyptian Religion*, 97.

17. Kemp, *Ancient Egypt*, 88.

18. Lewis, *Symbolic Prophecy*, 83–97.

19. Thomas, *Selected Poems*, 9.

20. St. Vincent Millay, "First Fig," 97.

21. Ritner, *Mechanics*, 17.

22. Hornung, *Conceptions of God*, 209.

23. Stone, *When God Was a Woman*, 214.

24. Ellis, *Feasts of Light*, 122.

25. Lotterhand, *Thursday Night Tarot*, xix.

26. Klemp, *Spiritual Laws*; Eckankar website, "A Glossary of ECK Terms," last modified June 5, 2017.

27. Talbot, *Holographic Universe*, 2.

28. Moss, "Wake Up and Dream," *The Robert Moss Blog*, last updated November 25, 2016.

29. Naydler, *Shamanic Wisdom*, 251–55.

30. Ellis, *Imagining the World*, 107–12.

31. Dunn, "Me and My Shadow: The Shadow as Part of the Ancient Egyptian Individual," TourEgypt website, last updated June 21, 2011.

32. Budge, *Book of the Dead*, 78–79.

33. Naydler, *Temple of the Cosmos*, 188–89.

34. Watson, *Nature of Things*, 124.

35. Cirlot, *Dictionary of Symbols*, 93.

36. Ellis, *Imagining the World*, 237–38.

37. Ellis, *Imagining the World*, 13.

38. Lichtheim, *Ancient Egyptian Literature*, vol. 1, 169–85.

39. "New Horizons may have seen a glow," 10.

40. Ellis, "Sekhmet, Bast, and Hathor," 204.

41. *A Course in Miracles,* 1.

42. Pumphrey, *Names and Power,* 3.

43. Hornung, *Conceptions of God,* 89.

44. Snyder, "The Apocalypse of Peter (Gnostic)."

45. Janesdaughter, "Say My Name That I May Live," Fellowship of Isis Central Archive website, last updated September 27, 2019.

46. MacManus, *Story of the Irish Race,* 8.

47. Ralph Blum, *Book of Runes,* 25.

48. Hornung, *Conceptions of God,* 76.

49. Konstaple, "About the Nine Spiritual Bodies," Constable Research B.V. website, last updated August 1, 2009.

50. Bailey, *Externalisation of the Hierarchy,* 676.

51. Lichtheim, *Ancient Egyptian Literature,* vol. 3, 142–51.

52. Davis, *Magic Staff,* 234–37.

53. Faulkner, *Ancient Egyptian Pyramid Texts,* 155.

54. Richardson and John, *Inner Guide,* 82.

55. Lotterhand, *Thursday Night Tarot,* 145.

56. Scully, *Sekhmet: Transformation in the Belly,* 79–84.

57. Gandhi, *Young India.*

58. Davis, *Magic Staff,* 263.

59. Hope, *Way of Cartouche,* 133.

60. Bailey, *Treatise on Cosmic Fire,* 536–49.

61. Forrest, *Isis Magic,* 305.

62. Mead, *Thrice-Greatest Hermes,* 345.

63. Brady, *Brady's Book of Fixed Stars,* 334.

64. Pinch, *Handbook of Egyptian Mythology,* 190.

65. "Salawa," Cryptid Wiki website, last updated February 20, 2017.

66. Hornung, *Ancient Egyptian Books,* 123–25.

67. Faulkner, *Ancient Egyptian Pyramid Texts,* 61.

68. Ellis, *Feasts of Light,* 1–5.

69. "The Science of Sirius," The Human Origin Project website, last updated September 27, 2019.

70. Bailey, *Esoteric Astrology,* 197.

71. "Schumann Resonance Today—Update," Disclosure News Italia website, last updated September 27, 2019.

72. Regula, *Mysteries of Isis,* 66.

73. Forrest, *Isis Magic,* 66.

74. Faulkner, *Ancient Egyptian Pyramid Texts,* 55.

75. Budge, *Osiris and the Egyptian Resurrection,* 93.

76. Gibran, *The Prophet,* 5.

77. Sauneron, *Priests of Ancient Egypt,* 38–39.

78. Sauneron, *Priests of Ancient Egypt,* 28–50.

79. Veggi and Davidson, *Book of Doors,* 181–82.

80. Budge, *Book of the Dead,* 443.

81. Cirlot, *Dictionary of Symbols,* 284.

82. Mei, *Ancient Mysteries.*

83. Cirlot, *Dictionary of Symbols,* 14–15.

THE LAYOUTS

1. Greer, *Tarot for Yourself,* 194.

2. Van den Dungen, *Ancient Egyptian Readings,* 184.

3. Lamy, *Egyptian Mysteries,* 9.

BIBLIOGRAPHY

A Course in Miracles, combined volume. Mill Valley, Calif.: Foundation for Inner Peace, 2007.

Aragorn, David. "Eclipse over Amarna: Beginning of the End for Akhenaten in his City of Light?" Earth Mystery News website, last updated August 22, 2017.

Andrews, Ted. *Animal-Speak Pocket Guide.* Jackson, Tenn.: Dragonhawk Publishing, 2009.

Assad, Tarek. "Sleep in Ancient Egypt." In *Sleep Medicine: A Comprehensive Guide to Its Development, Clinical Milestones and Advances in Treatment,* edited by S. Chokroverty and M. Billiard. New York: Springer, 2015.

Bailey, Alice A. *Esoteric Astrology.* New York: Lucis Trust, 1934.

———. *Externalisation of the Hierarchy.* New York: Lucis Trust, 1957.

———. *A Treatise on Cosmic Fire.* New York: Lucis Trust, 1962.

———. *A Treatise on White Magic.* New York: Lucis Trust, 1934.

Blavatsky, Helena Petrovna. *The Secret Doctrine: The Synthesis of Science, Religion, and Philosophy.* 2 vols. Pasadena, Calif.: Theosophical University Press, 2014.

Blum, Ralph. *The Book of Runes.* New York: St. Martin's Press, 1982.

Brady, Bernadette. *Brady's Book of Fixed Stars.* York Beach, Maine: Samuel Weiser, 1998.

Budge, A. E. Wallis. *The Egyptian Book of the Dead: (The Papyrus of Ani) Egyptian Text, Transliteration and Translation.* New York: Dover, 1967.

———. *Egyptian Hieroglyphic Dictionary.* 2 vols. London: John Murray, 1920.

———. *The Gods of the Egyptians.* 2 vols. New York: Dover Publications, 1969.

———. *Osiris and the Egyptian Resurrection.* New York: Dover Publications, 1973.

Cirlot, J. E. *A Dictionary of Symbols,* 2nd ed. Translated by Jack Sage. New York: Dorset Press, 1971.

Clark, Rosemary. *The Sacred Tradition in Ancient Egypt. The Spiritual Practice Restored*. Saint Paul, Minn.: Llewellyn, 2000.

Clement, Stephanie. *Meditation for Beginners: Techniques for Awareness, Mindfulness and Relaxation*. St. Paul, Minn.: Llewellyn Publications, 2003.

Clemmons, Maureen, and Daniel Cray. *Soaring Stones: A Kite-Powered Approach to Building Egypt's Pyramids*. El Segunda, Calif.: Delcominey Creations, 2017.

Davis, Andrew Jackson. *The Magic Staff: An Autobiography*. New York: J. S. Brown and Company, 1857.

Dunn, Jimmy. "Me and My Shadow: The Shadow as Part of the Ancient Egyptian Individual." TourEgypt website. Last updated June 21, 2011.

———. "The Sekhem-Scepter, A Symbol of Power and Control." TourEgypt website. Last updated June 21, 2011.

Ellis, Normandi. *Awakening Osiris: The Egyptian Book of the Dead*. Grand Rapids, Mich.: Phanes Press, 1988.

———. *Dreams of Isis: A Woman's Spiritual Sojourn*. Wheaton, Ill.: Quest Books, 1991.

———. *Feasts of Light: Celebrations for the Seasons of Life*. Wheaton, Ill.: Quest Books, 1999.

———. *Imagining the World into Existence: An Ancient Egyptian Manual of Consciousness*. Rochester, Vt.: Bear and Company, 2012.

Ellis, Normandi, and Gloria Taylor Brown. *Invoking the Scribes of Ancient Egypt: The Initiatory Path of Spiritual Journaling*. Rochester, Vt.: Bear and Company, 2011.

———. "Sekhmet, Bast, and Hathor: Power, Passion, and Transformation through the Egyptian Goddess Trinity" in *Goddesses in World Culture*. Vol. 1, *Asia and Africa*. Edited by Patricia Monaghan. Santa Barbara, Calif.: Praeger, 2011.

Ellis, Normandi, and Nicki Scully. *The Union of Isis and Thoth: Magic and Initiatory Practices of Ancient Egypt*. Rochester, Vt.: Bear and Company, 2015.

Faulkner, Raymond O. *The Ancient Egyptian Book of the Dead*. London: The British Museum Press, 2010.

———. *The Ancient Egyptian Pyramid Texts*. New York: Oxford University Press, 1998.

Forrest, M. Isidora. *Isis Magic: Cultivating a Relationship with the Goddess of 10,000 Names*. St. Paul, Minn.: Llewellyn Publications, 2001.

Fox, John. *Poetic Medicine: The Healing Art of Poem-Making.* New York: Jeremy Tarcher, 1999.

Frankfort, Henri. *Ancient Egyptian Religion: An Interpretation.* New York: Harper Torchbooks, 1948.

Gandhi, Mohandas Karmachand. *Young India Magazine,* October 22, 1925.

Gardiner, Alan. *Egyptian Grammar,* 3rd ed. London: Oxford University Press, 1957.

———. "The Graffito from the Tomb of Pere," *Journal of Egyptian Archaeology 14,* 10–11. Birmingham, Ala.: The Egypt Exploration Society, 1928.

Gibran, Khalil. *The Prophet.* New York: Alfred Knopf, 1923.

Greer, Mary Katherine. *Tarot for Yourself: A Workbook for Personal Transformation.* Franklin Lakes, N. J.: The Career Press, 2002.

Hauck, Dennis. *The Emerald Tablet: Alchemy for Personal Transformation.* New York: Penguin Putnam, 1999.

Herodotus. *The Histories* (Book II). Translated by Aubrey de Sélincourt. Edited by John Marincola. London: Penguin Group, 2003.

Hope, Murry. *Practical Egyptian Magic.* New York: St. Martin's Press, 1984.

———. *The Way of Cartouche: An Oracle of Ancient Egyptian Magic.* New York: St. Martin's Press, 1985.

Hornung, Erik. *The Ancient Egyptian Books of the Afterlife.* Translated by David Lorton. Ithaca, N.Y.: Cornell University Press, 1999.

———. *Conceptions of God in Ancient Egypt: The One and the Many.* Translated by John Baines. Ithaca, N.Y.: Cornell University Press, 1996.

Houston, Jean. *The Passion of Isis and Osiris: A Gateway to Transcendent Love.* New York: Random House, 1995.

Janesdaughter, Laura. "Say My Name That I May Live." Fellowship of Isis Central Archive website. Last updated September 27, 2019.

Jung, Carl Gustav, and Sonu Shamdasani. *The Red Book.* New York: W. W. Norton, 2009.

Kemp, Barry John. *Ancient Egypt: Anatomy of a Civilization.* London: Routledge, 1991.

Klemp, Sri Harold. *The Spiritual Laws of Life.* Chanhassen, Minn.: Eckankar, 2010.

Konstaple, Hans. "About the Nine Spiritual Bodies." Constable Research B. V. website. Last updated August 1, 2009.

Lamy, Lucie. *Egyptian Mysteries: New Light on Ancient Spiritual Knowledge.* New York: Crossroad Publishing, 1981.

Lesko, Barbara S. *The Great Goddesses of Egypt*. Norman, Okla.: University of Oklahoma Press, 1999.

Lewis, H. Spencer. *The Symbolic Prophecy of the Great Pyramid*. San Jose, Calif.: Supreme Grand Lodge of the Ancient and Mystical Order of the Rosae Crucis, 2015.

Lichtheim, Miriam. *Ancient Egyptian Literature*. Vol. 1, *The Old and Middle Kingdoms*. Berkeley, Calif.: University of California Press, 1975.

———. *Ancient Egyptian Literature*. Vol. 3, *The Late Period*. Berkeley, Calif.: University of California Press, 1980.

Lotterhand, Jason C. *The Thursday Night Tarot: Weekly Talks on the Wisdom of the Major Arcana*. North Hollywood, Calif.: Newcastle Publishing, 1989.

Lucretius. *On the Nature of Things*. Edited by Robert Allison. London: Arthur L. Humphreys, 1919.

MacManus, Seumas. *The Story of the Irish Race: Popular History of Ireland*. New York: Devin-Adair Company, 1980.

Massey, Gerald. *The Egyptian Book of the Dead and the Mysteries of Amenta*. London, T. F. Unwin, 1907.

Mattson, Jill Ingborg. *The Lost Waves of Time: The Untold Story of How Music Shaped Our World*. Oil City, Pa.: Wings of Light, 2016.

May, Rollo. *The Courage to Create*. New York: W. W. Norton, 1975.

McGrath, Sheena. "Seshat: Mistress of the Books." *We Are Star Stuff* (blog). Last updated October 28, 2017.

Mead, G. R. S. *Thrice-Greatest Hermes*. Vol. 1, *Studies in Hellenistic Theosophy and Gnosis*. London: Theosophical Publishing House, 1906.

Mei, Armando. *Ancient Mysteries: Collection of Author's articles published on the main specialized journals. New proposals unveiling the mysteries of the past*. Armando Mei, 2016. PDF ebook.

Meyer, Marvin W. *The Gospel of Thomas: The Hidden Sayings of Jesus*. New York: HarperCollins, 1992.

Meyer, Marvin W., and James M. Robinson. *The Nag Hammadi Scriptures: The Revised and Updated Translation of Sacred Gnostic Texts Complete in One Volume*. New York: Harper Collins, 2007.

Moss, Robert. *The Dreamer's Book of the Dead: A Soul Traveler's Guide to Death, Dying and the Other Side*. Rochester, Vt.: Destiny Books, 2005.

———. *Dreaming the Soul Back Home: Shamanic Dreaming for Healing and Becoming Whole*. Novato: Calif.: New World Library, 2012.

———. *The Three "Only" Things: Tapping the Power of Dreams, Coincidence, and Imagination*. Novato, Calif.: New World Library, 2007.

———. "Wake Up and Dream." *The Robert Moss Blog*. Last updated November 25, 2016.

Naydler, Jeremy. *Shamanic Wisdom in the Pyramid Texts*. Rochester, Vt.: Inner Traditions, 2005.

———. *Temple of the Cosmos: The Ancient Egyptian Experience of the Sacred*. Rochester, Vt.: Inner Traditions, 1996.

"New Horizons may have seen a glow at the solar system's edge," *Science News* 194:5, September 15, 2018.

Ouspensky, P. D. *In Search of the Miraculous: The Teachings of G. I. Gurdjieff*. Orlando, Fla.: Harcourt, 1977.

Pinch, Geraldine. *Handbook of Egyptian Mythology*. Santa Barbara, Calif.: ABC/CLIO, 2002.

Pound, Ezra. *Literary Essays of Ezra Pound*. New York: New Directions, 1935.

Pumphrey, Nicholaus Benjamin. *Names and Power: The Concept of Secret Names in the Ancient Near East*, master's dissertation. Graduate School of Vanderbilt University, May 2009.

Regula, DeTraci. *The Mysteries of Isis: Her Worship and Magick*. St. Paul, Minn.: Llewellyn, 2002.

Richardson, Alan, and Billie Walker John. *The Inner Guide to Egypt: A Mystical Journey Through Time and Consciousness*. Woodbury, Minn.: Llewellyn, 2010.

Ritner, Robert K. *The Mechanics of Ancient Egyptian Magical Practice*. Chicago, Ill.: The Oriental Institute of the University of Chicago, 1997.

"Salawa," Cryptid Wiki website. Last updated February 20, 2017.

Sauneron, Serge. *The Priests of Ancient Egypt*. Translated by David Lorton. Ithaca, N.Y.: Cornell University Press, 2000.

"Schumann Resonance Today—Update." Disclosure News Italia website. Last updated September 27, 2019.

Schwaller de Lubicz, R. A. *A Study of Numbers: A Guide to the Constant Creation of the Universe*. Rochester, Vt.: Inner Traditions, 1986.

———. *Symbol and the Symbolic: Ancient Egypt, Science, and the Evolution of Consciousness*. Rochester, Vt.: Inner Traditions, 1981.

———. *The Temple in Man: Sacred Architecture and the Perfect Man*. Rochester, Vt.: Inner Traditions, 1981.

"The Science of Sirius Mythology and Our Two Sun Solar System." The Human Origin Project website. Last updated September 27, 2019.

Scully, Nicki. *Sekhmet: Transformation in the Belly of the Goddess*. Rochester, Vt.: Bear and Company, 2017.

Snyder, Jackson. "The Apocalypse of Peter (Gnostic)" in *Secret Sayings of the Savior: All the Extra-Biblical Teachings of Jesus from Diverse Ancient Sources*. Jackson Snyder Bible: Scripture, Commentaries, Antiquities. Vero Beach, Fla., 1990–2012. Also accessible on the Jackson Snyder Bible website. Last updated September 27, 2019.

St. Vincent Millay, Edna. "First Fig" in *The Penguin Anthology of Twentieth Century American Poetry*. Edited by Rita Dove. New York: Penguin Books, 2008.

Stone, Merlin. *When God Was a Woman*. New York: Houghton Mifflin, 1976.

Talbot, Michael. *The Holographic Universe*. New York: HarperCollins, 1991.

Taylor, Jeremy. *Dream Work: Techniques for Discovering the Creative Power in Dreams*. Mahwah, N.J.: Paulist Press, 1983.

———. *The Living Labyrinth: Exploring Universal Themes in Myths, Dreams, and the Symbolism of Waking Life*. Mahwah, N.J.: Paulist Press, 1998.

Temple, Robert K. G. *The Sirius Mystery:* New York: St. Martin's Press, 1976.

Thomas, Dylan. *Selected Poems 1934–1952,* revised. New York: New Directions, 2003.

Van den Dungen, Wim. *Ancient Egyptian Readings*. Brasschaat, Belgium: Taurus Press, 2018.

Veggi, Athon, and Alison Davidson. *The Book of Doors: An Alchemical Oracle from Ancient Egypt*. Rochester, Vt.: Destiny Books, 1995.

Watson, Lyall. *The Nature of Things: The Secret Life of Inanimate Objects*. Rochester, Vt.: Destiny Books, 1992.

Wilkinson, J. G. *The Ancient Egyptians: Their Life and Customs*. New York: Crescent Books, 1988.

INDEX

Page numbers in *italics* indicate illustrations.

ab. *See* ib

abtu fish, 146

abundance, 14, 26, 46, 245, 294

Akashic Records, 4, 59, 216

akh, 41–44, *41,* 88, 199, 254, 268

   nine points, 44

Akhenaten, 46–47, 71, *72,* 94

Akhet, 45–48, *45,* 279

   nine points, 47–48

Alchemical Healing, xviii

alchemy, 14, 149

Alexander the Great, 50

altar, 113, 252

Amen, 48–51, *48, 49*

   nine points, 50–51

Amenhotep III, Pharaoh, *159*

Ammit, 221

amulets, and hieroglyph work, 25–27

Amun. *See* Amen

Andrews, Ted, 13

animals, 13

ankh, 8, 26, 52–55, *52*

   nine points, 53–55

Anpu (Anubis). *See* Anubis
   (Anpu)

an-t fish, 146

Anubis (Anpu), 23, 55–59, *55, 67,* 162

   nine points, 58–59

Apocalypse of Peter, The, 191

Aquarius, 255, 260

Aries, 259

arit, 59–62, *59,* 264–65

   nine points, 61–62

Arjuna, 45

Ark of the Covenant, 145

aromatherapy room, *114*

art, 2–3

artistic higher self, 273, 278

Asar. *See* Osiris

ascended masters, 195–97

ascendant, 260, 262

Asclepius, 89, 246

Aset, 220

Assiah, 271

Ast. *See* Isis (Ast)

astral realm, 133, 263

astral travel, 249

astrology, 35, 258–69

Aten, 70–74, *70, 72*

   nine points, 73–74

atom, 75

attention, 13–14

Atum, 23, 74–76, *74,* 125, 268–69, 278, *283*
   nine points, 76
Awakening Osiris, xi

ba, 20, 77–79, *77*
   nine points, 78–79
Bailey, Alice A., 196, 210
banjo, 165
Bast, 121, 213
beautiful child, 167
becoming, 148, 149
benben, 79–82, *79,* 267
   nine points, 81–82
Bes, 127
birth, 126–27
black arts, 14
blank, 82–83, *82*
   nine points, 83
blue lotus, 168, 209–10
body language, 62
boldness, 176
bread, 123
breath, 101, 125–28
breath of God, 125–28
Briah, 271
Buddha, 45, 133

caduceus, 87, 89
calendars, Egyptian, 230–31
Cancer, 259
candles, 101, 248
Capricorn, 260
carnelian, 14
cedars of Lebanon, 235
Celtic Cross Reading, 35
Center/The Imperishable Stars, 260, 269

cheriheb, 243
chi, 137
Christian references in book, 36–37
clairvoyance, 132
Clark, Rosemary, 43
Clemmons, Maureen, 49
cobras, 60–61, *61,* 245–48
colors, 183
Communion, 122–23
compassion, 109, 130
consciousness, 269
constellations, 195
Conversational Reading, 284–85
   sample reading, 284–85
cooperation, 187
Course in Miracles, A, 189
cow, 119
Creation, 3–4, 13, 80, 81, 89, 101, 125–26, 179, 188, 254
creative outpouring, 272
creative power, 249, 273, 279–80
creator self, 277–78
crested lapwing, 186
cube, 32

Da'at, 276
Daily Numerology Reading, 285–87
   sample reading, 286–87
darkness, 294
dark night of the soul, 157
Davis, Andrew Jackson, 196, 207, 244
Day of Reckoning, 186
dead, the, 156–57, 191–92
death, 74, 142–47, 201, 227
decks
   Hieroglyphic Oracle Card Deck, 316
   oracle deck, xiv–xv, 18–19, 38

Dendera Zodiac Layout, 258–69, *261*
  houses, 259–60
  sample reading, 262–69
descendant, 260, 262
desert, 93–94, 95, 220
designer, 273, 277–78
destiny, reading for, 287
determination, 278–79
Devil, 222
Dharmakaya, 195
divination, tools for, 258–95
djeba, 30
djed, 26, 84–87, *84*, 195
  nine points, 86–87
Djed Pillar, 269
Djed Pillar Spread, 269–80, *275*
  sample reading, 276–80
Djhuty. *See* Thoth (Djhuty)
DNA, 7–8, 87, 195
Dogon, 231
doorway, 59–60
Downey, Robert, Jr., 122
drawing hieroglyphs, 15–16
dream guide, 22
dream interpreters, 21
dream journal, 22
dreams, 21, 42, 66, 133–36
  and invoking hieroglyphs, 19–22
  lion fountain dream, 12–13
  Prospero's coat dream, 18
  of snakes, 248
dser, 93–95, *93,* 277
  nine points, 94–95
Duamutef, 31
duat, 96–98, *96*
  nine points, 97–98

dung beetle, 148–51, 263, 281. *See also* kheper
Dunn, Jimmy, 140–41
Durdin-Robertson, Lawrence, 291
Dylan, Bob, 103

Earth, 160, 234–35
East/Ascendant, 260, 267–68
Eden, Garden of, 86
Edfu, 110
Egyptian Book of the Dead, xi, 42, 64, 91, 92, 149, 200, 247
eight (number), 32–33
elements, 31
Elijah, 196
El Kab, 93–94
Ellis, Normandi (author), xi–xvii, 4–5
Eloquent Peasant, The, 153
Emerald Tablet, 89–91
emptiness, 83
Ennead, 33, 111
  Great Ennead, 187
Ennead (Journey) Reading, 287–91, *288*
  sample reading, 289–91
Episcopagan, xii
eternal life, 52
eternity, 101
Eve, 246
eye, 134
Eye of God, 132
Eye of Horus, 25

Feasts of Light (Ellis), 174
feathers, 152, 155
Fellowship of Isis, 291
femininity, 53, 118, 120, 239
fire, 112–15

fire altar, 112–13, 143, 146

First Time, 4, 254

fish, 143, 146, 147

five (number), 31–32

flood, 170

fohatic power, 210

form, 272

Forrest, Isidora, 238

forty (number), 28

four (number), 31

Four Sons of Horus, 31

Freemasons, 180

future, 284

Gandhi, Mahatma, 45, 206

Gardiner, Sir Alan, 16, 53

Geb, 23, 31, 96, 98–100, *98,* 173–74, 287, 289

   nine points, 99–100

gematria, 28–29, 33–34, 182

Gemini, 259

geometry, 29

glamour, 277

God, 6, 8, 9, 30, 46, 50–51, 54

god consciousness, 11, 88

gods and goddesses. *See also* neteru Ennead, 33

God's Wife, xii

Golden Rule, 54

gratitude, 131

gravesites, 124

gravity, 234

Green Man, 99, 165, 234

Gurdjieff, G. I., 3

h (letter), 6–8

Hamlet, 60

Hanukkah, 113

Hapi, 31, *256*

Harmonic Convergence, 46

Hathor (Het-Hor), 115–21, *115,* 213, 284

   temple of, *118*

Hauck, Dennis, 91

hawk, 107

healing, 26, 92, 100, 208, 256

   amulets and, 25–27

heart, 129–31, 152, 278

Hebrew scriptures, 37

heh, 100–103, *100, 268*

   nine points, 102–3

Heka/heka, xiii, 1, 6–10, *7,* 103–7, *103, 104,* 190, 279

   nine points, 105–7

Heket, 8

hem netjer, 243

hero, 107, 108

Herodotus, 42

hero's journey, 264

Heru (Horus). *See* Horus (Heru)

het (khet or khat), 112–15, *112*

   nine points, 113–15

Het-Hor. *See* Hathor (Het-Hor)

Hidden Messages in Water, The (Emoto), 188–89

hieroglyphic oracle card deck, 316

hieroglyphs, xv–xvii, 38–257

   amulet work with, 25–27

   birds and, 41

   drawing, 15–16

   hieroglyphic thinking, 38

   introduction to, 1–10

   invoking while dreaming, 19–22

   as key to consciousness, 13

   listed and described, 38–257

meditation and, 15–18
motives for using, 17
numerology and, 27–36
as oracle, 18–19
painting of, 14
ritual work with, 22–25
as sacred words, xiv
translation of, 5–6
unique magic of, 11–37
vocalizing, 16–17
highest ideal, 272, 280
Hod, 273
Hope, Murry, 210
Hornung, Erik, 105
Horus (Heru), 23, 107–11, *107*, 184, *217*, 264, 287, 294–95
nine points, 110–11
temple of, *114*
hotep, 26, 121–25, *121*, 266–67
nine points, 124–25
Hovis, Lexy, 40
Hu, 125–28, *125*, 227
nine points, 127–28
Hughes, Langston, 66

ib, 26, 128–31, *128*, 278–79, 284
nine points, 130–31
ibis, 41, 43
if, 134
imagery of hieroglyphs, 39–40
imagination, vi, 277
Imhotep, 91, 125, 167, 208
immaculate conception, 158–60
Imperishable Stars, 260, 262
Imsety, 31
imum coeli (IC), 260, 262
incarnation, 146

Inner Guide to Ancient Egypt, The (Richardson), 202
inspiration, 175, 272, 280
intention, 13–14
intuition, 62, 98, 110, 136
Ir-is, 263
ir-ma'a, 21–22, 132–36, *132*
nine points, 135–36
irony, 251
ir-rswt, 133
Isis (Ast), xii, 3–4, 23, 35, 64, 67–70, *67, 85,* 109, 117, 190–91, 220, 280, 287, 290, 293
as cobra, 84
and Nephthys, 162
nine points, 69–70
as Speaker of Spells, 11
Israel, 190

jackal, 55–58
Jacob, 134, 190
Jesus, 36, 71, 94, 105, 123, 137, 177, 191, 196–97
Jobs, Steve, 278
John, Gospel of, 3, 13, 126, 179
Jones, Deborah, 131
Judaism, 36–37, 271

ka, 8–9, 136–39, *136*
nine points, 138–39
Kabbalah, 271. *See also* Qabalah
kapet, 143
karma, 130, 235
Keats, John, 223
Kemp, Barry, 80–81
Kenhirkhopeshef, 134
kh, 88, 142

Khaemwast, 20, 196

khaibit, 139–42, *139*

nine points, 141–42

khat, 142–47, *142,* 285

nine points, 146–47

kheper, 23, 26, 147–51, *151,* 277, 293

nine points, 150–51

Khepera, 263–64, 281, *283*

King Arthur's round table, 122

Kirlian photography, 274

Klemp, Sri Harold, 126

knot of Isis, 237

knots, 237–38

knowers of things, 186

know thyself, 62

kundalini, 84–86, 115, 210, 247

Lamy, Lucie, 32

lands of Egypt, 234

lapis lazuli, 14

Lascaux paintings, 2

law of environment, 14

law of unity, 174

layouts, 258–95

Conversational Reading, 284–85

Daily Numerology Reading, 285–87

Dendera Zodiac Layout, 258–69

Djed Pillar Spread, 269–80

Ennead (Journey) Reading, 287–91

Ogdoad Reading, 291–95

Sphinx Reading, 280–85

Tree of Life Spread, 269–80

leadership, 177

lector-priests, 191, 243

Leo, 259

Libra, 260

life, purpose of, 167

life force, 129, 137, 247. *See also*
kundalini

light, 71, 182–85, 294–95

lion, 182, 206

lion bed, 145–46

Lotterhand, Jason, 205

lotus, 209–11

love, 54, 129–31, 130, 131, 150, 194, 235

Lucretius, 75

Lukashevich, Cosima, 2

Luxor Temple, *159*

Ma'at/ma'at, 3–4, 23, 122, 151–56,
151, 153, 154

laws of, 154

nine points, 155–56

mace, 205

magic, xiii, 1, 103–5, 190. *See also*
Heka/heka

Malkuth, 273

manu, 156–58, *156,* 267

nine points, 157–58

Mary, Virgin, 67, 78, 158

Matrix, The, 200–201

Mattson, Jill, 128

May, Rollo, 2

meditation, 43, 91, 139, 157, 178, 198,
201–2

breathwork and, 127

and emptiness, 83

hieroglyphs and, 15–18, 38

outdoors, 73

medju neter, 3, 11

Mehen, 29

Meretseger, 246

Meri, 158–61, *158*

nine points, 160–61

metaphysics, 172–73
midheaven (MC), 262
money, 263
monotheism, 72
Moses, 36–37, 89, 94, 137, 271
Moss, Robert, 22, 133, 134
mouth, 200
Muhammad, 189
mummies, 26, 129
Mysteries of Isis, The (Regula),
   237
myth, 6

names, 189–91
natural laws, 152–54
Nebhet. *See* Nephthys (Nebhet)
nefer, 29–30, 164–66, *164*
   nine points, 165–66
Nefertum, 23, 165, 166–69, *166*
   nine points, 168–69
Negative Confessions, 130, 154
Neith, 173–74, 237–38, 245
Nekhbet, 141
Nephthys (Nebhet), 23, 161–64,
   161, 287, 291
   nine points, 163–64
Neter, 172
neteru, xii, 6, 18–19
   families of, 23
Netzach, 273
Nile, 94–95, 231–32, 253, *256*
nine (number), 33
nine points, rationale for, 40
North/IC, 260, 268
North Star, 262
nu, 169–71, *169,* 277–78, 294
   nine points, 170–71
number magic. *See* numerology

numerology, xv, 27–36, 192–93
   Egyptian use of, 29–35
nun, 255
Nut, 23, 31, 96, 98–99, 171–75, *171,*
   182, 265, 287, 289
   chapel of, *173*
   nine points, 174–75

obelisk, 80
Oedipus Rex, 280–81
Ogdoad, 32, 169, 182
Ogdoad Reading, 291–95, *292*
   sample reading, 292–95
om, 235
one (number), 30
Opening the Mouth, 193
Opet Festival, 119, *119,* 177
oracle, xii–xiii
   hieroglyphs as, 18–19
oracle deck, xiv–xvi, 18–19, 38
   creating, 19
   purchasing, 316
oral tradition, 189
oral transmission, 28
order, 131
Orion, 172, 197
Osiris (Asar), 23, 63–66, *63, 85,*
   123, 165, 232, *242,* 265–66,
   287, 290
   Anubis and, 56–57
   and djed symbol, 84–87
   as firstborn, 234
   first step in Egypt, 254
   nine points, 65–66
   and Set, 220
   spell over, 238
   and Tree of Life, 269
Oxyrhynchus fish, 145

papyrus, 209
passion, 111
past, 283–84
past, present, future reading, 282–84, *283*
paut, 65
Pawah, 46–47
peace, 106, 122–24, *124*
per-ā, 175–78, *175,* 265
    nine points, 177–78
per ankh, 216
pharaoh, 20, 108, 111, 176
Philip, 197
Philo of Alexandria, 246
phoenix, 41–42, 46, 80–84, 254
physical self, 273, 277
physics, 172–73
Pisces, 260
Pleiades, 218
plinth, 152
portals, 199–203
    creating, 202–3
power, 17, 122, 252
present, 284
priest, 240–43
projects, 274, 292
protection, 224–25
psychic self, 273, 277
Ptah, 23, 87, 179–81, *179,* 262–63
    nine points, 180–81
Pumphrey, Nicholaus, 190
purpose of life, 167
pyramids, 80–82, 267
Pyramid Texts, 5, 80
Pythagoras, 27–28, 180

Qabalah, 85–86, 271
Qebehsenuef, 31
Qur'an, 189

Ra (Re), 23, 181–85, *181, 283,* 287, 289, 293
    nine points, 184–85
Ram Dass, 234
Ra-t, 184
Re. *See* Ra (Re)
Red Land, 93–94
Red Tent movement, 237
Regula, DeTraci, 237
rekht, 186–88, *186*
    nine points, 187–88
ren, 188–94, *188*
    nine points, 193–94
Renenunet, 246
Restau, 133
Richardson, Alan, 202
ritual work with hieroglyphs, 22–25
Robertson, Lady Olivia, 291
Rohn, Amy Auset, 39
rune stones, 192

Sagittarius, 260
Sahara, 115
sahu, 140–41, 194–98, *194*
    nine points, 197–98
salawa, 221
Sanat Kumara, 196
Saturn, 221–22
scarab, 148, *150*
scepter, 180, 250–52
Schucman, Helen, 189
Schwaller de Lubicz, R. A., 16, 52–53
scientist, 273
Scorpio, 260
scribes, 10, 187
scroll, 9–10
Scully, Nicki, xvii–xviii, 27
seba, 199–204, *199*
    nine points, 203–4

seeds, 10
seeing, 132–34
Sekhem, 26, 204–8, *204, 207*
    nine points, 206–8
Sekhmet, 23, 121, 143, *144,* 167–68,
    205
self, 273, 278
sephiroth, xiv, 23, 271–73
serpent, 245–48
se-shen (lotus), 209–11, *209*
    nine points, 210–11
se-sheshet, 212–15, *212*
    nine points, 214–15
Seshet/seshet, xi–xii, 4, 23, 215–19,
    215, 217, 279–80
    nine points, 218–19
Set, 23, 94, 219–23, *219,* 287,
    290–91
    nine points, 222–23
Seti I, *85, 153, 207*
seven (number), 32
Shabaka stone, 179
shamanic flight, 20
shamans, 26, 133, 201
Shambhala, 45, 47
Shemsu Hor, 109
shen, 26, 224–26, *224,* 266, 294–95
    nine points, 225–26
Shu, 287, 289
Sia, 226–29, *226*
    nine points, 228–29
sins, seven social, 206
Sirius, 57, 163, 230–32
Sirius Mystery, The (Temple), 231
sistrum, 212–14, *213*
Siwa Temple, 50
six (number), 32

Sky Walkers, 195
sleep, 134–35
snake, 86, 245–48
Sobek, 262
solar angel, 17
solar boat, 287–88
solar system, 184
Sopdet, 229–33, *229,* 278, 294
    nine points, 232–33
soul, 20, 77–79. *See also* ba
sound, 16–17, 188–94
South/Midheaven, 260, 268–69
space, 196, 293
speech, 126, 188–94
spells, 189, 191
Sphinx, 126, 280–82, *282*
Sphinx Reading, 280–85
    sample reading, 283–84
spinal cord, 84
Spirit, 137–38, 252, 268–69
spiritual awakening, 168–69
Srogi, Rev. A. Win, 285
star gate, 199–203
stars, 96–97, 120, 172, 216
Stone, Merlin, 116
success, 70
symbols, 3, 5–6, 13, 22

ta, 233–36, *233*
    nine points, 235–36
Tai Chi, 128
Tauret, 262
Taurus, 259
Taylor, Jeremy, 22
Tef-Nut, 287, 289
Teilhard de Chardin, 45
teleportation, 196–97

Temple, Robert K. G., 231
temples, 14–15, 87, 117, 149, 184, 199–200, 216
ten spiritual bodies, xiv–xv, 23–24
Teresa of Ávila, 45
thet, 236–39, *236*
  nine points, 238–39
Thoth (Djhuty), 3–4, 23, 88–92, *88, 90,* 216–17
  invoking, 38
  and Isis, 68
  nine points, 91–92
  purifies priest, *241*
thoughts, 1–2, 272, 279
three (number), 10, 30–31
throne, 68
time, 89, 102–3, 196, 293
Tipareth, 273
tools for divination, 258–95
Treatise on Cosmic Fire, A (Bailey), 210
Tree of Life, xiv, 85–86, 101, 216, 269–72
Tree of Life Spread, 269–80, *275*
  sample reading, 276–80
Trinity, 30, 81
truth, 181
turquoise, 14
Tuthmosis IV, 281, *282*
two (number), 30
Two Ladies, *246*

Unas, 134, 228
understanding, 44, 272
Union of Isis and Thoth, The (Ellis and Scully), 77
Unnefer, 165
Upuat, 56
uraeus, 247

Venus, 53
Virgo, 259
virtues, 272, 279
Vishnu, 210
vision quest, 113
vocalizing hieroglyphs, 16–17
vowels, xiii, 192

wab, 240–44, *240*
  nine points, 243–44
wab priest, 240–43
Wadjet/wadjet, 26, 245–50, 293
  nine points, 248–50
water, 188–89
Watson, Lyall, 143
waz, 26, 250, *250*–53, 267–68
  nine points, 252–53
West/Descendant, 260, 268
willpower, 272–73, 278–79
Wisdom, 272
Wolsiffer, Meg, 40
womb, 201
Word of God, 3, 11, 13, 126, 179, 191
  and hieroglyphs, 1–10
words as magic, 1
Words of Power, 189–94. *See also* hieroglyphs; Word of God
worry, 122

Yesod, 273
Yetzirah, 271

Zep Tepi, 4, 253–57, *253*
  nine points, 255–57
zodiac, 258–69
  ceiling at Dendera, *259*

HIEROGLYPHIC ORACLE CARD DECK

Throughout this book, I have suggested that you create your own oracle deck, imbuing the cards with your own energy and deepening your understanding of the multiple meanings of the sixty hieroglyphs presented in this book. If you prefer not to draw the oracle cards yourself, you can purchase *The Oracle of Seshet* deck of hieroglyphic oracle cards directly from me at **https://normandiellis.com/books**

MA'AT

HET

ZEP TEPI